*Is There Time
for a Winner?*

'IS THERE TIME FOR A WINNER?'

SHEFFIELD WEDNESDAY'S 2022/23 PROMOTION MIRACLE

ALEX MILLER AND JOE CRANN

FOREWORD BY BARRY BANNAN

www.verticaleditions.com

First published in the United Kingdom in 2023 by Vertical
Editions, Unit 41 Regency Court, Sheffield, S35 9ZQ

www.verticaleditions.com

Follow us on Twitter:
@VerticalEds
@AlexMiller91 @YesWeCrann

Cover images by Harriet Massey
(front) and Steve Ellis (rear)

ISBN 978-1-908847-29-4

1

A CIP catalogue record for this book is available from the British Library

Printed and bound by Jellyfish Print Solutions, Swanmore, Hants

CONTENTS

PROLOGUE

The ball beats the Barnsley goalkeeper to a sound that seems to reverberate that way only at the home of football. Sheridan, Waddle; to those in the stands, only Sheffield Wednesday legends of old have sparked its unmistakable timbre. It's a delicate crash of ball on net, a momentary flicker as it peels down the goal, a half-second of breathlessness and then pandemonium from the terraces, the individual sound of fathers hugging daughters, brothers embracing sisters and grandparents lifting their grandchildren to create the crash of a sea of 44,000 sunburnt revellers.

Wednesday's players race off in directions unknown. Blood runs cold and adrenaline runs amok. At the midway point between the corner flag and the Owls' technical area at Wembley Stadium, players meet substitutes in unruly rejoice. Barry Bannan looks to his public to punch the air, a bibbed Aden Flint raises his hands to his head and within microseconds they're joined by backroom staff who, it was later joked, surely should have known better. It felt to those present that the entire Sheffield Wednesday world was there, joined in unison at the breaking of a scoreline that many had given up on and that had looked destined for penalties. Wembley Stadium shook with pandemonium. Wembley was blue and white and Wednesday were going up.

At the centre of the stadium, though, and with the world in cacophony all around him, one Wednesday figure stood cold, motionless. Darren Moore stared across the pitch with perspiration glistening from his head and put his hand to his chin in a pose well-known to the thousands deep in guttural euphoria. He closed his eyes for just a moment, took a breath and motioned to his colleagues in quiet, heartbroken desperation.

Because as all those around him had darted into mayhem, he'd soon spotted that the linesman's flag had been raised, cruelly delayed by the presence of VAR ruling no League One figure was accustomed to. Will Vaulks' stunning 107th-minute goal had been ruled out, his gymnastic celebration executed for naught. Marvin Johnson was the first member of the pitchside melee to spot the flag and broke the news to his teammates. One by one, the Owls stared across the pitch, open-mouthed in disbelief. Vaulks' initial ball over the top had been delayed a moment as he struggled to drag it out of his feet on the dry, late-May pitch and Jack Hunt hadn't quite managed to hold his run. Hunt, off the bench and darting towards a second moment of immortality in a fortnight, had been ruled offside. His well-placed ball back inside was scrubbed out of the history books. A heartbroken Vaulks had belted home the best Wembley goal never scored.

The formality of a VAR check confirmed the truth and, with only 13 minutes of added time left on the clock, Wednesday would have to go again. The sinking feeling permeated the London air like a puncture as Barnsley supporters stole that feeling of jubilation and sucked it into the West Side of the ground – the one with all the good pubs, we were told – realising Luca Connell's misdirected effort moments earlier would not prove fatal. The sinking feeling set in. With time running out, the biggest South Yorkshire derby of all-time would remain 0-0. The 2023 League One play-off final was destined for penalties.

The match had been low on quality, headlocked in long-ball tactics and a desperate feeling of uncontrolled to-and-fro. Neither side had truly taken grip of the match, but although some would later laugh it off as a stinker, there were more than enough moments to fill a highlights package. It had been gnarled, gritty, exhausting, but full of moments. Both keepers had made excellent saves; Cameron Dawson a man inspired, Harry Isted a man possessed. Barnsley had a very strong penalty shout rejected and later bemoaned a decision when a key midfielder was shown a red card on just 49 minutes. Both sides had hit the woodwork and down to 10 men, it was the Tykes that had stepped into the occasion as the Owls failed to expose their numerical advantage. Barnsley had been better in the second half since the sending-off. Wednesday had the better of extra time.

In the stands 44,000 Wednesdayites vastly outnumbered their red-clad counterparts, but in truth had quietened a touch as the game grew old, locked in fear by the possibility of another near-miss by a club that, historically-speaking, had made near-misses something of a forte. The feeling was that, having failed to grow in stature after Adam Phillips' red card, having had such a classy goal scrubbed off and having celebrated appropriately, it would have been 'Very Wednesday' to have to face a slow march down Wembley Way with sunken shoulders, dads explaining to the children they had lifted into the air so joyfully in the wake of Vaulks' strike that this was what it means to be Sheffield Wednesday; bridesmaids with running mascara. Never, ever the brides.

It had been a hard road to this point. Relegated two seasons earlier in no small part due to a points deduction slapped on them while the club scrambled to recover from an outlay that contravened EFL rules on profitability and sustainability, Moore was the seventh manager to take to the Hillsborough hotseat since their last Wembley appearance – eight including a stand-in during a Covid pandemic that had beaten the life out of the club and left it broken.

That last Wembley appearance had taken place on May 28, 2016, when Carlos Carvalhal's Owls came within 90 minutes of achieving a place in the Premier League, but lost 1-0 to Hull City. That result, the spending that facilitated it and a play-off semi-final defeat to Huddersfield Town the following season, left a hangover that seven years on had not been eased. Broken was the word Moore chose several months previously when describing the club he had taken on, with players not having been paid on time, a transfer embargo preventing punches in the fight. No playing style, no heart. Rudderless.

The drop to the third tier cut deeply but delivered cause that Wednesday could use it to take breath and recover. Moore had at one stage been gravely ill, fighting for his life while his players had been fighting for a survival of a very different kind. Long-serving players had moved on and a slate had been at least partially wiped clean.

The pain of a last-gasp play-off semi-final defeat 12 months prior to Wembley had left some calling for the manager's head, and a summer turnaround of personnel in the changing room left uncertainty. Wednesday signed players unfashionable but with the cuts and bruises and hairy chests to stand up in the big moments. Record-breaking runs followed, famous nights under the lights bombing the richest club in the world out of the FA Cup to scenes nobody at the time felt would be surpassed for years to come. Half a season unbeaten proved not to be enough as Plymouth Argyle and Ipswich Town bulldozed through the final stages of the campaign to capitalise on a Wednesday wobble. A club-record 96 points would have been enough to achieve automatic promotion in any English league in history, but Wednesday finished third. Bridesmaids.

And then came Peterborough. Peterborough away. Peterborough at home. They had achieved play-off immortality already, dared to dream against Posh and somehow pulled off the seemingly-impossible. But in the Wembley stands, energy sapped by the sun, Wednesdayites knew it would count for bugger all if they didn't find a way past their South Yorkshire neighbours.

Barnsley fail to clear the ball and it falls only to a Sheffield Wednesday midfielder granted a yard of space by a Tykes defence suddenly exhausted. "Dele-Bashiru," the commentary rolls as the maligned youngster takes a touch and thunders the ball side-foot into the instep of his veteran teammate, Lee Gregory. A touch, a twist, a turn, some space. A twist, a turn, some more. Wembley frozen, almost silent but for a heartbeat, Gregory looks inside and, with the world agog, lines up a cross with his weaker left foot.

"Is there time for a winner?"

FOREWORD
BY BARRY BANNAN

It's hard to put into words what Sheffield Wednesday's 2022/23 season means to me. When I first came to play for this club I didn't even expect to be here eight or nine years later. To be honest, I just expected to come and play a few years and move on, because that's just what happens in football these days. So for me to have been here so long, and to experience the highs and lows that I have – from our first Wembley trip, to the honour of being handed the captaincy, to being relegated to League One ... it had been a rollercoaster of emotions.

The relegation hurt me more than anything I have experienced in football. Being handed the armband for such a big club was such a massive thing for me, so to be part of the team that let this club down was something that stuck in my heart and in my head – right up until winning promotion back to the Championship at Wembley. All that emotion, that hurt that I had felt up until that point, all came out under the arch that day. It wasn't just getting promoted to the Championship; it was much more than that for me. It was something that I felt I had to put right. It was personal.

On the pitch after the game, there was a huge sense of relief, but all the negative things that had been said, about us as a team and me personally, also came back to me. You remember when people wrote you off, the things they've said on social media that they think you don't see. In that moment you can take it in and say: 'Yes, we've proved the doubters wrong'. Emotion takes over, you think of your family in the crowd, and I think I might have still been on the pitch now if big Dom Iorfa hadn't come over and picked me up off the turf! It was time to reflect on what happened, because I couldn't believe it – over the last few years it felt like we were not meant to do that sort of thing. I've seen other teams do things like that, but in my experience with Wednesday it always seemed to be us conceding those goals, or trying – and failing – to hang on.

But this team was different. We went behind quite a lot and came back because the mentality was just so much stronger. I think it's what got us over the line in the end. My seasons before at Wednesday hadn't been what I'd wanted them to be. In many ways they were a failure really because we're a big club who are expected to win games and get promotions. That season was about putting all that behind us and showing everybody that this group of boys had got the mentality to go on and win things. I had my own vendetta and I'd built it up in my head as a revenge mission, but you can't do it on your own and everybody needs to buy into it. And we can take all that forward now.

When you're on a 23-game unbeaten run, you don't need to think too much because it just happens and happens, but when you suffer adversity, that's when you see the real side of people. When we came out the other end of our bad slump, that's when I knew that there was something special about this team. You can only be as good as the people around you and even after we had the run when we didn't win any games, we still managed to finish the season well. Even though we didn't make automatic promotion, I'd seen that we had the fight and the mentality to go strongly into the play-offs.

It wasn't just the players, though. Turning up to Middlewood Road towards the end of the season, it was in the staff members, too; the media team, the catering staff, the security staff, everyone. They all wanted it so badly. Everybody at the training ground was relying on us, so they were spurring us on as well. I think about 90 per cent of the people here – which I've only discovered over time – are Wednesdayites. It's not just a job; they actually support the club. They're not only colleagues, they are fans and our friends. Connecting the way that we did in the last couple of years, we've become so close, so a defeat becomes a case of letting everyone down. When you do well, they're all buzzing. Everyone was in it together.

It would've been easy to throw in the towel and say that it was done when it went out of our hands, but I'm always one to never admit it's over until it's over. Even at Shrewsbury, when we needed people to drop points that day, I was adamant that somebody was going to score and keep us in the hunt. It never happened, of course, but regardless I wanted us to make sure we were in the best possible position for the play-offs.

Winning at Wembley was the best moment of my life in football. That day you could see what the fans mean to us as players and what this club means to me since I've come here. They've been great to me and I've loved every minute. I'd always said I wanted to get the club back where we belong. And at the party afterwards it was obvious that it was a real collective – the whole club, everyone. We all want to be at higher levels, not just us out on the pitch, and it was that togetherness that got us what we wanted.

I think I was still replying to messages after the civic reception at the town hall a few days later when I was on my way to Dubai on holiday. Monday I couldn't go near my phone; on Tuesday I was hungover; Wednesday was the town hall; and on Thursday I was hungover again. On Friday I flew out and it was only once I was on holiday that I managed to finish getting back to people.

One thing that amazed me was that I was bumping into people on holiday who are Premier League players and they were all asking me what it had been like. So many people watched it and they were saying how much they couldn't believe what had happened against Peterborough and then at Wembley. The first thing they ask about is the semi-final and it's going to be that way for years to come – it's history. We'll get that when we're 50.

César Azpilicueta got talking to me – he'd watched it and said he'd never seen anything like it. I was turning to my wife and saying: 'This is a Champions League winner who's watched our games!' I think everybody who loves football will have been rooting for us because they like to see comebacks, but it was only when I was speaking to those sorts of people that I realised how big it all was. You don't think: 'What the hell have we just done?' until a bit down the line when you've got the Chelsea captain talking to you about it.

I remember thinking before Wembley that it might be my last chance to win something as a captain, to go into history for a club I love and will always come to support – if I'm not still working for them, of course! I knew if I could help to get us over that line, then I'd be remembered forever, so to win something as captain – especially with the way we did it – was incredible.

I've always touched on it, but the fans are the reason why this club is so good. You can get fans who hammer you, it happens everywhere, but the vast majority are unbelievable and for what they did for us, they're the real heroes. I know we went and did the job, but without them this club would be nothing. People come and sign here because they've been to Hillsborough or they've played in front of these fans and it leaves a mark. They're the thing you remember. As captain and on behalf of the players, I'd like to take this opportunity to thank them personally – especially the ones reading this book. They're the ones who got us across the line when we needed them the most and they can keep doing that for us going forward.

Watching that chance that Barnsley had late in the game, I could see what was happening and could sense how it was going to play out. I knew I couldn't get back in time. When he missed, it was as if we'd scored. But even if he hadn't, then I think we'd have got a goal anyway. After what happened in the semi-final, it really felt as if we were destined to win that game. To turn that around in the way that we had, we were never going to be denied... because there's always time for a winner.

Enjoy the book. WAWAW?

Barry Bannan, 2023

ONE

THE MAKING OF THE MAN

Darren Moore looked out over Sheffield Wednesday's Middlewood Road training complex from the window of his office – his hands on his hips, wide of chest, eyes looking out onto his new manor. It was March 1, 2020, and in Wednesday he had taken over a club in relegation freefall. After a second-half capitulation two days earlier had seen them go from 2-0 up to lose 3-2 at Luton Town, the Owls were drowning in the Championship danger zone. Wednesday were six points off safety and had lost their last four matches. They were fighting relegation with a points deduction that had been cut from 12 to six in November – the club still argue it should have been eradicated altogether – and with players who, frankly, looked exhausted and at several stages devoid of scrap. As rebuilding jobs go in football, it was up there.

One of Moore's first engagements had been to call their talismanic club captain Barry Bannan in for a one-to-one meeting in an attempt to scratch the surface of what change was needed. Moore was told the team had lost its way – not news, you'd have thought, to a manager who had been stationed only half an hour or so away at Doncaster Rovers – and that for years they had lacked any tangible playing style or identity. Moore's first media engagement was positive and engaging and while there was no sense of resignation with regard to their relegation battle, the general theme hinted at the bigger picture. It's not hyperbole to suggest that there was a soul of a football club to resuscitate.

Just five matches into Moore's reign, he too fell to ill-health. He'd caught the Covid-19 virus that had left terraces cold and barren for over a year, depriving Wednesday's already point-shorn relegation scrap of vital cashflow streams and its passionate fanbase. Returning after three matches to the touchline for a bitterly cold 2-0 home defeat to Swansea City, he fell into complications. Remarkably, for a player of such a long and successful playing career, Moore is a relatively-severe asthmatic, a status that put him in an at-risk category. With that firmly in mind, Rovers circulated quotes at the outset of the pandemic making clear that their then-manager was especially mindful of the coronavirus' growing risk. It proved prophetic.

Two days on from the Swans defeat he woke struggling to breathe, his body under attack. He contracted pneumonia, pleurisy and blood clots on his lungs. Moore spent time in an intensive care unit fearing he might die, his terrified family unable to visit him, desperately leaning on his faith for support and guidance. For four hours, three cardiac nurses stood over his body and there were 48 hours in which his survival was far from guaranteed. Speaking in a candid and emotional interview months later, Moore remembered his mum being "in bits," his 11-year-old daughter "petrified."

A strong man in body and mind, he recovered. Going against medical advice, he stepped back onto the touchline at Derby County for Wednesday's last match of the 2020/21 season in which any one of the bottom four teams – Wycombe Wanderers, Rotherham United and Derby themselves – could have gone down. Numerical gymnastics flooded the afternoon as goals flew in in all three matches. Wednesday rose out of the bottom three for the first time in months only for a matter of seconds, before a Martyn Waghorn penalty shunted them back. It was his double and a goal from on-loan Manchester City man Patrick Roberts that cancelled-out the efforts of Sam Hutchinson, Callum Paterson and Julian Börner. Wednesday drew 3-3, Derby stayed up and the Owls finished bottom of the table to become a League One club. A win – even one more goal – would have saved them.

The relegation battle had been a torrid time, with players paid late on several occasions as Covid, as it had so many others, tore through the fabric of the club. In the following months and years, players with relegation now etched into their CVs would be at pains to remind anyone listening that they had been relegated by virtue of their points deduction – an extra six would have had them safe.

Moore faced the music of the media in the moments after relegation was confirmed, clearly still gravely unwell, exhausted, at times short of breath. He had lost weight, his face gaunt. He was a husk of the strapping former Premier League captain known to the world, a fitting human reflection of the institution he was in charge of repairing. "The hard work starts now," he said in his closing gambit, before trudging away down the Pride Park tunnel to the galling strains of Derby supporters celebrating in the car park outside.

Who knows what Moore thought of when looking out of that Middlewood Road window at the outset of his Hillsborough journey? Perhaps he was thinking tactical thoughts, considering the best way to use Bannan, Josh Windass, Adam Reach. Perhaps he was thinking of his move from his place in Boughtree to Sheffield – without his family – a move he said he wanted to make in order to get a better sense for the feel of the city and the fanbase. Perhaps he stood there, 46 years of age, thinking about the life that had led him to this club, this office, this window.

Although always a generous interviewee, Moore is a private, humble figure, often coming across a little uncomfortable when asked questions designed to scratch the surface of Moore the man. For such a high-profile football figure, it's a life the general public know little about.

***

Darren Moore was born on April 22, 1974 as the fourth of six children in a fiercely tight-knit Caribbean family. The Moore family lived in Handsworth, a working class area of inner-city Birmingham set between the stadiums of West Bromwich Albion to the west and Aston Villa to the east. An area rich in the sights, sounds and community of genuine cultural diversity, Handsworth is home to a vast community of Caribbean descent having played host to the immigrants that were welcomed in the post-war effort. In the following decades and alongside people from across the world, particularly South Asia, Caribbean workers were recruited directly from the West Indies to work in the city's munitions factories, foundries and car plants. It's an area rich in culture and served to provide the streets walked on in the early years of great artists, performers and thinkers, from Joan Armatrading to Benjamin Zephaniah and Jamelia, from Steve Winwood to Tony Iommi.

It's an area not without its challenges. For many people of a certain age, mention of Handsworth conjures images of bitter 1981 riots that took place alongside widespread unrest in a number of areas – including Toxteth in Liverpool, Chapeltown in Leeds and Brixton in London – largely in response to the "stop and search" policies in the early years of Margaret Thatcher's government that saw police target and marginalise young, black men. Further riots took place in the area in 1985, 1991, 2005 and 2011. Great work and investment has been undertaken in recent years to lift the profile of the area. It remains a proud and dynamic community.

It doesn't take too much of a leap to suggest that it is on those streets that much of Moore's personality traits were born. In a rare interview touching on such personal themes in the wake of the 2022/23 season, he described a tight-knit town united in struggle, success and empathy. He spoke of a real sense of righteousness, of genuine community and of against-all-odds mentality and spirit.

Christianity was there in his up-bringing as a child but was not necessarily a huge driver for him personally – he would find a true connection with God and faith later in life. As a young boy of athleticism, competitive instinct and single-figure age, his driver was sport. But not necessarily the sport you'd think. If you were a young man growing up in a UK West Indian community in the early 1980s, there's a strong chance your heroes were not called Robson, Keegan, Sansom or Hoddle. It was more likely Lloyd, Holding, Marshall. It could have been Haynes, Greenidge, Roberts. The West Indian cricket team of the time is still regarded as one of the greatest of all-time and it was that team that took Darren Moore's affections. That was until one afternoon when his dad called him into the lounge from a knockabout cricket match on their street. West Brom, a club whose Hawthorns ground proudly stood no more than two miles down the road, were playing on the television.

"It looked to me like the pitch was a stage and the players were performing on this stage," Moore said four decades on with a quiver of wonder in his recollection of the memory. "It was like theatre. I said to my dad: 'I'm going to do that.' It was the team that had Cyrille Regis, Brendan Batson and Lawrie Cunningham. My dad was so interested in them because we were relating to the three black players on the pitch at the time. He wanted me to see it. He spoke to me about the three black players. I wanted to be them. I must have been eight or nine. That has lived with me since then.

"It inspired me. From then, the cricket bat went down and the football came out. From then, it was just football, football, football. I had a real desire to play to the best of my ability for my school team and from there I went into my local team and then into the district. I was gravitating upwards in football because I had a vision in my head of that game that my dad had shown me."

His interest in other sports would remain. Blessed with natural talent, an early eye for tactical advantage and huge physical attributes, he could turn his hand to cricket, rugby and basketball. He'd develop a huge interest in boxing and American football. But it was football, proper football, that had his heart after watching Regis, Batson and Cunningham do their thing. Football, to a young Darren Moore kicking a ball around in the railway arches leading into New Street station, was everything.

From James Watt Primary School, he graduated to Holyhead Secondary, where West Brom would often train on their all-weather training facility. Moore would pass up on lunch to sit in the cold, watching the likes of Don Goodman going through their preparations and making mental notes of what he could work on when he got home to his football that evening. The school would offer up free tickets as part of their agreement with the club and he became a West Brom fan. On weeks the Baggies played away, he would head to Villa Park and marvel at the talents of Paul McGrath; he, too, a centre-half of enormous ability.

Growing into his teenage years and much to his frustration, he was ignored by West Midlands academies, but did find himself of interest to an EFL club who had achieved great success in hoovering up overlooked talent from the region. It was over three hours and nearly 200 miles away. It was third tier Torquay United, who had taken the likes of Lee Sharpe on a Youth Training Scheme and sold him soon afterwards for a record fee to Manchester United.

Moore made the move south a couple of months after turning 16. The following March, aged 17 and quietly going about his business doing jobs ahead of an evening match, he was called into the office of Yugoslavian manager Ivan Golac – they're ahead of their time down there – thinking he was in trouble. Future Leicester City and Scotland defender Matt Elliott had gone down injured and, with an hour's notice, Moore would start at the heart of defence. Ironically, the match was against Birmingham City. He was praised for his calmness and tenacity by reporters who, just a couple of hours earlier, had been scrambling trying to find out who the hell he was. Only a last-minute goalkeeping error cost Torquay a point in Darren Moore's debut outing.

On a personal level, the move south was a challenging switch that again tested the depth of character in a young Moore. He was a tall but gangly figure, some way removed from the barrel-chested man mountain that would grace the Premier League and international football in the coming years. One person who spent time around the club describes a youngster many didn't necessarily think would make it, an "awkward player not always in control of his arms and legs. Put it this way, he didn't catch the eye." Those within the club, however, saw something deeper. They saw a steely determination and will to succeed, the green shoots of a professionalism that would see him become a captain, coach and manager later in life.

Neil Warnock was the man to bring him in as a first-team regular, when he arrived on an ultimately successful relegation rescue mission in March 1993, a year on from that whirlwind debut. When Moore won the club's young player of the year award later that year, Warnock demanded he make the awards speech himself, such was the regard he held him in. A year on, a 20-year-old Moore was controversially sent-off in a 1994 play-off semi-final tie at Preston North End, swinging his arm at Paul Raynor, missing by a foot and watching on in horror as the burly midfielder went down like the proverbial sack of potatoes. A red card was shown and Torquay lost 4-1, surrendering a 2-0 first-leg lead and crashing out. Asked about the incident by Wednesday-nosed journalists nearly three decades on, it was clear it had left scars. For many years it would be the joint-heaviest first-leg lead ever overcome in the play-off format; 29 years, in fact.

In these early days of senior exposure, a chant that would follow him throughout much of his playing career emanated from the terraces. Frank Bruno was in the latter stages of his glittering heavyweight boxing career and was a black man, large enough for Torquay fans to launch into chants of "Bruno, Bruno" in appreciation of a successful Moore header or block. It was a chant Moore didn't revile at – he loved his time at the club and shared a hugely positive relationship with Seagulls supporters who meant no harm – but it's fair to say he didn't like it at all. The generous way to put it is perhaps that it was a chant "of the time."

Moore left Plainmoor for his first move to South Yorkshire in 1995, earning Torquay a fee of £62,500 from Doncaster Rovers. He took with him more than a start in professional football, but a start in life. He'd fallen in love with a Paignton girl who would later become Angela Moore and the pair remain steadfast. He made firm friends with fellow players Paul Hall, who would go on to play for the likes of Portsmouth and briefly on loan for Sheffield United, and future Hull City and Notts County man Duane Darby, the latter who joined him in the Doncaster move. The trio share an active WhatsApp group to this day. It was at Torquay that Darren Moore, literally and figuratively, went from boy to man.

Moore's playing career was up and underway. Filled out to a frightening six-foot-plenty and suitably fearsome in his approach, he was no-nonsense, aggressive and played with a fierce determination. He was no sprint champion in his younger years but read the game seconds ahead of his opponents. Even in his early twenties he began to exude leadership skills and at Belle Vue, pulled a captain's armband over his bulging bicep for the first time. It was a difficult period for the club – Doncaster's owner Kevin Richardson was facing charges that he'd deliberately burnt down a stand and it was claimed by manager Kerry Dixon that he was demanding he pick the team, too. Aged 25, Moore left for Bradford City, swapping the fourth tier for the second, for a healthy profit in June 1997.

A key part of a vast transfer investment aimed at achieving promotion to the Premier League, Moore found promotion and fan favourite status at Valley Parade. But most importantly – and most pertinently, in terms of the development of the human being that years later would stand at the window of his office looking out at Middlewood Road – it is where he truly connected with Christianity, thanks to a man he would later bring to Sheffield Wednesday. In a difficult first season in West Yorkshire, he found Wayne Jacobs. And then he found God.

"I always believed in the Lord, but I had in my head and my heart that playing football and serving the Lord was impossible to do," Moore, who car-shared with Jacobs to and from training, later said. "It was always one or the other. I thought that once I had decided to play football and become a professional, that that was it. Wayne Jacobs showed me that the Lord had a part to play in our everyday lives. We used to share conversations about scripture, words of the day. We'd share prayers in the car. What people don't realise is that at that time at Bradford, I was fearful of my ability to play at that level. I felt I was a League One or League Two player. To be in the Championship? Vying for a spot in the Premier League? Could I really do that?"

Moore felt he could discuss this crisis of confidence with Jacobs, who invited him to his house and to a 'Christians in Sport' meeting where he was met with a room of fellow pros at different stages of their career. The guest speaker for the evening was Graham Daniels, an ex-Cardiff City and Cambridge United player who would later become a director with the U's. Daniels quoted a line in the bible that altered everything: "God does not give us a spirit of fear, but of love and a sound mind." They were words that would change the course of Darren Moore's life.

"I remember thinking: 'Goodness, that's me.' I was full of fear," he reflected. "I'm six-foot-three, but I felt eight foot tall coming out of the meeting. We drew the next game 2-2 and we went on an incredible run from there, us growing as a group of boys. I put all that down and give all the glory to the Lord Jesus because I'm almost convinced, I'm assured that without him playing that part in my life and my career that it would have been impossible to achieve what I achieved that season."

Bradford were promoted that season and despite Moore playing 44 times as a key man in the side overseen by Paul Jewell – later one of his predecessors in the Wednesday hotseat – it became clear he wasn't seen as good enough to make the leap into the top tier. Jewell signed David Wetherall and though Moore stayed on until November, desperate to get a chance and prove himself, it wasn't to be. He'd move to Portsmouth in 1999 for £500,000.

"It was a gut-wrenching feeling. From my dad showing me that first game, I had a dream to play at the highest level the country had to offer," he said. "Once we had been promoted, I was one step away. It wasn't to be the case, it was snatched from me. It was there, I could touch it. It was hard, very hard. I held on at Bradford for months but wasn't given the opportunity. I felt like potentially my dream had gone. It was hard, but leaving was something I had to do."

Lesser men may have crumbled. But with a renewed faith behind him, he made a success of a feted spell at Pompey, in which time he made two appearances for Jamaica. He would go onto lead group meetings with a large group of fellow Christian colleagues, often just 20 minutes or so before matches. This was a practice common in the locker rooms of the US but in the rough and tumble of an English football changing room, it took a certain inner-confidence, now seen as typical of Moore, to put it into place. Through Moore's guidance Linvoy Primus, his roommate and centre-half partner at Pompey, went through a similar journey of religious discovery to Moore's through Jacobs. It's something Moore takes great pride in. He was a million miles from the nervous and self-doubting player that had confided in Jacobs just a year or so earlier.

In press conferences years later as manager of Sheffield Wednesday, Moore would touch on matters around his faith sparingly, happy to discuss its impact on him though not quite in the depth of detail laid out in this chapter. In his highest and in his lowest moments at Wednesday – and there would be a few – it is his faith in God that he would lean on. The sense is that the faith gives him a calmness and clarity to his work and delivers a humbleness rare in the game. His favourite passage of the bible is Psalm 91:1-2: "Those who go to God Most High for safety will be protected by the Almighty. I will say to the Lord: 'You are my place of safety and protection. You are my God and I trust you.'"

Moore's tag as "the nicest man in football" is one sometimes used as a criticism by those who take up the notion that niceness can't succeed in such a cut-throat industry. With a glowing playing career and burgeoning reputation as a manager, he was busily going about disproving it. It should be said that there is a rarely-seen edge to Moore – albeit a soft one – and that behind the scenes he can delve into fury when the time is right. Wednesday players still remember a 5-0 defeat at Sunderland in January 2022 as an evening that saw Mr Nice Guy blow the doors off the changing room with an angry post-match summation.

It was in the early stages of Moore's third season at Portsmouth that the dream ticket landed. Gary Megson – another one-day Owls predecessor – lifted the phone to offer him the chance to step into the footsteps of the men that made him lay down the cricket bat as a young boy in awe. Nearly two decades on from the wide-eyed discovery of Messrs Regis, Batson and Cunningham, Darren Moore would sign for West

Bromwich Albion as a 27-year-old in September 2001. What's more, he'd all but secure promotion to the Premier League and his status as a top flight player in the penultimate match of the season. Moore was outstanding in securing a clean sheet in a 1-0 win at, of all places, Bradford City.

His career from there is well-documented. He became a feared Premier League and second-tier opponent that would bounce between the top two divisions with the boing-boing Baggies, where he featured in five seasons, and later three with Derby County. He'd become a legend at the Hawthorns, so much so that a visit with the Rams saw West Brom supporters sing his name before the match had even kicked off. Having grown up a couple of miles from the ground, it was a moment that he felt had seen him come full circle. He had family and friends in the crowd. Locked with emotion, he prayed.

He'd return to South Yorkshire – not for the last time – for a two-season stint at Barnsley before enjoying a swansong sojourn at Burton Albion, leaving in February 2012. Offers from Mansfield Town, Telford and Tamworth were tabled, but he chose to retire aside from a single appearance for Wellington Amateurs, in a semi-final played as a favour to their manager, a friend he had played with when they were children. They won. Moore later joked he had needed to take "several paracetamol" after the match, such were the signs from his body that it was time to hang up his boots for good. He left behind a career of nearly 650 professional appearances.

What next, then, for Moore? A good talker, he toyed with media appearances, taking the mic as a summariser on Barnsley with *BBC Radio Sheffield*. His philanthropy was something he would take great pride in, later walking the Great Wall of China with his great pal Primus to raise money for children's causes. He has raised thousands of pounds for Christian Aid and Oxfam and worked as an ambassador for West-Midlands based Inspire Afrika. He found joy in cycling, taking on a 100-mile ride around the Midlands for a leukaemia charity alongside his former West Brom teammate Ben Foster, and became an ambassador for the Kaleidoscope Plus Group, who champion mental health and wellbeing. With roles at the Professional Footballers' Association, becoming a champion for Kick It Out and other anti-racism programmes as well, he was a busy man.

But it was in coaching that he would re-launch his career, heading back to West Brom as a professional development coach in the summer of 2012, soon after his retirement as a player. Coaching is something that had always intrigued him and towards the end of his career Moore found himself paying close attention to team meetings and tactical sessions that he wasn't even directly involved with, desperately soaking up every drop of information he could glean from a wide range of managers. He'd near-completed his badges while still a player at Barnsley, two years ahead of his decision to knock playing on the head.

A brief time at Blackburn Rovers on the coaching staff of Michael Appleton came and went before West Brom again opened their doors in September 2014. From there he never looked back, building a steadfast relationship with future Owls colleagues in Jimmy Shan and Jamie Smith and sharing a bond that was as tight as you'll see in football. He'd later describe his relationship with Smith as "almost telepathic," one often looking over during matches to offer a suggestion that had already entered the other's head.

"He's my right hand, isn't he?" Moore would later say. "We've both had the same coaching background, we've both watched and helped each other develop through the academy at West Brom. He's hardworking and he's a wonderful personality that the players respect and get on with. First and foremost he's a top, top coach, a really good coach who loves his time on the grass. I often say, if you could push his bed on the middle of the pitch, he'd sleep there. He just loves it and that's him.

"He's very switched-on and I think it works because we've both had a similar coaching background at our previous club. We think the same and we see the game in a certain way. We can see things and challenge each other, respectfully, but we challenge each other on things we say and see. That's healthy, it's great for us as individuals and coaches."

Rising through the academy system and twinning coaching jobs with a three-year stint as the club's loans manager, among other roles, Moore saw different sides to the backroom of a football club, working and developing countless players who, if not at the Hawthorns, made it at different EFL clubs alongside the likes of Shan and Smith. His talent was rewarded in what had long since felt a natural progression in 2017, when he was elevated to the first-team coaching staff under Alan Pardew. A year later, he'd be in the top job as caretaker boss in what was an impossible task, with the Baggies cut well adrift at the bottom of the Premier League. He'd enjoy success against all odds, embarking on a five-match unbeaten run, winning at Old Trafford and at St James' Park while earning home draws against Tottenham Hotspur and Liverpool. He'd get the job full-time but was cruelly axed in March the following season with the club sat fourth in the Championship table. Amid a public pursuit of Alex Neil, Shan replaced him after Moore gave him his blessing. Moore left with a win percentage of 47.9 per cent, West Brom finished fourth and rivals Aston Villa went up through the play-offs.

In a rare display of ruefulness, he'd later say: "I thought to myself that the club was going to appoint someone with wealth and experience to get them over the line, but because they didn't do that I think they should have just left me in place to get on with it. It didn't finish the way it should have done that season and decisions at the top proved it was the wrong decision at the time."

All roads were leading to South Yorkshire once more. Wasting no time, he'd take up the Doncaster Rovers job vacated by Grant McCann in July 2019 and on a modest budget would take Rovers to a ninth-place finish in a season cut short and decided by a points-per-game model in the first months of the Covid-19 pandemic he would later fall into a very personal battle with. The following season he had them battling towards the top of the table at Christmas. Interest from Sheffield Wednesday after the sacking of his former West Brom colleague Tony Pulis was first reported in January 2021.

Moore made clear to friends he had been flattered by reports of interest from Wednesday but played down the likelihood of the move coming to fruition. Under caretaker boss Neil Thompson the Owls were battling hard against relegation from the Championship under impossible circumstances. But as Wednesday's fortunes downturned and the likelihood of relegation spiked, their interest became clear to Moore on Friday, February 7, 2021. It was the day before Thompson's final match as stand-in, that 3-2 defeat at Luton Town.

Doncaster lost 2-1 at Ipswich Town that day and some present recall a sense of distraction from Moore, understandable given the now-clear circumstances. Moore had asked Rovers for permission to speak to Wednesday and was told in no uncertain terms that while they could do little to stop him, there would be no way back should he decide to go ahead.

The lure of Wednesday was too much. By Monday, he was stood looking out of the window of his new office. He'd been led there by Handsworth, Cyrille Regis, play-off red cards, Wayne Jacobs, Premier League snubs, Portsmouth, West Brom and Derby. There'd been coaching joy and coaching heartbreak, God and Doncaster.

Middlewood Road was his new place of work.

TWO

NOT QUICKLY ENOUGH

Ahush of despair around Hillsborough. Shell-shock. The sound only of jubilant Sunderland fans in the top of the Leppings Lane End and the untamed celebration of their manager Alex Neil from the opposition technical area. Veins bulged from his neck as he clenched both fists, elbows at his hips, his North Lanarkshire roar bursting into the south stand without apology. In the home dugout? Pained, gut-punch dejection and little movement apart from a water bottle thrown in disgust from the bench. Neil's was a roar that consigned Sheffield Wednesday to another season in League One.

When Lee Gregory had directed Marvin Johnson's cross home 19 minutes earlier, it had felt as though it would be Sheffield Wednesday that would go on to Wembley for a League One play-off final match-up against Wycombe Wanderers. One goal down from a laboured first leg at the Stadium of Light, Wednesday had clawed and scrapped their way to parity. With the Hillsborough crowd alive and with momentum seemingly edging one way, it was the Owls that had the game in their grip.

But this was Wednesday. And it was the 93rd minute. And as former Owl Danny Batth – a player who had come close to returning to Hillsborough just a few months earlier – launched a ball over the top to lively winger Jack Clarke, there seemed to be too much space to work with. Mid-season signing Nathaniel Mendez-Laing failed to track back, leaving Jordan Storey exposed. Patrick Roberts got the run on a flat-footed Liam Palmer. Clarke crossed, Roberts scored. Sunderland led 2-1 on aggregate with seconds to play. For all their rising from a summer of madness, for all the building of their form towards the end of the 2021/22 campaign, Wednesday were done. Wednesday had failed.

That their gut-punch concession was down to individual lapses in concentration, that it had come late and that it had passed-up a lead, was no shock. These were themes returned to time and again throughout the analysis of Wednesday's shortcomings and though fightback wins had returned – their 3-1 win at struggling Doncaster Rovers was their first victory from behind in six long years and was followed by similar tricks against Cheltenham Town and on the last day against Portsmouth – there was no doubt that these frailties had cost them a sustained tilt at automatic promotion.

The play-off bout with Sunderland had been a tight and edgy two-legged affair, far removed from the 3-0 Wednesday win at Hillsborough and a 5-0 night of terrors at the Stadium of Light earlier that season. The first play-off leg in the north-east saw the Owls forced back with Clarke and Roberts finding joy out wide, a theme that would repeat at Hillsborough. Much was made of Darren Moore's decision to select Liam Palmer ahead of Jack Hunt on the right, in what was perceived as a negative move and restricted their ability to break from the Black Cats' claws.

To come away with a one-goal deficit from that chastening evening was seen as something of a result for Wednesday, especially given that their home form was the best in League One – Sunderland were second – and had seen them lose only twice at Hillsborough in the season proper. A points-per-game ratio of 2.3 at S6 breathed confidence that Wednesday could overcome the first-leg deficit and book their ticket to the Big Smoke. Though it was a tight, three-day turnaround, it also gave more opportunity for Barry Bannan and Josh Windass to better recover from injuries that had clearly hampered them up north.

That their two most effective attacking players were playing all-but-crocked at the most important stage of the season felt typical of Wednesday's recent luck. It came in differing circumstances; Windass had been able to play only 368 minutes of football all season, having had to undertake surgery on a hamstring injury sustained at West Brom in pre-season. Bannan, a near-ever-present, had gone down late in that final game against Pompey and trudging from the Hillsborough pitch, wore a look of ashen realisation that this was a seismic moment – not only in his personal promotion ambitions, but those of the club as well.

That the deciding goal in the Sunderland second leg came as it did

– with 93 minutes on the clock – was no surprise. That Roberts was one of the men to enact the misery, having scored the Derby County goal that sent Wednesday down a year earlier, less so. These acts of unimaginable cruelty just seem to happen to that football club. It was the Wednesday Way. Painful though it was to witness, the strides taken by the club in 12 months or so had been inarguable.

***

After relegation, the clamour for change had been immediate. But one certainty, in the hours after the final whistle at Pride Park, was that Moore would be the man tasked with leading Wednesday's resurgence. He'd been brought in with one eye on the possibility of his League One experience being needed and within hours of relegation being confirmed, Dejphon Chansiri backed him publicly in an official club statement. The Wednesday chairman also said that he took "full responsibility" for everything that happens at the club, apologising to the fans for what they'd seen play out over the course of the 2020/21 campaign. The focus now, he said, was about moving forward.

"We must pick ourselves up from the floor and move forward in a positive way," Chansiri said. "We have had plans for both scenarios and now our immediate future is clear, we can start to put those plans into place. I can pledge that as chairman, I will give everything I can and offer as much support as possible to everyone as we try and achieve promotion at the first attempt. There are issues we must address in the short and long term and some things will not happen overnight."

Within two weeks the retained list was confirmed and no fewer than 10 senior players were to be released over the summer, a number of whom had played their part in those two unsuccessful play-off attempts a few years before. There would be no sentiment. Moore continued a post-Wembley '16 clearout that Garry Monk had started, and in turn saw the club's wage bill fall off a cliff. In total 14 players would leave before Wednesday's stint in the third tier began, including several who had cost the club a substantial amount in transfer fees and wages over the years and moved on for nothing. Between Jordan Rhodes, Adam Reach and Joost van Aken alone there was a reported £16m in transfer fees forked out.

In an interview in mid-May, in his office at Middlewood Road, the

Owls boss was looking more like himself, fuller of face and with an infectious enthusiasm at the prospect of what he called a "rebuild" at S6. He spoke of implementing a style that would start at academy level, his excitement to see Hillsborough full for the first time, and a need to "come together as one." Look forward, not backwards, he said. Not everyone was convinced.

In a candid interview with *BBC Scotland* during the European Championships in 2021, fresh from relegation and with Wednesday under a transfer embargo for the late filing of their accounts, captain Bannan admitted: "It's been tough. Last year was a hard year, we had a points deduction so we were on the back foot straight away and we ended up getting relegated – which is never great at any part of your career, especially when you're a bit older as well... It's a bit up in the air at the minute, there's a lot of people leaving behind the scenes and stuff, so it's not a great place to be – but once I get back in and have talks, we'll find out what I'm going to be doing next season."

It was a position Wednesday would recover from. With news of the embargo having been lifted arriving as football fans up and down the country sang the national anthem ahead of England's Euros semi-final win over Denmark on July 7, the Owls went to work. The new faces to survive through to the 2022/23 season included a bulk of the squad; free agent former Fulham and Everton youngster Dennis Adeniran, released Huddersfield Town bit-part Jaden Brown and a very familiar face in Hunt, who returned to S6 after three seasons at Bristol City. With the deal done, Hunt phoned his wife Cara and told her in an emotional call: "We are going home. To Hillsborough." Moore also persuaded Swansea City's George Byers, Marvin Johnson – a free agent having left Middlesbrough – and Stoke City forward Lee Gregory to drop down into the third tier.

With the likes of Moore's big-name former West Brom charge Saido Berahino – he who had once commanded a £20m bid from Tottenham Hotspur and was being talked up for England recognition – alongside mysterious Dutch attacker Sylla Sow from RKC Waalwijk and Everton loanee Lewis Gibson, the squad looked strong and with no transfer fees shelled-out, had been put together on a wage budget of £10.9m – an encouragingly sharp drop on the £21.1m spent in 2020/21 relegation campaign. January loanees Harlee Dean and Storey would arrive to strengthen an injury-torn defence as well as the Owls' promotion credentials. Arsenal youngster Tyreece John-Jules played only 18 minutes for Wednesday before the injury curse struck. All would come and go, leaving with a mixed bag of report cards.

There were bumps in the road, obviously, with Paul Williams leaving his role as first team coach, a Julian Börner saga that would eventually see him return to Germany with Hannover 96, and that serious hamstring injury that ultimately kept Windass out for around four months. It would prove to be a pivotal moment in his Owls career as he ended up signing a new contract the following month. Not many realised at the time how important that particular signature would prove to be in Wednesday's mission to get back into the Championship. Liam Palmer and Dominic Iorfa would also pen new deals, with Bannan having done so as recently as the previous February.

The hole that Williams' departure had created was filled by former Queens Park Rangers and Nottingham Forest coach Simon Ireland, to be put in charge of set pieces among other things, in early August while Moore's confidant Wayne Jacobs was called to offer his services in and around the camp. Adriano Basso had joined as goalkeeper coach. Liam Dooley, promoted to the role in May, was continuing his work as chief operating officer alongside Chansiri and general manager Alastair Wilson. A lucrative, long-term kit deal was signed with Macron, season ticket sales were up on the days before Covid and hospitality boxes were selling better than before, too. Hard work from dugout to training pitch, from recruitment room to boardroom, was laying foundations for success, it seemed.

A whistling start to the season saw Wednesday continue their off-field momentum and go top of the table in August, but proved all too fleeting. They conceded late to draw at Ipswich and to lose at home to Oxford. Late concessions in draws at AFC Wimbledon, at home to Lincoln and away at Cheltenham Town came within a fortnight and in an unbeaten run of 11 league matches, of which they drew seven. In away matches only four teams – AFC Wimbledon, Gillingham, Ipswich and Fleetwood – conceded more goals from the 81st minute onwards than Wednesday's eight. Doncaster – relegated alongside Gillingham and AFC Wimbledon – had the same tally as the Owls. A failure to defend set pieces was apparent as they shipped 19 – the fourth-worst tally in the division that contributed 38 per cent of their 50 goals conceded, the highest ratio in the league. Individual errors were bemoaned constantly.

For all the quality in the Owls squad, it all pointed towards a soft underbelly and it was those clutch statistics that laid bare the reasons behind their failure to sustain a tilt at the automatic promotion places. They faced immense adversity, a Covid outbreak that served to further squeeze an already congested fixture schedule, the absence of their manager in January after another, albeit far less serious, personal scrape with the virus, and injuries. There were lots of injuries.

When Adeniran succumbed to a hamstring issue in a miserable, rain-drenched 3-0 FA Cup defeat at Plymouth in November, he joined Johnson, Sam Hutchinson, Iorfa, Windass, Gibson and Gregory on the medic's table and left a crestfallen Moore describing an injury crisis unlike any he had seen in 30 years in football. Moore would embark upon an investigation into the causes of injury concerns that had plagued Wednesday for years, making tweaks to training routines, bringing in sports scientist Rob Lee and introducing yoga to life at Middlewood Road in an attempt to stem the flow.

"It's a concern and something we need to look into," he said. "We can't allow it to keep happening. Today was a bridge too far in terms of the players at our disposal. The bigger concern for me is getting a couple of players back and making sure we keep them back. That has to be the procedure now." Chey Dunkley, Mendez-Laing, Shodipo, Dean, Byers and Storey would also be faced with weeks at a time out across the course of the season.

All that said, the season was a long way from joyless. Though the stretch for automatic places eventually secured by Wigan Athletic and Rotherham United were never truly in reach beyond those first sunny weeks – the Owls fell five points short despite faltering late-season form from the promotion pair – a fourth-placed finish was brought about by exceptional post-January form. Wednesday lost only three times from that late defeat at Oxford on January 22, winning 14 of their last 20 matches and scaling the top of the league's form tables. They hammered Cambridge United 6-0, put five past Burton Albion and four past Plymouth and Cheltenham as they built an enviable home record at Hillsborough.

Recovering lost ground, a classy win at third-placed MK Dons saw 5,600 travelling Wednesdayites witness one of the greatest goals in the club's history when Bannan lobbed Jamie Cumming from 40 yards. They conceded late, obviously, in a 3-2 win. It left them seven points back with four to play and though that late dart at the top spots was effectively ended with defeat at Wycombe Wanderers leaving two to play, a comeback win at Fleetwood Town and a 4-1 last-day win over Portsmouth gave them sparkle and joie de vivre heading into the play-offs, despite concern after Bannan's late hamstring trouble. It's where they'd meet Sunderland.

**

The atmosphere was bubbling inside the Stadium of Light as almost 45,000 took to their seats, goosebumps raised as Elvis Presley's *Can't Help Falling In Love With You* burst from the crowd and a huge cat's eyes tifo spread out across the east stand. Between them, Sunderland and Sheffield Wednesday had 10 First Division titles between them, five FA Cups and two of the vastest fanbases in European football. And yet here they were, locked in a mission to climb out of the third tier; Sunderland at the fourth time of asking, Wednesday the first.

As expected, it was a cagey affair, Neil's side desperate to end their all-too-long stay in League One and the Owls looking to make sure they didn't end up with one of their own. The hosts were the better side and Wednesday, accused of being too cautious, never really got going as they seemingly sought to get the job done on home soil. It almost worked, but in first half stoppage time a mistake from Hutchinson let Ross Stewart in to top up their sky-stretching season tally of individual mistakes. He finished his chance at the second time of asking and as the whistle was blown on a fraught second half, it was advantage Black Cats.

Bannan had made it through 90 minutes in the first leg, but hadn't looked himself. Windass had come off the bench for the last half hour but looked a long way off the pace. The hope was that the three days before the decisive leg would do them good, with indications showing Windass would start as the Owls kicked open the doors of the last chance saloon.

At an apprehensive Hillsborough, Sunderland sought to slow the game down at every opportunity and largely kept Wednesday at arm's length. With Mendez-Laing and Callum Paterson stripped off and ready to come on, Moore was forced to change his mind after a collision that left Hutchinson bloodied and bruised – the player walking off the field a bandaged warrior, to the sound of four corners of the stadium singing his name, in what would be his last action in an Owls shirt. After 207 appearances for the club it was a very 'Sam Hutchinson' way to bow out, and a moment that further separated Wednesday's direction from the oh-so-nearly of 2016.

Time drifted away, chances few and far between, and then Bannan saw it. That pocket of space behind the defenders, the slightest of gaps that he had to find. Bannan slipped through to Johnson, Johnson centered for Gregory and in a breathless flurry, Wednesday were level. They had found a way and with 15 minutes left to go, it looked like they'd need half an hour more to settle this one. The fourth official held up his board – 10 minutes added.

It was still tight, but there was that growing sense that if a winner was to come, then it'd be the hosts that got it. They had the momentum, they had home advantage, but they also had left a gaping bit of space down their right hand side for Clarke to run into. He drove at Storey, 90+3 showing on the clock over his shoulder, and crossed into the six-yard box. Roberts' finish, Neil's roar. The net rippled and Sunderland had stolen the ticket to Wembley. As time would prove, injury time goals at the Leppings Lane end in a play-off semi-final are rarely forgettable.

The dissections would follow, questions again would be asked of Moore, his suitability for the job and his future at the club. Bannan, honest as always, admitted afterwards: "It is going in the right direction, but it is not going quick enough... We wanted to get promoted this season, but we failed. We have a big summer ahead now. We know we are not far away now and it is just about the right recruitment." He made clear he was going nowhere.

Moore, crestfallen, was going nowhere either, but many would be. "It's the end of a journey," he told his players in the changing room in a post-match debrief wrapped in emotion. The start of the next journey was just around the corner.

THREE

TRAMLINES ON TOUR

Browns Sports Resort is set in a sleepy and exclusive enclave in the hills above Vilamoura in Portugal, quietly separated from the unbuttoned linen shirts and yachts of the popular holiday destination by a 15-minute spaghetti of winding uphill roads and baking tarmac. Portuguese palm trees line streets of cracked pavement before the sort of property owned by middling 1980s pop stars whose skin has long since turned a rich mahogany. Sun-battered golfers take taxis to and from their accommodation in town, the grass lining the swimming pools is thick and the hiss of crickets provides a calming soundtrack. Think Ray Winstone's gaff in *Sexy Beast*, with significantly less swearing.

It is at Browns Sports Resort that Sheffield Wednesday's 2022/23 season truly got under way. As is standard procedure for professional football teams of a certain level, warm-weather training is the order of July and in sky-high temperatures Moore and his staff were handed the opportunity to work with their new squad non-stop and intensively, utilising the facilities available to them; including a small plunge pool, gym with boxing ring and punching bags, tennis courts and games rooms.

The bulk of the work took place on a small, but nicely-formed two-pitch facility set a short wander out from the centre of the resort. A water station and a run-of-the-mill B&Q canopy set-up provided players with a spot to take snap breaks in short, sharp sessions. An initial inspection of the playing surfaces on arrival ended with Moore speaking to resort staff to request that they were heavily watered before the next day's training. By the time they'd completed that first session, it was more of a demand.

The weather was hot, but the satisfaction of Wednesday players with regard to the facilities was a little lukewarm. The food was okay, but required something of an improvement after a couple of days and there were complaints that the air conditioning in their rooms was temperamental – a long way from ideal for professional athletes trying to recuperate after high-intensity sessions in incredible heat.

Set at the top of the facility at Browns is a dining-room adorned in framed shirts signed by the teams of several sports who have utilised it before, from Heineken Cup-winning rugby sides to the England cricket team. At meal times players sat across two large tables in groups, sharing jokes and grazing from a buffet-style table of lean meats and pasta salad. The food was replenished whenever the Wednesday manager noticed a buffet tray laid empty. Even in the comparatively stress-reduced confines of warm-up July, his eye was all-seeing.

Next door to the dining-room at Browns sat a heavily air-conditioned, darkened room that the Owls had decked out for team meetings and analysis. It was designed to double as a work base for the club's media team and two journalists lucky enough to have been invited, on Moore's say-so, to observe part of the week's training. On more than one occasion the media mob were greeted with polite smiles and invited to leave while Moore, Jamie Smith and his coaching team plotted the embryonic stages of promotion through laptops and projector screens. There was much work to do, it seemed.

Football as an entity has become more professional during the past couple of decades and the days of these trips being exercise-interrupted stag dos were left in the 1990s; players came and went from the bar area clutching bottled water while watching the British Open on TV. Popular goalkeeping coach Adriano Basso engaged Cameron Dawson in conversation over a cold beverage and two players chatted with journalists about the potential signing of Hull City forward Mallik Wilks, a transfer link reported in the local media a couple of weeks earlier. The mood in camp was relaxed, but while the players rehydrated themselves and recovered their bodies by the pool, the staff were hard at work analysing, analysing, then analysing the analysis. Barry Bannan commented on just how hard the backroom staff were working as Moore led them into yet another evening meeting.

Much of that work was spent watching video analysis of the sessions filmed on a drone operated by the club's head performance analyst Richard Stirrup, a former non-league player of some repute with

Stocksbridge Park Steels and Sheffield FC. Stirrup had first appeared at Middlewood Road as a youngster on a scholarship before heading to university, later returning to work his way through the Owls ranks behind the scenes. Alongside him was the baby-faced Liam Bracken, who cut his teeth in short spells at Sunderland and Sheffield United, then trod a similar path through roles in the Wednesday youth ranks and acted as Stirrup's partner-in-crime.

Wednesday shared use of Browns' football facilities for part of the week with Rochdale's youth side – although, as the senior patrons, they more or less had the run of the place – and the Lancashire youngsters completed the bulk of their work on a pitch set away from the area used as base camp by the Owls. What caught the attention of a few of the players a little more was the presence of heavyweight boxer Dillian Whyte, using the resort's gym facilities fresh from a sixth-round defeat to Tyson Fury in front of 94,000 fans – the largest attendance for any boxing match in the 21st century.

Whyte, a tentative Crystal Palace supporter of no huge passion, owned property in the area and double-taking Wednesday figures were told that he trained there regularly, in his own area of the gym, away from the more fleeting guests. A day or two into Wednesday's time at the facility, the man they call 'Body Snatcher' asked kitman Ash Holland whether he had any spare kit he could have as a memento. Footage of Whyte sparring in an Owls singlet later went viral on social media.

Wednesday's match programme for the week-long trip was carefully designed to test them immensely as they took a step up in volume both on the training ground and in match scenario, with fixtures against Championship side Middlesbrough and newly-promoted Premier League outfit Bournemouth a tough proposition no matter the friendly circumstances. In July 2022 the football world was still emerging from the clutches of the Covid-19 pandemic, as was Portugal itself; the public were instructed to wear face masks while using taxis and in many shops including chemists, where they were strictly compulsory by law.

That was partly the reason why matches were therefore scheduled to be played behind closed doors and in an effort to prevent vast crowds of dedicated Wednesday fans gathering at their training complex, Browns was not publicly named as the venue with all photographs and videos published during the week checked and double-checked for signage or revealing features. Hundreds of hardy Wednesdayites made the trip to Albufeira anyway in the hope that match details would be released late in the day. On the evenings of both matches rumours swarmed the holidaying fans and many arrived at incorrect venues. One or two groups who had collected correct information were turned away.

The Boro match was a particularly closely-guarded secret. Manager Chris Wilder – a die-hard Sheffield United fan and former Blades boss with no small history of needle in matches against Wednesday – arranged the match with his old Bradford City teammate Moore, but on the condition that no reporters were present and the match was treated as completely unofficial.

Huge efforts were made to keep the game hush-hush for a variety of reasons and it was suspected that Boro had some trialists on board whom they'd sooner keep away from the eyes of public consumption. It came as something of a surprise to Wednesday then when Middlesbrough's club website previewed the run-out in a piece containing approved Wilder quotes two days beforehand. The outing was spread across four 30-minute periods where subs came and went and a 1-0 win for the Championship side was described as unremarkable by one of those present. Footage of a raking Bannan pass was later leaked on social media. It's hard to keep secrets in football.

It was noticed in training sessions that a lot of work was put into the 'overloading' of areas of the pitch with carefully marked out sections of the training area signalling specific positions players should take up in opportune moments. Small-sided matches were designed to encourage playing out from the back – a tactic Moore had preferred throughout his time in management and for which Wednesday received some criticism from supporters the previous season. The message was clear: Wednesday would elect to play once more and Moore's coaching principles – far removed from his own past playing style some would describe as "rough and tumble" – would stay true.

Reasons for some of the intricacies of his set-up – his desperation for the in-possession balance of left-footed players playing on the left of a back-three saw winger Marvin Johnson employed there for much of the previous season, for example – were made clearer close-up and with the benefit of audible instruction in a training scenario.

At that point Moore was in the early stages of recovery from knee surgery, delayed on his orders so as not to take time away from his work and from a desire to press on in the transfer market early on in the summer. It had been noticed from early on in his Wednesday reign that he walked uncomfortably and it since became clear he had been in grave discomfort as the weight of his considerable frame took toll on his knees during a mammoth playing career. In pre-season back home a golf buggy was procured to assist his getting around and was fitted with a specialist licence plate reading 'GAFFER 1.' It wasn't long before some of the squad's cheekier personalities hijacked the cart and took it for a spin.

The Wednesday boss spent much of the Owls' training sessions in Portugal sitting in the shade and watching on as right-hand men Jamie Smith and Simon Ireland oversaw drills and barked orders at players. Anyone stumbling across the session unaware would have done well to pick Moore out as the main man as another coach, Wayne Jacobs, strolled between the drills to offer words of encouragement, lending a keen eye on quality of touches and speed of passes. In terms of dynamic there was one moment that stood out. A breakdown of an Ireland drill that some players appeared struggling to grasp flickered frustration from a couple of younger ones. Enter Moore. Struggling to his feet, his voice bellowed across the facility with an air of domination and every player stopped without skipping a beat. Silence. Message put across, the work improved. It was an impressive moment that showed his grip on the squad.

The night before journalists were welcomed into the inner-sanctum, Wednesday's players were allowed to drink in some of the local night-life – quite literally. The marina in Vilamoura is the largest in Portugal and is on the upmarket side of your regular Iberian holiday night out, with a few jolly Irish bars sprinkled among the swanky cocktail joints and restaurants designed not to embarrass clientele with boats bigger than your average Hillsborough home left floating on the water. Bannan later described these nights out as hugely important for team-building and welcoming new faces into the fold. Some drink and some are teetotal, but all are encouraged to get involved in the banter of a night on the town. The players headed out for a meal – paid for by Bannan – and the night was spent largely at a live music bar; a good time had by all. Michael Smith announced himself to his new teammates as good craic, holding court, as did David Stockdale.

The age-old football rite of passage of initiation was fulfilled when new signings were instructed to stand on a chair and sing to their new teammates, completely acapella. Seven new signings meant plenty of entertainment, to the point that the evening was later cheekily christened as 'Tramlines on Tour'.

Eye-witness reports signalled a sense that, while Simon Cowell should rest his head easily enough for fear of lost millions, the standard was more than reasonable. Stockdale belted out Bon Jovi's *Livin' on a Prayer* with a level of enthusiasm with which Wednesday fans would soon come to associate him and Reece James did his boy-band jawline justice with a rendition of Ben E. King's *Stand By Me* that had his new colleagues on their feet from his first dulcet note. Not for the last time that season, a half-injured Will Vaulks sang Robbie Williams and six-foot-six Ben Heneghan took on *Ain't No Mountain High Enough* – originally recorded by Marvin Gaye and Tammi Terrell – in a performance loosely awarded a silver medal behind James.

Heneghan was Wednesday's first signing of the summer, one that was met with a mixed reaction from Owls supporters not long since used to flashy, multi-million pound additions designed for Championship domination. A man mountain centre-half brought in to help solve a weakness at defending set-pieces and crosses that cost them a sustained tilt at automatic promotion the previous season, the former Everton and Stoke City youth product had battled his way back from non-league football with Chester to play starring roles in the colours of Motherwell, Blackpool and then AFC Wimbledon, a side relegated from League One a few weeks earlier.

No stranger to the city, Heneghan had previously played for Sheffield United, but found himself cut adrift by Wilder from the outset, used as a pawn at the centre of a transfer power wrangle between dug-out and boardroom. The fact is that Wilder never fancied him, but a then 23-year-old Heneghan was not given chance to prove himself in red and white and played a grand total of only 59 minutes for United in a cup match before he was shoved out on loan to Blackpool. It was felt by those close to the defender that the Blades' boss had cruelly and deliberately shunned him from the outset to show the bosses upstairs that, as far as the transfer market went, it was his way or nothing. His first Owls media engagement would come and go with Heneghan falling well short of saying he had anything to prove to the people of Sheffield although he did raise a smile when teed-up on which was the bigger Steel City football club. "Come on man," he said with a knowing smile. "There's no question."

Next to arrive – the next day, in fact – had been Stockdale. At 36 years of age and by his own admission bereft of the sort of six-pack footballers are meant to shovel under their shirts these days, the former Premier League goalkeeper was known as one of the game's true personalities, a whirlwind chatterbox with a wicked sense of humour. A joker off the pitch, his career to date had been anything but a joke as he gathered four promotions, a call-up by Fabio Capello to the England squad and hugely successful times at Fulham, Brighton & Hove Albion – where he had been the goalkeeper when Wednesday knocked them out of the Championship play-offs in 2016 – and more recently Wycombe Wanderers.

With academy graduate Joe Wildsmith having left the club for Derby County after 11 years at Middlewood Road, it became clear the veteran stopper would battle it out for the No.1 shirt with Cameron Dawson, recently returned from a promotion-winning loan spell with League Two runners-up Exeter City. Stockdale spoke of that battle and vowed to help to improve Dawson, a lifelong Wednesdayite 10 years his junior and not without his doubters after an up-and-down career with the Owls.

Coming to the end of his time with Wycombe, Stockdale had privately told those close to him that he felt he had one more EFL promotion left in him, one he almost achieved before falling at the final play-off hurdle in Wembley defeat to Sunderland. He had been training only twice a week with his former club, travelling back and forth to Buckinghamshire from Leeds under his great pal Gareth Ainsworth. He'd be 37 in September and backed his body to cope with the increased workload of a day-in, day-out programme. He faced question marks about his age on Twitter with a smile, posting images of zimmer frames and old-man emojis.

"The chance to play for a club as big as Wednesday, it was a bit of a no-brainer for me," Stockdale said at his unveiling. "When I knew it was settled, I spoke to the gaffer and it was a done deal. As soon as we had our little chat, it was dead on for me. The first thing I said to him was that I wasn't here to waste time: I'm here to win trophies. I spoke to the gaffer and I set it out – promotion is my aim. It was last year: it was the year before. I'm not here for money, I'm not here for fame and I'm obviously not here for fashion. I'm here for medals and that's my one drive."

Stockdale's commitment to offering the benefit of his experience made itself apparent from Portugal. Aside from a stellar start to life in training – one senior player's response to a poolside question over how the new man had settled in was simple: "What a goalie!" – it was noticed that after one session the 36-year-old had delayed a cool shower to stay behind and assist Basso with a private session aimed at improving the footwork of teenage goalkeeper Pierce Charles, a hotly-tipped young-ster signed from Manchester City the season before who was quickly building a reputation as one to watch within the walls of Middlewood Road.

Moore had made it clear that Wednesday would be operating mainly in the free-agent market and that he was seeking to build a squad of League One experience. While the additions of Heneghan and Stock-dale were assumed not to be breaking the bank in terms of wages, mid-field man Vaulks was seen as a more ambitious addition after arriving from Championship Cardiff City to become the Owls' third signing. A seven-cap Wales international who had recently been married, he was another infectious personality who could have arrived at S6 much sooner had a then-managerless Wednesday not plumped for QPR's Massimo Luongo ahead of the then-Rotherham United man in the weeks between Steve Bruce's sudden departure and the arrival of Garry Monk in the summer of 2019.

Such is the soap opera of modern football, Vaulks had appeared to join in place of fan favourite Luongo, a fierce cog in Wednesday's second-half renaissance in 2021/22, but one who had had his time at the club torn to shreds by repeat injuries. It was midway through the Scouse timbre of Vaulks' first press conference as an Owls player that the club announced they had ended negotiations to extend Luongo's time at Hillsborough – an announcement that seemed to take the Aus-tralian by surprise as much as anyone – and, faced with conversation about his ability to step into a midfield three alongside George Byers and Bannan, the new signing came out swinging.

"I've not had one single conversation or question about the previous player or about whether I can do what he does or whatever," he said, with a little scorn that would soon become clear was out of character. "I'll be honest, it hasn't even crossed my mind that I'm trying to replace someone. I am myself and I offer something that only I offer because we're all different players. They did have a settled midfield three and I just want to prove the manager right for bringing me in here."

In recent seasons the fanbase had not been especially accustomed to Wednesday getting their business done early and Moore took the lead in working tirelessly, alongside head of recruitment David Downes, to get players in ahead of their trip to Portugal. Michael Ihiekwe and Smith arrived from Rotherham United the day after Vaulks with a tornado of controversy following them from down the Parkway. And in the days leading into their departure for the Algarve two more would arrive. Akin Famewo, a 23-year-old defender signed for £50,000 plus a handful of potential add-ons from Norwich City, was a player not many knew about, but had become the first player to be signed for a fee by Wednesday since Callum Paterson nearly two years previously. A left-footed centre-half of sell-on potential and melodic surname who had captained Norwich's under-23s in recent campaigns, he was, in fact, a player Moore had been tracking for some time.

Fellow defender James, he of boy-band sound and vision, booked the final fresh ticket to Portugal, having sealed a season-long loan move from Blackpool after a Championship season ruined by a knee injury. No tracking was necessary by Moore on this one with the pair having worked together to excellent effect at Doncaster Rovers after James' successful turns at Sunderland and Wigan Athletic. A Manchester United academy graduate who had shared changing-rooms with the likes of Paul Pogba, the 28-year-old had played in a variety of positions under Moore at Rovers and together with Jamie Smith, they shared a strong working relationship. Indeed Wednesday could have signed him a year earlier had they not been stalled by registration embargoes, allowing Blackpool to steal a march.

"The gaffer was a big pull to come," James said soon after his arrival before admitting his knees had "gone to jelly" when lining up as an opposition player listening to Wednesday fans sing *Hi Ho Silver Lining* in years gone by. "I'd played for him before and knew what he was about – and obviously the size of the club. It's an unbelievable club to play for. It doesn't belong in this division and you see that game after game with the support that we've got. It's incredible and I think it's something that any player would love to be part of."

More signings would arrive as Wednesday turned into the season proper. Tyreeq Bakinson, a gangly, talented central midfielder aged just 23, arrived for a cut-price deal, having been shunned at Bristol City by former Owls captain Nigel Pearson. Media reports of interest in Charlton Athletic targetman Jayden Stockley, Birmingham City's centre-half captain Harlee Dean – who had been on loan at S6 the season before – and QPR's out-of-favour striker Macauley Bonne all came and went as other targets were secured around them. Deji Sotona, Paudie O'Connor, Alfie May, Marko Marosi, Haydon Roberts – Wednesday are a club never far from the transfer gossip pages.

What later became clear – in a *Sky Sports* documentary series following the progress of Salford City – is that Wednesday were contenders for the signing of Brandon Thomas-Asante, one of the brightest young attacking talents in the EFL. He signed for Championship promotion hopefuls West Brom and would go on to score nine goals in an eye-catching debut season. Taylor Richards, a young Brighton & Hove Albion midfielder who had scored 10 times in a season under Moore at Doncaster, had come close before QPR swooped late to take him to the Championship. It is believed Richards was the player Moore later referred to when discussing a "top target" the club missed out on.

"We just missed out on an excellent player and I'm really sad we didn't get him," he said. "It's not to say the players that we've got won't excite the Wednesday fans, but this one would've been the real icing on the cake. I thought we had it done, but then one of the big Championship clubs came knocking and sometimes you can't knock the player for that really. It was done – nearly. For us to miss out on that one was a shame. He was a good talent, but that's the way it is."

First reported at the start of June, the quest to sign Mallik Wilks rolled on and on. Messageboards were packed with supposed sightings of the Hull man in Sheffield city centre and social media flooded with replies of "Wilks Update?" to any tweet or story posted by local reporters.

Early in the summer it was decided that talented young defender Ciaran Brennan would continue the development of an 18-match Wednesday career to date by heading out on loan to League Two Swindon Town. He'd spend pre-season with the Robins, where, it was hoped, he'd play the majority of the season and return to S6 ready to make a more permanent mark on the first team he had grown up supporting.

There was interest in enigmatic Dutch bit-part Sylla Sow and reports of clubs eyeing academy graduate Alex Hunt, who, it transpired, was free to leave for pastures new after experience-building stints on loan at Grimsby Town and Oldham Athletic the previous season. Chatter about Championship interest in key figures Fisayo Dele-Bashiru, Lee Gregory and Byers also bubbled in the background of a busy summer.

The fixtures in Portugal had not been Wednesday's first in pre-season. A sunny sojourn at non-league Alfreton Town registered a goalless draw of little adventure, with the Owls lining-up separate teams in the halves and largely going through the motions of a first summer run-out with Heneghan, Ihiekwe and Smith given the chance to pull on their new colours for the first time. Although there was a frisson of excitement, in that it served as the first official engagement of Wednesday's season, such was the relative boredom of the afternoon that the main talking-point had been the absence of ringmaster Darren Moore.

It was decided that the touchline facilities at Alfreton were not conducive to the recovery of a six-foot-four man mountain who could at that stage barely walk unaided, so Jamie Smith, as he had done so often in the past, took on managerial duties. Dominic Iorfa earned credit for his 45-minute brawl with former Lincoln City handful Matt Rhead, Dele-Bashiru played with an intensity that he would take into the season proper and youngster Hunt looked visibly beefed up in the middle of midfield. It was all fairly gentle.

Moore did reappear on the touchline six days later as Wednesday's friendly programme kicked up a touch at Harrogate Town although he was still in strife with his knee – to the point that, having headed towards the exit of the ground, the walk back to engage in media duties was deemed too painful a prospect and Smith filled in again. A confident performance in which Vaulks and Famewo were welcomed into the fold was perhaps overshadowed by the presence of an over-sugared handful of Spa Town ultras based behind one of the goals, young teen-agers clad in Stone Island jackets whose Christmas Lynx you could smell from 50 yards. It was an amusing distraction from a worthwhile run-out in which James impressed from left-back, in which Smith opened his Owls account from the penalty spot and in which Josh Windass curled an early right-foot strike into the top corner of the Harrogate net to signal the sort of quality that meant that he was publicly pursued in one of the most 'out-there' transfer sagas in Wednesday's recent his-tory.

Argentine side Atletico Talleres were a side likely not thought of outside the world of computer games in South Yorkshire before the summer of 2021. But with Windass' former Rangers manager Pedro Caixinha in situ with the Cordoba side, they were a club rarely far from the pages of the *Sheffield Star* for several weeks, launching a hefty six-figure bid to take the Spanish-speaking, Hull-born forward to South America the season after hamstring surgery had reduced his contri-bution to the 2021/22 season to only 12 appearances. Wednesday re-sisted, despite both Caixinha and club president Andrés Fassi choosing to speak about their interest in signing Windass non-stop and on loud speaker for much of the summer – a tactic that irked both Chansiri and Moore throughout. The Owls had rejected a strong bid from Millwall the previous summer and there was a school of thought outside the walls of Hillsborough that, given the 28-year-old's recent injury strug-gles, it might be a deal worth considering. Moore later said the bid had not got close to their valuation of the attacker, who had signed a new contract with the club less than a year earlier, and later expressed disappointment in what he saw to be a deliberate attempt to unsettle Windass.

Back to Portugal, Wednesday were lining up for a friendly far more official than their defeat to Middlesbrough. In surroundings far more plush than the admittedly slightly-dated Browns Sport Resort, back-room staff and journalists arrived at a Bournemouth training base, paid for in no small part by Premier League riches, long before the Wednes-day team. A half-hour delay became an hour and there was growing concern that the match was in danger of being reduced from a 90-min-ute affair, with the Owls' flight home leaving that evening. A previ-ously tight turnaround time was looking fraught. While they waited,

Bournemouth players were instructed to roll their legs over exercise bikes that looked out onto a stunningly-curated playing surface. Former England striker Peter Crouch arrived to watch the match, for a reason nobody quite feels sure of.

Staff at the facility – not Wednesday's, it should be stressed – told those waiting that the Owls' team bus was held up by road closures brought about by local forest fires that have blighted the incoming air traffic for a week. The flames had at one stage covered 74,000 acres of land, claiming homes and the life of one pilot who was killed when his fireplane crashed. Such was the intensity of the fires that ash fell from the sky dozens of miles away, including on the training bases of both Wednesday and Bournemouth, causing both sides to cancel evening training sessions and instead take on a fitness session indoors. The breathing conditions were rendered unsafe for professional athletes and on the evening in question two young Owls players received a stern word from goalkeeping coach Basso for playing basketball outdoors.

As it transpired, the delay was not down to forest fires. Wednesday's coach had broken down as they travelled from Browns to the match, a front wheel collapsing on a pothole after the bus driver had taken a wrong turn. Wednesday's players were instructed to walk uphill in the direction they came from, up a winding path for anywhere between 10 and 20 minutes depending on who you ask. It transpired they were to be picked up by the Bournemouth coach. It was a situation that sparked no little frustration from senior players on board – particularly given that, in the season before, they had opened up life in League One by having to battle through crowds of fans outside The Valley after running into traffic issues on their way to a draw with Charlton Athletic.

The Owls arrived in time to take in a brief warm-up before a spirited 2-1 defeat to the Championship title-holders, Dele-Bashiru continuing his eye-catching pre-season form with a calm finish to reduce the arrears. Wednesday were perhaps the better team on the day, holding much of the possession for the first hour and only conceding due to a Lewis Cook effort that cannoned off the legs of Byers before a well-taken goal from £20m former Liverpool striker Dominic Solanke.

Byers and Heneghan caught the eye, Heneghan for the main part wrestling internationals Solanke and Keiffer Moore with the competency of a dad breaking apart a fight between children. Playing the last half-hour in place of Stockdale, Dawson made a classy point-blank save from the head of Jefferson Lerma as the scrap for the gloves took a turn. Vaulks was absent and would have to wait for his first Owls run-out, rejoining full training only midway through the trip after picking up a niggle before Alfreton. What appeared slightly more concerning was the absence of new man Smith, who watched on from the sidelines, having picked up a thigh problem while on tour.

"We come out of the Portugal trip really pleased," Moore said in a rushed media debrief before scrambling off to Faro airport. "We got some really heavy work done and the players will benefit from it. We're pleased to complete the programme and hopefully we've got nothing too serious with the players, which is pleasing. We move on now and we're on to the fast-forward button – the season is only a few weeks away."

That fast-forward button was pressed on a 2-0 Hillsborough defeat to La Liga side Rayo Vallecano that came and went with little incident or consequence, the only real talking-point being the presence of legendary Colombian striker Radamel Falcao in the Spaniards' attack. But in making the trip to reigning League One champions Wigan Athletic, in what was the side's final friendly outing ahead of an opening-day match up with fellow third-tier big boys Portsmouth, old concerns flared. In an insipid performance the Owls went down 4-1 – Heneghan netting the opener – in a match in which they struggled to defend crosses.

With the media fixated on an inability to defend balls coming into the box as they had last season – particularly from set-pieces – Moore would spend a portion of his pre-Pompey press conference calmly hiding frustration in explaining the fundamental differences between defending wide areas in open play and defending dead-ball situations. What matter the results in pre-season? Little, it was very fairly argued, in a ream of comment pieces. But with only a win at Harrogate to show for a whirlwind few weeks in the sun, Sheffield Wednesday entered the season with a few minds to convince about their title credentials.

The fun and sunshine of Tramlines on Tour was behind them. The real festival would begin on July 30 at a sold-out Hillsborough.

FOUR

BEGINNINGS

It was almost 6pm and there was plenty of daylight left in the evening. Darren Moore had just finished his post-match duties and stood in the middle of the pitch at Hillsborough, chatting to the club's ground staff. Beneath his feet the grass was pristine, still in the early stages of the season before League One boots trampled it to pieces, and the sun shone on him just the way it had on his players all afternoon.

Sheffield Wednesday had just put Forest Green Rovers to the sword at S6 to continue their almost-perfect start to a fast-paced campaign in the third tier and things couldn't really be going too much better for the title-chasing Owls. With 12 goals in six league games Moore had them well on track – the Midas touch even reaching defender Liam Palmer, scoring in back-to-back matches for the first time in his career. For some, "HMS Piss the League" had well and truly set sail.

Travel back a month, though, and most Wednesdayites will admit being a bit fraught. The season had started with a bang as Marvin Johnson put them 1-0 up against Portsmouth in front of 26,000 fans, but twice Wednesday were pegged back and they came within 10 minutes of losing the opening game before a Fisayo Dele-Bashiru rocket secured a point with his first brace in blue and white. The point wasn't bad, but the manner of the goals was worrying.

Despite fielding three giants in central defence in an attempt to cut out the errors of the previous campaign, and the recent friendly against Wigan Athletic, all three of Pompey's goals were cut from the same cloth as so many of those that had eventually led to Wednesday missing out on promotion in their first season back in League One.

Big Ben Heneghan and former Rotherham captain Michael Ihiekwe joined Dominic Iorfa in defence and with over 18 feet between them,

Moore had hoped for some dominance in the air – with the experienced David Stockdale, and his almost 20 years in the game, marshalling from behind to try and make sure they didn't give away any silly goals. But none of them dealt with three balls into the box from Portsmouth's right-hand side, and frustrations were clear to see as teammates in blue and white vented at each other in scenes reminiscent of so many seen before. New signings, more height, same outcome. The manager wasn't pleased.

It was a broken record of sorts as he admitted: "We need to cut the mistakes out." It had been said time and time again, but, with new signings through the door, patience was needed – Heneghan and Ihiekwe required time to settle and Iorfa had to get used to fresh faces. "If you cut them out, then it means you're going to have clean sheets – and there are parts in games and from set-plays when we have to be better at it," Moore added. "When I look at the game in those transitional periods, it's where we have to be better. It needs to be harder for those chances to come against us. We have to get back and work at them. They were avoidable – I could see that in real time. So I have to look back at it, analyse it and learn from it really, really quickly."

Conceding three goals, especially as they had done, certainly wasn't in Moore's plans as they got the season under way, but again they'd dug in to get something after falling behind, continuing to buck a trend that had plagued the club for so long before his arrival. MK Dons awaited them next, a side who had suffered the same fate in the play-offs just a few months earlier, and fans would be making their way to Milton Keynes in their thousands – many wearing the new yellow kit designed to invoke memories of the glory days of old; of David Hirst, Roland Nilsson and John Sheridan.

The travelling support made up about half the crowd inside Stadium MK and they made all the noise in Wednesday's first game on the road. But while a 1-0 win – courtesy of a Josh Windass penalty – was welcomed, the victory was overshadowed by the sort of bad luck to which Owls fans had grown all too accustomed. Akin Famewo, making his debut for the club with his left foot bringing balance to the backline, started solidly. As a young, athletic and intelligent defender he looked more than competent for about half an hour. But there would be no dream debut for the former Norwich City man.

It looked innocuous at first, the defender clearing the ball away from Louie Barry by the Wednesday box, but he dropped to the floor immediately, grasping at his left leg just metres away from the Wednesday faithful. With the Dons on the attack he got to his feet not once, not twice, but three times, almost reaching out towards the bench on the second in an attempt for help. Watching on, former Owls striker and now in-house pundit John Pearson said: "Famewo's in deep trouble." But nobody watching knew just how bad it would be.

As he limped off, one arm around club doctor Richard Higgins and the other around physio James Starmore, that was his last involvement of 2022. He would not start again for five months. The 23-year-old was just planting down some roots for the first time in years after loan spells with St. Mirren and Charlton Athletic and would have to lean on others after a horror start to life at S6 had left him with his own personal mountain to climb.

"Honestly it was one of the most heartbreaking moments of my career," he recalled. "I'd just arrived at this massive club, I was so excited to start my journey here and then it was one big boundary… I knew on the pitch that it was a bad one because I've never experienced that kind of pain – I've never had an injury that bad. I knew it was going to be lengthy, but I just got my head down and kept working. I didn't watch football for a couple of weeks, though, because it was painful to watch – I obviously supported the boys and that, but it was painful not being involved."

And Palmer, thinking back, explained how that win – under the circumstances – felt such a big one. "It was one of the toughest games of the campaign and they went on to have a horrible season, but they played some good stuff and it was a real backs-to-the-wall performance from us. Not many will remember it, but I could see the togetherness, the determination not to concede, was strong that day."

Though victorious, two games into the campaign and Wednesday had already been dealt a huge injury blow. Michael Smith, who joined from Rotherham with Ihiekwe, had picked up a knock after the first game and missed five more: Dennis Adeniran was still on the mend from the season before. For all the talk of fixing the injury issues, there is no remedy for misfortune. That didn't mean Moore wasn't going to try, though, and he'd already decided to bring in some outside help in order to help give them at least a better chance of avoiding the sort of pile-up from the year before.

Claudia Brown has been around professional football for a while now. She's come a long way from her days in local government when she worked in public relations, but she's more than earned her stripes in football – working for West Bromwich Albion, Doncaster Rovers and Port Vale, training with renowned sports yoga teacher Sarah Ramsden, who made her name at both Manchester City and Manchester United. Brown first met the Owls boss during her time working in the Midlands – almost by accident, as it happens.

"I had absolutely no plan to get into football, but just before I'd finished my course with Sarah – I think I had one session left – she got a call saying that the woman who was looking after West Brom was leaving," said Brown. "So I ended up there with the first team, working with players such as Craig Dawson, James McClean, Rickie Lambert, Jonas Olsson, James Chester and this man kept looking through this pane of glass in the door during sessions. It was putting me off and I didn't know who he was, but then one day he came in and introduced himself. He just said he wanted to see how things were going. So I went and asked the guy at reception: 'Who's this Darren who keeps looking in?'

"He said to me: 'Oh, Claudia, Darren's a bit of a club legend around here.' We've laughed about that since. But, yeah, he used to come in, say: 'Hi' and check up on how I was getting on even though it wasn't his job. It's just the way he is and I think he just likes to know what's going on."

Moore took Brown to Rovers with him and by the time that his second season at Wednesday got under way, he'd made sure that she was through the doors at Middlewood Road as well. The logic is that while yoga – which many players have used to elongate their careers – offers no guarantees in terms of preventing injuries, it can certainly improve the chances of avoiding serious muscle issues. And as far as the manager was concerned even the small wins were worth getting.

"What I've always said to the lads is that the more your muscles can be mobile, the more your joints will be able to work at their full range of motion," Brown said. "So the muscles will be more pliable and they move easier. So when you do get an injury, it may be that you recover quicker and you won't be out as long. But that comes only with consistency. Once a month for 20 minutes isn't going to help anybody, so I was running sessions every week and I'd give them homework sheets.

"It was about showing them the very weird twisting shapes that they do in games at speed and often with an opposition player on top of them – and explaining the stiffness and tightness that come with it. I showed them pictures of Mo Salah, Ronaldo, the England team doing yoga. Rugby teams, too. I wanted it to make sense why I was getting them to do certain positions. At the end of the season with the celebrations there was a bit of a do at the stadium and I got a lot of hugs after they'd had a drink. But I also got a lot of: 'I love you, Claudia, but I fucking hate yoga.'"

They might have hated it, but several still felt the benefits. The science around injury prevention is varied when it comes to yoga, but Brown tells a story in particular that shows how it can be of benefit. One Owls player, who had been having back problems for about a decade before her arrival, noted how much better he felt after being put on a specific programme – to the extent that he asked for more to keep it going. Another had been dealing with a variety of upper-body issues – but after a regime of work that was preceded by a statement of: "You're not going to like this," she got a hearty handshake and was told: "I'll give you your due: I feel fucking terrific." They wouldn't fix things straightaway, but progress was progress.

Injuries aside there were also two major losses away from the first team when young Isaac Holland and Tony Yogane left for Brentford B, the teenage duo being tempted away by the potential glow of the Premier League. The Owls received a decent fee believed to be about £1million, but losing two of their most talented youngsters – who had been playing well above their age group – certainly left a bitter taste for the manager and the chairman. But what could they do?

"We feel disappointed to lose those two promising players," Moore admitted as they made their way down the M1 to buzz with the Bees. "We wanted them to stay with us, but they have gone to the Premier League and we wish them well... The chairman and I are not particularly happy with the system in place. There will probably be other managers at lower-league clubs who will be against the system, but it is what it is. It doesn't serve a real purpose for us, but obviously it does for the teams operating in the higher echelons of the league."

Onwards, though. There was a hint of revenge on the menu as Wednesday faced Championship new boys Sunderland in the Carabao Cup. Victory, of course, wouldn't even come close to making up for the play-off heartbreak of the season before, but the game would at least offer Wednesday a chance to test themselves against a side who would eventually go on to secure another top-six finish in the division above.

Adeniran was back in the XI for the first night game of the season and he wasted no time in showing fans what they'd been missing as he ran out for the first time since January. Having worked the ball on to his weaker left foot with a little more than 15 minutes on the clock, he pulled back and fired one straight into the top corner to keep up the club's early goal of the season run after Dele-Bashiru's Pompey brace. He then turned provider, whipping in a delightful ball to put it on a plate for Sylla Sow to score what would prove to be his last goal in a Wednesday shirt. *Shake it up, baby...*

"The manager always told me to keep my head down and keep going," a smiling man-of-the-match Adeniran said afterwards. "Obviously I've been injured and in pre-season he said that I'd been doing well, so I just had to keep going and my opportunity would come. Hopefully tonight I've shown him what I can do... It was really a surreal moment with the adrenaline rush you get. I'd almost forgot how it feels to be scoring here, so it was such a fantastic moment for me scoring in front of these fans."

Given his immense popularity within the group, stand-in captain Palmer wasn't the only one pleased as he handed Adeniran his award. It had been a long and arduous road back to fitness for the 23-year-old, and to see him doing his thing again was the sort of moment that could hand a real boost to what was becoming an increasingly tight-knit Owls squad. He'd have to wait for his next appearance though, sitting out the largely uneventful 1-0 win over Charlton when Tyreeq Bakinson leapt highest to grab the winner at S6 and take Wednesday into second place.

Against the Addicks Stockdale had had to call on some of that gamesmanship for which he'd become so well-known at Wycombe Wanderers. While fans hated seeing it done to them, they absolutely loved seeing the experienced shot-stopper take that little bit longer with a goal-kick when he was on their side. Back-to-back shut-outs had meant that opening day against Pompey had been forgotten, and – true to form – Stockdale was more than happy to take the smooth with the rough. He'd been criticised and he'd been praised, but he was fine with both. "Not everybody is going to agree with how you played," he'd told the media after his first clean sheet. "But you've got to be a big man. You don't stay in football for 21 years without coming up against a few comments and if you can't read the bad comments, then don't look at the good ones.

"I took on board what people were saying, rightly or wrongly, and I go to my peers, the manager, the coaches and say: 'Right, what do I need to do?' Me and Cam Dawson sit down on a Monday and go through Twitter to see what people have been saying. And we've often sat there and had a good few laughs at the comments, but at the end of the day football is all about opinions. I read the bad and I read the good and if you can't stand the heat, get out of the kitchen."

On arrival at Hillsborough Stockdale had vowed to do his best for the team, whether he was playing or not, and right now he was between the posts rather than Dawson – although it had quickly become clear that his relationship with his teammate was a strong one, despite the fact that Dawson wasn't even eight years old when Stockdale made his professional debut in 2005. The former Brighton & Hove Albion man had made an immediate impact, both on and off the pitch, and the foundations of a Hillsborough fan favourite was clearly being laid.

Three wins, three clean sheets and the Wednesday train was rolling out of the station, but they'd have their work cut out at Peterborough United in their fourth league game of the campaign. London Road would prove to be a particularly unhappy hunting ground in 2022/23 – but that was nothing new, considering it'd been two decades since the Owls had last won there.

It was a game of little drama for about half-an-hour, aside from a huge Heneghan block to keep out former Owl Jack Marriott, but things would soon spice up, starting with Reece James' sending-off in the 34th minute. His tackle on Joe Ward was deemed as dangerous play and James later apologised to his teammates after making what Moore described as "the wrong decision." But it wasn't the dismissal that left the sourest of tastes; rather the incident that followed it. George Byers was sacrificed in the reshuffle after Wednesday went down to 10 men and, still waiting for his first chance to complete 90 minutes for the Owls that season, the popular midfielder clearly did not agree with the decision, slapping assistant Jamie Smith's hand away as it was offered on the touchline.

Moore's No.2 went after him and a few choice words were shared among all the shirt-tugging and pointed fingers before Dawson pulled his teammate away. The Wednesday boss never even turned around, his eyes fully focused on what was playing out in front of him.

As usual he batted the whole thing away post-game. He said he hadn't seen the incident, but insisted that he would put any fracas down to "frustration," adding that it was not something that he would be "alarmed by." A few days later the pair had hugged and made up after some chats behind the scenes and it was all swept away as a storm in a teacup. For those outside the inner sanctum, only time would tell if that was really the case, but in reality those involved had rapidly moved past it and on to the task at hand. Byers and Smith were having dinner together the next day.

"I was on the bench that night," Bannan recalled, "and it really was argy-bargy, to be honest. George was angry at coming off and, while I wouldn't say he was in the right, I'd probably be the very same. Nobody wants to be taken off that early into a game. When you're a winner, you want to try to stay on and win. They could probably have both dealt with it differently. George maybe shouldn't have been so aggressive coming off and Sivvy probably overreacted to what actually happened. But Sivvy is a lovely man, George is a great kid, and they made up after the game. They were arguing a bit in the changing-room and I basically told them to shut up and forget about it, which they did. It's football, it's changing-rooms, it happens every weekend in different places. We all want to win, they both had the right intentions and sometimes it blows up. It was heat-of-the-moment stuff and was over and done with soon enough. They care and that's what matters. You need that fire; you wouldn't be successful if you didn't." And so they moved on.

***

It was the morning of Wednesday's game against Bolton Wanderers and, as he and his teammates ate their breakfasts in the team hotel and discussed the best way to bounce back from the Posh defeat, club captain Barry Bannan decided to have a word with his manager. There was something that he wanted to suggest ahead of their trip to the University of Bolton Stadium, a decision that would see him relinquish the Owls' armband – for a day anyway.

Exactly 4,394 days had gone by since Wednesday's No.2 Liam Palmer had made his Owls debut, a bright-eyed academy graduate running out at Hillsborough in front of a little more than 7,000 people in the Carling Cup. Now, as he approached his 31st birthday, he was about to make his 350th appearance in Wednesday colours, joining an exclusive list of players to do so – and Bannan thought he deserved to lead the team out as he did.

So with the Lancashire sun beating down on one half of the turf, out he came – shoulders back, head high, armband wrapped around his left bicep. It wasn't the first time that he'd had the honour, but, as he turned and clapped the Owls faithful to his right-hand side, there will have been a different level of pride for this one. To play 350 games for one club in the modern era is no mean feat and, with the defender looking fitter than ever, there would be plenty more to come.

Behind him as he took to the field, eight players back, stood new arrival Mark McGuinness. The young former Arsenal man had arrived on loan from Cardiff City as a replacement for Famewo and Moore was wasting no time in getting him into the action. His capture went down as well as a pint of his namesake on a sunny Dublin afternoon and he could walk the walk, too. Wednesday were on to a winner.

Byers, just days after that coming together in Cambridgeshire, also started as proof that bygones would indeed be bygones. Football loves a narrative, so it felt written in the stars that Bannan's ball into the box would land at his feet about nine yards out. The net was still rippling as he started his sprint towards the away end with his arms outstretched. As he passed the halfway line, the travelling faithful knew what was coming. As he neared the edge of the Owls' box, his right hand to his head, Wednesday's No.14 motioned his increasingly familiar salute and all was forgiven.

This day was all about Palmer, though. The Owls stalwart bounded up and down the field like a man who'd spent the summer running 10 kilometres every day – a feat he'd completed in order to raise money for the cancer-battling son of his former Owls teammate Arron Jameson – and, when he got on the end of Windass' delightful through ball, there was going to be only one result. He wheeled away, in his retro Adidas Predators, ears cupped in an uncharacteristic jibe at the home support-ers, and his side were well on the way to victory. A goal, a clean sheet and three valuable points on the road – Palmer's milestone game had played out to perfection.

"I couldn't have dreamt for a better day, to be honest," he said with the broadest of smiles and a shirt with *Palmer 350* on the back in his hand. "I'd said in the pre-match press conference that I'd be happy with the three points, but I was half-lying really – I wanted it to be a good oc-casion, something that I remembered fondly." Sadly it was an occasion that his parents, Terry and Allison, missed because of a holiday, but he joked that they could go away more often if that was what happened when they did. They'd have plenty more to celebrate with him anyway.

Wednesday had ended Bolton's unbeaten start to the season and more good news was to come, especially for the journalists who were waking up and going to sleep with "Mallik Wilks update?" seared into their brains. The Hull City man had been part of one of the longest-running transfer sagas in recent times, with some fans saying they'd seen him driving around Sheffield and others insisting that family friend Josh Windass was in his ear about a move. As the end of August approached, there were concerns that it might not happen at all. On August 22, however, almost three months after interest was first re-ported, that key "Wilks update" arrived.

Victory over Rochdale in the Carabao Cup, which came at a price with injuries to Heneghan and Dele-Bashiru, was Wednesday's fifth in six games in all competitions. It became six in seven with a 5-0 ham-mering of Forest Green Rovers, in which Wilks almost scored on his debut with an overhead kick, and all was right with the world.

Next up: the only Yorkshire derby of the season. Barnsley at home.

FIVE

THE RUNNING BOY

Josh Windass is running. He's running alone, fast, heart racing, sweat dripping. He's running with a desperate anguish. It's dark and he's running through the streets of Menston, a quiet village in West Yorkshire that he calls home. He's running off the pain of a relatively-recently healed broken leg and the world-changing, slow-motion gut-punch of watching his dream fall away after a decade in which it felt inevitable. He's running to get himself back into football. He's running off the strain that befalls a family recently bruised by the separation of his mum Helen and footballer dad Dean. He's 18 years old, the running boy.

It's 11 years before this book's story unfolds. Windass, one of the most hotly-tipped youngsters in Huddersfield Town's academy since he was a little boy who balanced football with summers playing cricket and doing all the things a young lad does, was set to follow in the foot-steps of his dad, one of the great football personalities of the 1990s and 2000s and a player of underrated technical ability, having played in the Premier League with Bradford City, Middlesbrough and Hull City. Dean had a short 2002 loan stint at Sheffield Wednesday, a back injury curtailing his contribution to two pained appearances under Terry Yorath before he returned to Boro for treatment.

So he's running. Following his Terriers release, Josh had had trials with a number of clubs in and around Yorkshire, including Wednesday. One player who featured alongside him in one of the games remembers Windass "tearing it up" – but he got little joy in terms of offers to re-enter the life for which he had spent his childhood preparing. When one day Dean entered his living-room to find Josh laid on the sofa playing on the Xbox, he snapped and, sensing his son was feeling sorry for himself, got him a job with a pal on a building site, earning £50 a day.

It was an experience – although he may not admit it – that sharpened his focus even more and, after begging his mother not to make him get a "proper job," found himself sitting in his living-room staring back at a stranger.

Billy Miller was manager of Harrogate Railway Athletic, operating a division below Stocksbridge Park Steels in the Evo-Stik North Division One. With no cash, no car and no real offer of an immediate return to football, Windass had spied an opportunity. His policewoman mother worked in Harrogate and could provide lifts to and from training. He could play for them if the opportunity fit. Promised a clean slate, no pressure and complete freedom to move on as and when an opportunity arose to better himself, he signed. He scored nine goals, he played just about every game and within three years, via a stint at Accrington Stanley he says he owes everything to, he was playing in the No.10 role for Glasgow Rangers in front of 50,000 people. Wigan Athletic and Sheffield Wednesday – first on loan and then permanently – would follow.

"To be fair to the kid, he was always 100 per cent focused," Miller said. "Being released by Huddersfield would have come as a bit of a shock to him. But he knew exactly what he wanted to achieve and he used his time at Harrogate to find himself again as a footballer. He never missed training with us. He was always sharp and would stay on to do extra work on things like free-kicks and corners. In fact, he actually did his own summer camp, a two-week thing with a friend of his, right at the start of pre-season to make sure he was ready.

"You could see that Josh was always destined to go on and become better. We would normally train once or twice a week and we played 42 games during the season in the Evo-Stik North. It was an opportunity to re-evaluate and go again. At the end of that season, he got the chance to join Accrington Stanley and the rest, as they say, is history.

"Josh actually broke his wrist in his last game for us at Mossley. He went up for a header just before half-time, put his hand out as he came down, fell backwards and ended up breaking a small bone in his wrist. The physio and I took him over to the hospital in Manchester and sat with him for about nine hours while they re-set it all. Again, though, Josh has always had a really pleasant outlook on life. He was laughing and joking in the hospital bed. More than anything I am just so glad to see what Josh has achieved. It's phenomenal. All we did was provide a platform."

Tattooed and teetotal, Windass first arrived at Wednesday on deadline day of the 2020 winter window on loan from Wigan Athletic. There had been a "clash of personalities" with his Latics boss Paul Cook. A few months later, with a permanent September switch believed to be worth somewhere in the region of £500,000 drawn out in the wake of financial trouble at Wigan, Cook and Co. didn't allow Windass to train with them and he prepared instead on his own – running once more – at a lonely sports facility in West Yorkshire. "If I give too much detail on that one, there will be people out of a job for quite a long time," Windass later said on the acrimony of his Wigan exit. "So I'll just keep that one quiet."

Not one for boring press engagements, Windass speaks his mind on social media. It's an outlook and a way of doing things that can get him into the headlines from time to time. But it's refreshing, a shoot-from-the-hip approach that makes for more interest and insight for fans and media than most other players in the wider game, many of whom have been squeezed through the toothpaste tube of teenage training sessions as the media game got fractious. "Chest out" is his way. Why? Who knows? Is it bravado? How much of it is tongue-in-cheek?

Asked about the real Josh Windass, Cameron Dawson smiled. He joked that, when the forward was in his best form, the changing-room know about it – a PFA League One player-of-the-month award, handed over months later, would sit above Windass' locker in the changing-room for several weeks – but it was all in good spirit, Dawson said. Windass is a popular changing-room figure and above all he's a dictionary definition of a model professional who desperately wants to win football matches. "He's a great lad is Josh," Dawson smiled. "He's chirpy, he's loud and you normally hear him before you see him. He has his quiet days. What you won't see is that he works incredibly hard and he's a great professional, a really top professional, and he always puts it in in training. He works very hard."

Windass is not one particularly to hide his feelings on the pitch either. And as his No.11 shirt was indicated on the fourth official's board to signal his removal from the field a little more than an hour into their South Yorkshire derby defeat to Barnsley on September 3, he sunk his shoulders and made his way over to replacement Mallik Wilks. The Owls were 1-0 down thanks to Devante Cole's effort and within 10 minutes James Norwood had doubled the deficit. With Windass' workload still being managed after the decimation of the season before, he was taken off. And the crowd booed, as they did at half-time and again at full-time. The visitors had not been especially dominant, but in big moments they had been bigger, faster and stronger than Wednesday. Certainly more clinical.

Victory sealed Barnsley's first back-to-back successes at Hillsborough since just after the Second World War. It's a genuine rivalry, but one from which the Tykes certainly take more vigour than Wednesday, given the Owls' preoccupation with the Blades and Leeds. Norwood, who had sealed the match with a well-taken header, delivered a dollop of social-media hilarity a couple of months earlier when asked, as part of his opening media gambit at Oakwell, what his favourite joke was. "Sheffield Wednesday," he replied. In football folk can wait a very long time for the last laugh.

Post-match, it fell on new boy Michael Ihiekwe to face the media music as the mood of a desperate fanbase at a club such as Sheffield Wednesday, in a division such as League One, did its thing after a second defeat in seven league matches left them only third in the table. The frustration was in no way left only to the terraces either with strong words said between coaching staff and senior players in the dressing-room. Ihiekwe, easily one of the more experienced figures in a hugely-experienced group, stepped out to take responsibility on behalf of the players, admitting they had failed to carry out the instructions laid out to them by their coaches. Moore had said the performance had left them "scratching their heads" and that he could tell from an early stage that, for whatever reason, his side were far from their best. Partly in the guise of accelerating the integration of new faces and partly designed to work on the "Plan B" of high wingers and two front men who hadn't buttered many parsnips in the derby, an extra couple of double sessions were scheduled that week by Moore and Co. There may have just been a little frisson on punishment thrown in there for good measure.

"I think that as a collective we were a little bit off it for whatever reason. They frustrated us and it worked," Ihiekwe said. "They're a good team and they've come down from the Championship. Nobody has any given right just to go out and win games. They were a little bit more competitive, which isn't nice for me to say, but it's true, winning second balls and stuff. We need to look back at it and improve. The coaching can only do so much. We have to do it on the pitch. We had all the information and we watched them over the last few days. It just wasn't executed well enough today, we got in certain positions to do certain things and we didn't execute them to the best of our ability. When things like that are adding up and we keep doing it, the outcome is going to be the same."

On the audible frustration expressed by supporters during an insipid performance, Ihiekwe added: "That's part of being at a big club. At any level, if we're not playing to par that can happen. It's up to us on the pitch to keep going, to show personality and to keep improving in the game. The fans were frustrated because it was a local derby, but we are as well. We just need to keep going, play with confidence and improve."

Catastrophic though the level of concern was in some corners of the fanbase in the days after the Barnsley defeat, the wheels of the season stopped for no result and the club kept working to put the pieces together to improve on their third-place position and achieve an automatic return to the Championship. Moore had spoken about the desire to bring in a free-agent, third-choice goalkeeper despite his admiration for Pierce Charles in particular, but hadn't seen the opportunity arise in a long and winding summer transfer window. Adriano Basso watched on as six-foot-five former Wolves youngster Jamie Pardington featured for the under-21s in a home clash with Bristol City. Basso left even more assured that ultimate faith could be put in 17-year-old Charles as a third string regardless of his tender years – and indeed in Luke Jackson and Charles' fellow teenager Jack Hall as further back-up options.

Amongst the fall-out from the derby defeat, the scale of Dennis Adeniran's surgery-requiring injury became public knowledge – much to the apparent ire of some senior club figures – and, with the transfer window closed and all business done at first-team level, attention turned behind the scenes to finding a club for the likes of young defender Ryan Galvin to join on loan. He'd link up with National League Maidstone United, managed by Moore's former Doncaster Rovers teammate Hakan Hayrettin, the following week. Then, in and among the usual and often relatively mundane trappings of an average football season, the whole world stopped.

On Thursday, September 8, 2022, it was announced that Queen Elizabeth II had died peacefully at Balmoral Castle. It was news that sent the entire sporting world – or this little corner of it, at least – spinning off its axis, as only something as seismic as the death of a head of state after 70 years of service can do. Non-stop and heavily debated both sensibly and moronically in coffee rooms, on television and as always most prominently on social media, decisions were made as to which events should be cancelled first, and how quickly, as the country staged a weekend of mourning – whether they were indeed mourning or not.

Horse racing meets, the PGA Championship golf at Wentworth, Premiership rugby, the entire third day of the Lord's Test between England and South Africa, the Tour of Britain cycling event; all halted. When Friday evening EFL matches – Burnley v Norwich in the Championship and Tranmere v Stockport in League Two – were also postponed, it felt inevitable that the weekend's clashes would also suffer the same fate.

Inevitability is no guarantee, though, and, with Wednesday handed the longest trip of them all – a 300-mile, five-hour trip to Plymouth Argyle – they set off. "Further to discussions on Friday morning it has been determined that all EFL fixtures from 9-10 September will be postponed as a mark of respect … to the passing of HRH Queen Elizabeth II," read a statement released at a little after 11am, with the Owls a little over an hour into their journey. "This is aligned with the approach that the Premier League and the FA will take with their competitions this weekend."

The Owls instead hosted a double-session training routine that afternoon and backroom staff held a meeting to enact the programmes they had spent the last two days re-moulding in anticipation of a postponement. It would give them more time to shake off any lingering debris of defeat to Barnsley, at least. The club went quickly to work, too; their commemorative programme put together to mark the passing of the Queen included memories of her visit to Hillsborough Stadium – she opened the Kop in December 1986 and was said to have made reference to how much she enjoyed the club's name – was sold out in person and online and was the first to ever require a reprint, such was the demand.

The long trip to Plymouth would eventually be rescheduled for 24 days later – on a Tuesday evening.

"Baffling," posted former Rangers man Windass – rarely one to shirk his feelings publicly – on social media. "Thousands and thousands of people are now out-of-pocket because of non-refundable tickets and hotel bookings, and many other things. The country is already on its knees. I respect the Queen… Very much so. I don't respect forcing people to sit at home and be sad and lose out on hard-earned money. But that's just my opinion."

Given the week's gap between Barnsley and the postponement, Wednesday had 10 days then to do yet more early-season work with their squad. Ten days' conditioning for those who needed it and, after the double-sessions thrown on to acclimatise the newcomers, time for all that, too. Once it was made clear that the period of national mourning would last only a weekend, Morecambe would provide the venue and next test on a Tuesday evening still pleasantly warm despite the advent of September. It had been during a bitterly disappointing 1-0 August defeat at the Azuma Stadium the season before, that ended a remarkable start to the campaign and pushed Wednesday into a run of one win in six. Again the plucky Shrimpers set up to frustrate – and then some. As they had done the season before, Wednesday went into the final hour having not scored.

The Running Boy came into the foreground again. Wednesday were playing that variation experimented with previously, although this time they did it from the off with Mighten and Windass stationed wide on a midfield two packed-out with the technical ability of Bannan and two strikers, Smith and Gregory, ready for an aerial battle. It was one-way traffic – particularly when Dele-Bashiru replaced James to provide another physical body in the ever-retreating Morecambe resistance – and on 70 minutes Windass got Wednesday ahead with a well-timed header from Bannan's corner. The celebrations were of relief rather than jubilation in a match when the Owls plundered 32 shots at goal, compared with Morecambe's four, and enjoyed 72 per cent of possession.

Late on George Byers headed home a carbon copy of Windass' opener, Michael Smith did the business to convert a Windass assist and Wednesday walked away 3-0 winners, with the Shrimpers boss

Derek Adams hailing the quality of a squad and club that "shouldn't be in League One."

"You can't expect to beat a team like that when they're on form and tonight I thought Sheffield Wednesday were on form," he said. "They passed the ball, zipped it about, they had runners from defence and midfield and unfortunately they have such a strong squad." It was the sort of flattering post-match mantra Wednesday had heard time and again the season before.

Four days later Wednesday would get to pay their respects to the Queen their own way, at home to ambitious fellow promotion hopefuls Ipswich Town. Programmes shelled out in their thousands, a minute's silence was beautifully observed and the national anthem was blasted out at Hillsborough by *Britain's Got Talent* contestant Maxwell Thorpe. But the general atmosphere was anything but regal from thereon in as both sets of supporters expressed their disgust with the performance of the officials. At one stage managers Moore and Kieran McKenna were pulled together to explain that, if any further missiles were thrown on to the pitch, the match would be abandoned. Moore later expressed his relief in not having to navigate what would have been a "catastrophe" for the club. One photographer's display after the game showed one projectile to be lollipop-shaped.

As if it hadn't been clear at the outset of the campaign, it was by now that Ipswich would be one of the mountains that stood in the way of Wednesday's mission to rejoin the Championship. Alongside the rebuilding Derby County and Sunderland before them, Ipswich are one of England's most storied clubs and their third-tier expectation was married with ambition – and the funds to match. Wednesday, of course, were very much a part of that bracket, too.

Ipswich had fallen on hard times in recent seasons and were two years deeper into the third-tier mire than the Owls, having been relegated from the Championship in 2018/19. That ended a 63-year stay in the top two divisions that had welcomed a UEFA Cup win under the charming Sir Bobby Robson in 1981 and more recently, a sojourn back into that competition as recently as 2003. Finishes of 11th, ninth and 11th in their League One tour painted a picture of a fallen giant until US investment group Gamechanger 20 Limited rolled into East Anglia with visions of domination.

Paul Cook – he of the Windass arm wrestle – touted himself for the Wednesday job in the weeks leading to Moore's appointment at S6, but had come and gone at Portman Road before, in December 2021, a vision was put into place and driven by the talented Northern Irishman McKenna, plucked from the first-team coaching staff at Manchester United. He was quickly backed appropriately with a first-class, United-flavoured coaching team and a well-funded recruitment drive of Premier League quality. Leeds United left wing-back Leif Davis – turned down by Wednesday as a teenager – had arrived for an undisclosed seven-figure fee in the summer and later they'd have the muscle to go again in January, adding Everton striker Nathan Broadhead and Arsenal defender Harry Clarke for similar sums. They were not there, it was made clear, to mess about.

In McKenna, Ipswich had snared one of the brightest young coaches in the country. Relaxed and debonair at times, fierce, cold and cutting at others, he was a recognisable face to many even before his first appointment in management for his work at Old Trafford, having been promoted to one of Europe's most glamorous dugouts by José Mourinho at the age of just 32. He climbed further up the ladder under Ole Gunnar Solskjær and was a face shown weekly on *Sky Sports* as the man most often turned to when the Norwegian sought advice. His playing career had ended at Tottenham Hotspur aged just 22 after two years of surgery, training and desperation in the wake of a hip injury and it was that level of determination that had driven him to where he was, facing down Sheffield Wednesday as manager of one of the most ambitious, up-and-coming clubs in the country aged just 36. There was no doubt – to Wednesday and their title ambitions, Ipswich were a problem.

Although the bad-tempered match itself was in many ways nothing like that at Morecambe, it was a further display of the sort of gnarling, fighting spirit that would come to define the Owls' campaign, this time scrapping back against top-quality, third-tier opposition rather than battling their own "here we go again" demons against a team set up to irritate. That said, Wednesday would absolutely have preferred not to have found themselves 2-0 down with 15 minutes remaining thanks to Kayden Jackson's early strike and a seemingly match-settling Dominic Iorfa own goal on 70 minutes.

On so many occasions the previous season Wednesday were accused of slipping up on dry patches of ground, of making life hard for themselves when it needn't be difficult. "The Wednesday Way" was a phrase barbecued in negativity, wrapped up in decades of frustration and expressed a steadfast ability to step on a rake when the garden seemed empty. And it showed on the terraces as Iorfa – who would struggle for form in stages of the season, but seemed to rise to the occasion when the Owls needed him most – entered his own little *You've Been Framed* entry and sank to the knees when Wes Burns' seemingly-innocuous cross had collided with him to deflect the ball past Stockdale at the Leppings Lane End. A number of colleagues joined him in visible anguish. Wednesday don't come back from 2-0 down with 15 minutes to go, after all, and certainly not in such a gritty game in which six Ipswich players were shown yellow cards in the second half alone.

But they proved this time that they could bounce back. The match was the green shoot after the seeding of the previous season's comeback performances, the first fightback flower of spring that at the time nobody really seemed to notice. This squad were thrown together with hairy chests and bruises, winners' medals and – sorry lads – receding hairlines and a sense of responsibility that could win points from perilous positions. That's what had been said anyway. And on September 17 – for the first time this season – that true, snarling grit was hinted at as Marvin Johnson flicked Barry Bannan's smartly-taken free-kick into the back post for George Byers to knock home.

When Michael Smith nodded home Reece James' centre with only a minute remaining, there was more than a hint of offside as well as Wednesday mettle. Not that the manically-celebrating Owls fans cared a jot as Smith lifted a ballboy high above his head in celebration, something he later admitted he had no recollection of as adrenaline took over. In the circumstances Wednesday had achieved an excellent point against the league leaders.

Afterwards news of an injury to the indomitable Mark McGuinness – who had quickly become a fan favourite at S6 – was confirmed. A scan had revealed damage beyond what was first thought and he'd miss the next four matches. A blow and all of a sudden, with Akin Famewo out for the foreseeable future, Wednesday were a little light at the back again, having played out the Ipswich game with no recognised defender on the bench. One player who had alleviated the load on that front was James, who slotted in on the left of a back three for the first time in any sort of regularity in his career. Versatility was something for which Moore and Jamie Smith knew him from their shared time at Doncaster when the former Manchester United academy player had jumped into the middle of midfield with ease. Having been hurled into the spotlight with his red card at Peterborough so early on in his Owls career, the softly-spoken Lancastrian was quickly growing a love affair with the Wednesday fanbase.

Still, not much room for manoeuvre at the back then for a Hillsborough Papa Johns Trophy tie with League One colleagues Burton Albion three days later. The presence of the competition was a nuisance for most – it was nicknamed "the Pizza Cup" by those who looked upon it as such – but something to navigate while fringe players built their match sharpness. It was certainly seen as that by the meagre 4,577-strong crowd at S6 who watched on as the supporting cast again fluffed their lines. A 3-2 defeat left Wednesday bottom of a division containing slow-starting Burton, League Two Bradford City and Leicester City's under-21s. They were all-but out with the ignominy of welcoming the Foxes' young guns to come.

"I have a desire in my heart in terms of every game we play for Sheffield Wednesday, that we apply ourselves right and make sure we are in competition to win every game," Moore told reporters post-match with an air of genuine disappointment. Asked if he'd been let down by his fringe players, he responded with the air of a politician protecting the ineptitude of an under-performing Government department, but the mood was there for all to see.

The Burton performance, following the limp loss at Bradford, defeats at Peterborough and that bitter Barnsley result, left Wednesday fourth in the table on 17 points after nine matches – a single dip below the feted "two-per-game" figure fans and media used to determine the progress of a side craning for automatic promotion. They were four points behind early pacesetters Ipswich and Portsmouth – another monster of a club at third-tier level – with 37 matches left to play. But the social media dissenters had begun to clear their throats.

Such is the pressure and expectation to achieve with the weight of Waddle and Wembley on the modern blue-and-white-shirt, the expectancy levels blown up by the fortunes and promise of the megabucks early-Chansiri era. Moore would repeat, after just about every dropped point or poor performance, that there was an understandable expectation that his side should simply win every game. It was a line he delivered in a matter-of-fact way, almost with a shrug. It was a reality you feel he had come to expect, but clearly didn't sit lightly on incredibly-broad shoulders.

Amid it all were rumblings about the contract status of young Fisayo Dele-Bashiru, a hugely talented, dynamic midfielder whose early performances in the season had begun to tail off a touch as those of his rivals for the midfield places had grown. Talks had begun in the heart of his hot streak, but a stand-off concerning expected salaries was hedging Mexican – and weren't particularly impressing senior figures at the club. Moore would intimate a few weeks later that an agreement was growing close, but no dice. He'd later decide to shelve talks altogether, believing that the former Manchester City teen had lost focus.

Having been taken off at half-time in the Burton defeat, Dele-Bashiru was left out of the starting line-up when Wycombe Wanderers came to Hillsborough on September 24. The Chairboys, with David Stockdale between the posts, had reached the play-off final in the previous campaign and were known as a niggly side led by Gareth Ainsworth. With man mountain veteran Adebayo Akinfenwa having retired, a desire set in to move the club on to the next stage of their development and they were looking to "play more ball." Going 1-0 down at Hillsborough in the first minute to Joe Jacobson's own goal wasn't part of that plan.

One of the criticisms of Moore's tactics had been a "handbrake approach" to certain matches. What was already clear was that with wingers on board such as Mighten and Wilks, a different side had been shown with regard to selection in matches against the lesser teams in the division. With Wycombe in town – a team expected to challenge at the top of the division – Windass was played in behind the front two of Smith and Gregory as Wednesday went for it and returned a handsome, but hard-fought 3-1 win, Barry Bannan cancelling out Sam Vokes' equaliser in the first half before Callum Paterson sealed things with the final move of the game. What was impressive and hushed a few doubters was the Owls' management of the game and Moore commented that the performance had been "more or less perfect" in terms of the out-of-possession efforts.

The result moved Wednesday on to 20 points just 10 matches into the league season, their highest total at that stage of a campaign since the 1990/91 Ron Atkinson-led effort that ended in promotion from the Second Division and a famous League Cup win at Wembley. They'd gone third although they'd played a game more than those around them and were tootling along on that almost-obsessive "two-per-game" margin. But the feeling was that there was even more to come, that Wednesday hadn't quite hit their straps with a truly-settled midfield yet to be found, injuries in defence and a fresh injury concern to George Byers, who had picked up a foot niggle and sat out the Wycombe match. Initially it had been hoped that Byers would make a swift recovery, but he would miss nearly a month of action.

Luckily Will Vaulks was beginning to hit his straps. The dog-loving Wales international was later described – lovingly it should be stressed – as a mix of "a rabid mongrel and a changing-room spaniel" in one *Sheffield Star* column; the laugh-a-minute heart of all mischief behind the scenes, but a snarling, commanding presence on the field. A rare injury to his thigh in pre-season had robbed him of a smooth start to life at Hillsborough as Dele-Bashiru and Byers set up camp alongside Bannan in the engine room of Moore's plans. Starting his first league game in six weeks in a star turn against Wycombe thanks in part to Byers' absence, he'd played only 17 minutes of the previous five games. It was later admitted that Moore felt he needed time to bed in to how he wanted things done after Byers had been the man to leave the field early to no small acrimony in the madness at Peterborough. With the bit between his gnashers, the Scouse spaniel would go on to start all but four matches in the remainder of their League One campaign.

There weren't many finer Vaulks performances all season than that at Port Vale, up next in one of the more relentless periods of a relentless season. It was the first of eight matches in October and played out on a pitch more suited to rugby than football. A side without Gregory because of a late back tweak won another game that "they wouldn't have won last season." That was a phrase that would be pumped out by reporters and fans alike for months on end.

It was a horrible game broken up by one moment of quality, a Vaulks sidefoot in mid-tackle thunderbastard on the hour that blitzed past Jack

Stevens in Vale's goal and sparked a somersault celebration that all but surpassed the glamour of the goal itself. A social media video released by the club months down the line asked a flurry of Wednesday players what they felt was their goal of the season. In pretty handsome company Vaulks' Vale vapouriser won by a landslide.

Another win. Another hairy, scary, chest-beating win for a side who were developing a reputation for the battle. Four unbeaten and with results a-wobbling elsewhere, Sheffield Wednesday were third and now just two points of table-topping Plymouth Argyle, who had rallied to leapfrog Ipswich and a Portsmouth side on the start of what was to prove a debilitating tumble out of the reckoning – and one that would ultimately cost Danny Cowley his job as manager. Wednesday would head to Devon for the rearranged Plymouth match with top spot in their sights, momentum tanking nicely.

What of Plymouth then? A side built up by Wednesday cult hero Ryan Lowe and his assistant Steven Schumacher out of League Two in their debut 2019/20 season, they stayed up comfortably the year after and had flirted with the highest echelons of the third tier in 2021/22 before Lowe's departure to Championship Preston North End. Lowe had wanted to take Schumacher with him, but his fellow Scouser declined and took on the Pilgrims' hot seat himself. A run of one win in their final seven league matches – including a last-day 5-0 home defeat to Milton Keynes Dons – had the social media banter pages filled with depictions of a club who had bottled their big chance.

Like McKenna at Ipswich, Schumacher was a smart, savvy young manager in a division packed with them. Aged 39, he had been a midfield battler in a handsome EFL career at clubs such as Bradford City, Crewe Alexandra and Bury. Sitting top of the tree after 11 matches, it was clear that his side would compete again and in an attractive style; dynamic, swarming in their approach with Ryan Hardie, Niall Ennis and Swansea City loanee Morgan Whittaker offering defences no end of headaches. Bali Mumba and Finn Azaz – also loanees from Norwich City and Aston Villa respectively – added flair and pace.

Unlike most of the other early pacesetters in the table – Barnsley, Bolton Wanderers and Derby County featured on the fringes of the scrap – Plymouth were not a club to have tasted the riches of the Premier League. In fact, with a population of 262,000, they have the dubious honour of being the largest city in England to have never hosted top-flight football at all. Given the wide catchment area of Devon, they are a club with huge untapped potential, with a refurbished, sophisticated Home Park stadium easily of Championship quality and a Green Army of supporters who travel as well as anyone – incredibly so, given their geographical challenges. It was clear even in the early stages of the season that they were a club pointing in the right direction.

Wednesday set up for the clash with four at the back and Tyreeq Bakinson a surprise inclusion in midfield after playing just a solitary minute of the previous four league outings. Byers was still out with his foot issue and Bakinson's presence allowed Bannan to be pushed further forward into the No.10 role in which he operated so smoothly at the back end of the previous campaign. With Windass and Marvin Johnson high up behind Smith – Gregory was returning to fitness and Mallik Wilks was now out injured – it was another example of Wednesday's new approach to taking the game to those around them in the table.

To suggest the back-four system was cut open from the off would be an overstatement. But all-action Plymouth wasted no time in getting themselves into the game and, when Hardie bounded on to a well-picked clearance to form a one-man counterattack, his shot was bundled beneath the outstretched arm of David Stockdale to send the Green Army into raptures after just three minutes. Ben Heneghan and Michael Ihiekwe seemed to have done their jobs in forcing Hardie to shoot from a wide angle and both stood momentarily agog at the efforts of their goalkeeper. If the anticipation of the week's build-up had put a tingle in the Devon air even before the opener, the atmosphere in that moment was turned up to eleven.

So impressive it was then that Wednesday fired back immediately, Liam Palmer charging into the Plymouth box to find acres of space from a stunning Bakinson through ball to poke the ball past Michael Cooper – who had already developed a reputation as the division's best goalkeeper – and trigger a hush in Home Park. Wednesday had levelled things up and it was 1-1 after only seven minutes.

The match was a breathless example of two teams going at one another with attacking instincts on-point as both defences looked leggy at times by comparison. Cooper made a flurry of eye-catching saves, from Johnson, from Palmer, from Windass, who also hit the post as he continued his sprint towards fitness and form. Of Cooper's five saves on the night, four of them might adequately be described as "worldies" and the Owls had the better chances, even though Argyle racked up a whopping 24 shots to 13 and controlled 59 per cent of the ball.

On 73 minutes, with the momentum just having turned away from Wednesday a touch and with Moore staring across the pitch at an effort he felt had dipped dramatically, he turned to his coaching staff. It's not known exactly what was said, but a decision was made quickly. Bannan and Windass, Wednesday's two best and most attacking players, would be taken out of the action in a double substitution. Callum Paterson and Dele-Bashiru – two players known for their energy – would replace them.

That Plymouth seemed to seize the moment from that point may have been a coincidence. After all, Moore would later passionately state that he felt the double switch was not the moment that cost Wednesday the match. But it sure felt that way. Even though energy levels were dipping, players of the combined threat of Bannan and Windass deliver teeth to an away performance that was open and there for the taking. A point at Home Park would be a great result no doubt, given that Plymouth had won all five games there, conceding only in a 2-1 defeat to Ipswich. But whether it be tactical or mental, Wednesday's balloon seemed to deflate while those in green expanded.

Big forward Sam Cosgrove – a one-time Wednesday transfer target not too many windows back – was fresh off the bench and causing problems. He rose above Heneghan to put the ball over the line, although a feather touch from Stockdale and Ihiekwe's acrobatic clearance had the officials fooled – to the disgust of the home support. When Ihiekwe survived a penalty shout for a tumble with Cosgrove moments later, it seemed that the Owls would leave a thrilling, open match with a point.

Alas. In the final minute of normal time there was sluggish defending out wide, a slip and more slow work in the middle. Cosgrove rose above Heneghan again to head the ball confidently between Stockdale and the front post.

"The players just switched off at moments when they needed to keep their concentration really," said Moore, breaking from the routinely cool-and-calm, post-match press conference persona to describe his mood as "seething." He reviled at questions from reporters surrounding the double change, explaining his rationale in bringing on fresh legs.

Days later he would double-down with a sense of perplexity about the intensity of focus the decision had been given, both in the media and among the fanbase. "Irrespective of the result tonight it's still early in the season after 12 games," Moore continued. "But every game matters to us: we want the performance. I just thought tonight that the way they got the win might have been avoided."

It was an opportunity lost, as Plymouth extended their lead at the top of the table. After 12 matches the Owls remained third with 23 points, five back on the table-topping Pilgrims and four behind on Ipswich in second. Portsmouth were two shy of Wednesday in fourth, but had two games in hand. The itchiness, the nervousness of being Sheffield Wednesday in League One, was more than murmuring and the social media dissenters were growing in number again.

Heneghan, too, was one of a few players who would come in for criticism online despite a growing tally of statistics across several metrics that put him among the best-performing defenders in League One. "We know what social media is like, full stop, and we're playing in a very opinionated game," Heneghan later said with a smile. "Some are going to love you and some are going to hate you: that's just part of being a footballer. You see the best in the world get criticised, so some will say about someone playing in League One: 'He's decent' and others will say: 'What's he doing here?' Personally I don't go searching for all the talk but when you get the nice plaudits, you can't help but be happy with that and there'll be a few bad ones when you scroll down. It goes over my head. The fanbase is a totally different level. There will be more opinions and more voices. You have to take the rough with the smooth."

After shaking hands at the final whistle and sharing a word with Schumacher, who embarked on a four-corner tour of Home Park to drink in the enormity of a win that had taken his side to a six-from-six tally at home, Moore turned to his dug-out to embrace a new face in the world of Wednesday – an old friend brought in without a whirlwind of publicity, glitz or glamour just a few days earlier. The face would make a marked difference to Sheffield Wednesday's already-promising season. And his work had already begun.

SIX

"TOP DRAWER"

The pre-match press conference before Sheffield Wednesday's trip to Port Vale had been a fairly standard one. Conducted online via Zoom – as all standard media conferences had been since Covid got its claws into football in March 2020 – talking points had included George Byers' continued injury issue, the Wycombe win and the dynamic of the club's strikers. Standard, run-of-the-mill stuff. Whisper it quietly but despite best efforts, the nature of the beast means that pre-match pressers can get a bit tired and routine in the cut and thrust of a season.

After the final question had been answered and reporters had shuffled up their things and leaned into their laptops to say their thanks and goodbyes, Darren Moore quite unusually cleared his throat to speak again. "Lads, just to let you know while you're all listening in, we added a new staff member to the group this week," he said. "His name is James Shan and you'll be seeing him around the place." With that, armed with the knowing cheeky smile of a man who knew he'd left those on the call with questions left unanswered, he was gone.

Shan's arrival marked the end of Wayne Jacobs' time at the club. The long-time close friend of Moore and a lifelong Wednesdayite who had started an excellent playing career at Hillsborough, Jacobs had been balancing his coaching commitments with his tireless work running a Bradford children's charity. Such is the mark of the man that, when push came to shove, the charity work would come first. Sharing a word with a reporter some months down the line, Jacobs described the experience of working at S6 as "a dream come true."

Shan arrived as a free agent after his time as assistant manager of Rochdale had ended earlier that year. A talented coach who had started in the academy at West Bromwich Albion, he was co-manager when

Moore was handed his first proper coaching role with their under-18 side. Moore was late for their first meeting – an irony not lost on reporters who, from time to time, would have to wait for the start of those weekly press conferences – but they hit it off and helped one another's development no end. Shan was a talented player who missed out on a playing career despite trials with a number of clubs including Wednesday, but had quickly made his way through the coaching ranks at the Hawthorns with hard work and no end of talent. Moore, of course, had been a hugely successful player. Shan's strengths lay in coaching possession and Moore's career had been built on solid defence, so it proved to be a match made in heaven.

Like Jacobs and the other coaching staff he'd left behind, Shan had an existing relationship with the Owls' boss before he joined the club, a close one, and it became abundantly clear that the technical team were a band of brothers, each pulling in the same direction as their leader. Shan had known Jamie Smith since they were children, too, only a few minutes' drive separating the areas where they'd grown up. "Jamie lived in the posh bit, mind – and he's a bit older than I am," Shan would later quip with a wink.

His impact was huge and immediate. He quickly struck up a rapport with the playing staff – a few weeks in, Barry Bannan posted unprompted on social media to express how impressed he had been with Shan's work – and it allowed Wednesday to go at training in a different way from when Jacobs' charity commitments had rendered him unavailable. Shan's presence would allow for more detail and smaller groups working on more specific things. And his preference for snappy passing moves would enable Wednesday to improve on the ball, Moore said.

The fact is that Shan may never have stepped foot into the professional game were it not for a handful of "sliding doors" moments. Released by Walsall after an injury had made them take back a YTS offer, all those trials at all those clubs had taken a toll and he travelled to Perth, Australia to live with family. He spent a year surfing, working as an air-conditioning fitter and flipping shrimps on the barbecue. He returned home with the plan to gain a qualification as an electrician quickly before jetting back out and making a life for himself Down Under. The fate of football swung, though, and after glancing at a pitchside notice at Birmingham City's training ground – where he'd been doing some odd-job coaching work with an old coach of his – he applied on a whim. The rest, as they say, is history.

Early appearances in the Wednesday dugout at Port Vale and Plymouth under the belt, the 44-year-old was in the technical area when the Owls welcomed Cheltenham Town to Hillsborough on October 8. Reece James' rise and rise at S6 was rocked as he suffered a hip injury that would rule him out for the next six matches although the return of Mark McGuinness to the bench was a major positive in a defence that seemed to be ticking over nicely barring the odd individual mishap. Seven clean sheets in 13 league matches presented a pleasing statistic – although the best would be yet to come.

A 3-0 win was not quite as comfortable as the scoreline might suggest. Wednesday opened the scoring with a 30-yard Josh Windass free-kick in the third minute – the latest in the ever-growing list for their goal-of-the-season competition. But Cheltenham stayed in the game somehow, despite rampant Wednesday possession and 23 shots on goal. An attacking line-up was again named and Wednesday played with a degree of swagger, Lee Gregory perhaps the player who finished the game with a grimace after missing a couple of chances to get his campaign rolling.

One goal in 12 appearances had not been the start envisaged or expected from the man who had lit up the penalty area the season before on his way to becoming the club's top scorer. Not that many minded – his contribution to the attack was still of razor-sharp intelligence and his work rate sky-high. Bannan's match-settling second goal was football as performance art, the wee Scottish man sending the ball thundering into the top corner before Fisayo Dele-Bashiru finished things off in injury time.

The following weekend came a trip to a sunny, pleasant Cambridge and, as had been the case the season before, Wednesday's arrival had brought a sense of excitement to the ground. One parent sat within listening distance of the press box and had brought his son to watch Bannan alone even though neither were Cambridge United supporters. "Watch his first touch," he told his lad. "That's what I've been saying to you. It can go wherever you want it to if you think before the ball comes to you." Unlike the season before, however, the Owls dominated from start to finish, kicking off with Bannan stationed wide left and Windass on the right. Both found space and both punished it.

A 2-0 win will be remembered, though, as Gregory's day. A well-taken finish from a defence-splitting ball by Tyreeq Bakinson set Wednesday up and running in the sixth minute and, although Cambridge huffed and puffed, they could blow little down before the 34-year-old added his second to seal the game on with 13 minutes to go, deftly volleying Liam Palmer's cross home. The scoreline was shorn by an impressive Dimitar Mitov effort in the home goal and some less-than-clinical finishing, but it was another job well done and took Wednesday to 29 points from 14 matches, just a point shy of the automatic promotion places after Ipswich's shock defeat at Lincoln City.

Gregory's double was the perfect way for Wednesday to win, admitted Moore, who had spent the morning hoping for just that, given the importance of goals to his strikers. But Gregory is no fragile beast. "I don't know anything that's been said or whatever. I get enough stick from family and friends, so I'm all right with it," he joked with the smile of a man who had just scored twice in a match-winning performance. "It's down to experience maybe, I just brush all that off and I'm always confident I'll score. It's just a case of when. Even if you're not necessarily on the scoresheet, you can tell when you've had a good game and contributed in some way. We come out here to get promoted. If it means me doing the horrible side of the job, other players scoring and us winning, then so be it."

Like Shan, Windass and a number of other Wednesday figures, Gregory's road to Hillsborough was one less travelled. Not in a geographical sense perhaps – he grew up just a few miles away in a Sheffield United-supporting household in Batemoor – but his career had been one built from the ground up, having been released by them at the Lane as a wiry, 16-year-old right-back. He had been a trainee electrician who would enjoy the more than occasional evening at Sheffield nightclubs during the week, often clutching his older brother's ID for safe passage. "It was Leadmill sometimes on a Monday, Tuesdays in Crystal and Plug on a Thursday," he later remembered, although stressing he always kept himself in good nick thanks to the positive influence of his dad and brother. Riddled with self-doubt and having fallen out of love with the game, he needed an intervention from Alfreton Town manager Nicky Law to turn his head towards the possibility of a successful semi-professional career after at one stage giving up playing altogether.

"Growing up here, you're either red or you're blue," he said of a love for football that intoxicated him, as it does so many Steel City youngsters, from an early age. "It's as simple as that. It was nothing but football: nothing else mattered. If you didn't play football, you were the weird kid probably getting bullied because you didn't like football. I grew up on a massive estate in Batemoor and everybody just played football all the time. When I left Sheffield United at 16, I was done. I had been seven when I joined them and then they released me. They said I was too small, I was never going to grow and I was never going to be athletic enough. It broke my heart and I didn't play for ages."

After success with NCEL side Staveley Miners Welfare as he turned into his twenties and a "thanks-but-no-thanks" stint at Mansfield Town, Gregory was 22 by the time that National League side FC Halifax Town provided sanctuary and it was at the Shay that he partnered first future Leicester City and England striker Jamie Vardy up top and then Scott Hogan, who would play for Aston Villa and Birmingham City among others. His break into EFL football came when, amid reported interest from Birmingham City, Huddersfield Town, Milton Keynes Dons and Barnsley, Millwall won the day with a bid of about £250,000. It was quite a tale for a skinny apprentice sparky with a fake ID – and one with a bizarre driving character at the heart of the transfer.

Ian Holloway was Millwall manager but Gregory owes the move in no small part to Holloway's wife, Kim. With a Halifax game playing out in the background to marital life in the Holloway household one evening, she turned to her husband with a shrug and said: "You used to sign players like that." It planted a seed, a period of scouting took place and, after three failed bids, Millwall got their man in 2011, eight years on from his Sheffield United release and a life staring into plug sockets. A big-money, ultimately-unsuited move to Stoke City and a loan stint with Derby County acted as paving stones to Sheffield Wednesday and in the summer of 2021 Moore brought him back to his home city on a free transfer. Within a few weeks Wednesday fans were singing his name to the tune of Norman Greenbaum's *Spirit in the Sky*. Gregory is a fans' favourite with a great deal in common with those who adore him.

In midweek there was that Leicester City under-21s run-out, which proved to be something of a procession and attracted only 3,173 fans in what was one of the lowest showings ever recorded at Hillsborough. Academy man Will Trueman scored in a 2-0 win, though, as did Callum Paterson, who throughout the evening frankly looked like an over-competitive dad bullying his way around a school game. Given the designs on promotion and the fact that Championship teams do not play in the "Pizza Cup," it was hoped it would be Wednesday's final appearance in the competition for a very long time. And despite Moore's assertions that every game was for the winning, a few mid-weeks free from Papa Johns action couldn't be seen as a bad thing regardless of the day out at Wembley for the finalists. There were bigger prizes on offer.

Gregory scored early in a Saturday afternoon 1-1 draw at Lincoln City four days on from the Leicester game and, with an assist in the win over Cheltenham, he suddenly had four goal contributions in three outings. It was a timely return to form in front of goal and his song was never sung with more fervour than at Sincil Bank in a match that kicked off at 1pm on police advice after trouble in Lincoln city centre the season before. A draw at Lincoln was becoming something to be respected, the perennial "difficult place to go," with former Liverpool and Wolves winger Mark Kennedy making waves as their manager, having cut his teeth coaching in the academy at Manchester City. Lincoln were suddenly a steely proposition – particularly at home – and sat ninth in the division, having beaten Ipswich the week before. The fact is, though, that Wednesday could and perhaps should have taken the win as they spurned a host of chances. One player who will certainly look back at that October 22 afternoon with a cold shiver will be Ben Heneghan.

With Akin Famewo's long absence rolling on and on – although it had become clear that initial fears that his devastating injury would rule him out for the remainder of the season had proved to be pessimistic – and with Dominic Iorfa momentarily out of favour, Heneghan had risen to prominence at the very heart of defence. With Michael Ihiekwe one side of him and McGuinness the other, he was in a back three with huge aerial ability, handy enough on the ball and struck as a mean trio of nightclub doormen. But the fact is that there had been very little opportunity to form a settled line-up at the back. It seemed that, as one recovered fitness, another got injured. And it happened again as Heneghan twisted and turned and went down in innocuous fashion, mercilessly bayed at by Lincoln's crowd for "going down lightly." He'd actually decimated his anterior cruciate ligament and would miss the rest of the campaign, leaving Wednesday short at the back.

It was a desperately cruel blow for a softly-spoken, popular member of the changing-room who had fought tooth and nail after his release by Everton and Stoke City to battle his way back from non-league football with Chester, firstly with Motherwell. A move to Sheffield United had seen him shunned and, although his time with Blackpool and AFC Wimbledon had been richly successful, his shift to Sheffield Wednesday at 28 was one that he had said himself was something of a move back to the career trajectory of which he had dreamt. On first contacts, clearances and many of the "old-fashioned" central defensive metrics, he had performed at the top of the class. Surgery undertaken inside a fortnight, he flew to Dubai to find peace before embarking on a long and winding road to recovery at a cold and sometimes lonely Middlewood Road.

An eight-game October brought its challenges for Wednesday and, from the outside at least, a touch of fatigue. A 1-1 draw at home to Bristol Rovers was played out in front of the *Sky Sports* cameras and brought another goal for Smith – his third in League One for the Owls as he continued to grow into the season after a period of patient fitness-building that had seen him "butt heads" with coaching staff. But it also brought boos from pockets of a Hillsborough crowd frustrated at more lost ground on Plymouth and Ipswich. After 16 games Wednesday had lost one of their last nine, but were eight points back on the Pilgrims in pole position. Five separated them from second-placed Ipswich. A relentless pace was being set and no matter the reminders of the season being a marathon – it was still October after all – the prospect of another campaign in League One was clearly gnawing away at many in the stands.

"We have got to win every game here," Moore said in response to questions about the boos. "We know it doesn't always work like that, but we have got to win every game here. I understand it. As a manager I understand the heartache of this place over the years; years and years of heartache, long before I was here, in terms of where the club once was and what some of these fans have been used to. There is expectation with what the fans feel about League One, but we have to do it together and I am totally with them and I understand it.

"The boos come from frustration because they want it so badly, but we all want it so badly. If you look at the home record this year, it has been excellent. We know we have to keep performing. The fans know the potential of the players. They have seen the level of performance of the players. Just stick behind them and go from there." Although delivered in Moore's relaxed tone, all wry smiles and calm, it was about as direct a call to action for supporters as he would deliver all season… that wasn't broadcast on a big screen at Hillsborough, at least.

The Owls boss had also discussed a frustration in his side not quite making the most of the chances he felt they were creating. The long and arduous pursuit of Mallik Wilks had not yet begun to pay off with injury slicing into his involvement and while Gregory, Smith and Windass had offered stellar performances, no Owls figure had yet taken on the responsibility of becoming the first Wednesday player since Neil Mellor 11 seasons earlier to score 20 goals in a single campaign. Moore laid on extra shooting drills in training in an attempt to help to facilitate an improvement he maintained was in the post.

As if by magic, it worked. A 4-2 home win over Burton Albion was just the ticket, but exposed the fine margins in which football operates. Had they been any more devastating in their approach than in previous outings? Perhaps not, but more cut-throat certainly. Bannan, Smith and Wilks put them 3-0 up before the hour and Dele-Bashiru made it four on 75 minutes before a Brewers double straddled a missed penalty by Gregory. It had been Wilks' first league goal for Wednesday – he flanked Smith with Paterson as Windass, Byers, Gregory and Vaulks were rested – and he also claimed an assist. When Alex Mighten scored his first Owls goal in a routine FA Cup first-round win over Morecambe the following weekend, with Windass bagging the other, it felt as if Moore's new pace pair were beginning to get going.

Seven games unbeaten and only one defeat in 13 meant that momentum was growing at Hillsborough all over the field and off the pitch the club, so often criticised for losing talented young players to the system after signs of promise, seemed to be looking to get their house in order. Goalkeeper Pierce Charles signed his first professional deal, having been involved in a great deal of first-team training and the club having persuaded him that it was the environment to invest himself in.

While it also served to fend off increasing interest of the England youth ranks for whom Charles also qualified, Moore had half a hand in his friend, Northern Ireland manager Ian Baraclough, taking him on an experience-building senior international trip. Contract offers were also tabled to Rio Shipston and Sean Fusire, two confident young players expected to make waves. Sam Durrant, a 21-year-old attacking midfielder brought in from Blackburn Rovers, was signed on a deal until the end of the season. Sheffield United winger Hassan Ayari was brought in on trial, although nothing materialised from it.

What was by now clear, six weeks or so into his time at Sheffield Wednesday, was that Jimmy Shan's presence was making itself felt. Speaking to a reporter at Cambridge's Abbey Stadium before that 2-0 win earlier in the month, one senior Wednesday player said he only wished Shan had become available earlier, such was the impression he had made on their campaign in those early weeks. "Top drawer" was the expression used to describe him.

As with Moore and Smith, Shan would travel between his home in the West Midlands and South Yorkshire, staying in hotels and returning whenever the monstrous mid-season schedule would allow. His young sons attended matches whenever possible but, in a candid interview with the *Sheffield Star*, Shan revealed the human side to life as a football coach. His biggest break yet had been a three-month, 12-match run as caretaker manager of West Brom following Moore's sacking in March 2019. Feeling conflicted about taking on the opportunity given the position of his great friend, he had accepted the role only after an hour-long conversation in which Moore had encouraged him to do so. Shan won seven and drew one of the 12 matches and before and after every one, the first person to text him with best wishes, congratulations and commiserations was Moore.

"My youngest son was born on the Thursday and then on the Saturday, 6:30pm, I was caretaker manager of West Brom," Shan said. "That was a crazy period of my life. For the first few games I was just being told to do the next one, do the next one. I was telling my wife our lives could really change because there was massive speculation that Alex

Neil was going to take the job and that would have had an impact on us financially as a family. The bottom line is that if Alex had come in, I might have been out of work. It was a strange situation to be in. The downside was that ultimately I didn't really have an initial bond with my newborn baby because I was never there. I was only 20 minutes away in terms of the commute, but there was so much time and effort going into planning games that people just don't see. I wasn't able to form that bond truly until the end of that season.

"I love the game, but I hate the industry," he continued, his face cold and serious. "Things can be out of your control and it has such an impact on your life and your family's finances. You go two or three games when you're not successful and you get beaten and you never know what's round the corner. But in that period I probably wouldn't work any differently from when I'd been successful. And ultimately when the players cross the white line, you have as a coaching staff to put a lot of trust in them to execute the plans and the instructions they've been given."

SEVEN

WINTER WONDERLAND

Sheffield Wednesday and the Premier League? It's complicated. Not in a strictly footballing sense, of course. In a footballing sense the relationship is pretty simple. Having been a founder member of the 1992 rebrand that changed everything, things started really rather nicely; they got better, but then they, well, didn't. Swirling debts, a catalogue of bad decisions and the knock-on effects of an Italian temper conspired to dump the Owls out of the top tier – and the riches that come with it – just five months into the new millennium as *Sky Television* put their foot down on broadcasting domination and plundered the league into unimaginable wealth. The Carlos Carvalhal flirtation with a return came and went in the early stages of Dejphon Chansiri's own spell of financial splurge and by November 2023 Wednesday were in the third tier for the third time since they'd last been in the first.

But the thing is that, despite the yawning chasm between relegation in May 2000 and the modern day, the feeling hasn't subsided that the top division is where Wednesday truly belong. That's not only in the fanbase, but among pundits and ex-players selecting the make-up of their dream Premier League and reaching for Wednesday's presence in a grasp for glorious nostalgia. Any conversation surrounding promotion from League One was not far behind comments that suggested that once that business was out of the way, it was time to kick on and go for "the actual prize" almost immediately. For many the blood-and-guts bunfight of a third-tier promotion scrap was a mere step at the bottom of the ladder. It's a mindset Wednesday players and coaches have had to deal with for good and for bad. Whether it's a healthy mindset for a club to have after 23 years is a matter for debate.

So curiously framed then are cup clashes between Wednesday and sides currently operating in the Premier League. The megaclubs? For sure, recent matches against Manchester City, Chelsea and Arsenal had been given a full-mashing "David-versus-Goliath" billing. But what of the lower top-tier sides, those no more steeped in heritage than Wednesday themselves, with more modest fanbases?

Wednesday had been drawn to make the long trip to Southampton in the third round of the Carabao Cup on November 9 and found a club in a spot of disarray, bottom of the Premier League and in a state of flux after Ralph Hasenhüttl's sacking just a couple of days earlier. Having achieved the back-to-back promotions that Wednesday so rabidly craved, the Saints were in the final month of an 11-year top-tier stint that had taken them to Europe and four times to Wembley. No matter their current issues, Southampton represented a hell of a scalp. Reacting in a confused way to pre-match questions about whether he would be tempted to rest key players with more pertinent battles to face in the league, the sense was that Darren Moore had smelt the whiff of opportunity.

He named a strong side and was bold in his approach, Wednesday hungrily pressing and outmuscling their opponents from the first minute. When Josh Windass smashed Fisayo Dele-Bashiru's through ball past Alex McCarthy in the Saints goal on 24 minutes, with two divisions and an ocean of investment separating the teams, it had been Wednesday that had appeared the more confident, the sprightlier, the more competent on the ball. Incoming Saints boss Nathan Jones – then still technically the manager of Luton Town – watched on from the stands and may well have wondered the scale of the job at hand as the Owls swaggered their way around St. Mary's in a whirlwind first half-hour. Later Moore stopped his post-match interview to congratulate Jones on landing the gig.

As had been the necessity for several weeks, the Owls boss had shuffled his pack a touch. The decision to play Callum Paterson as a right wing-back was a surprise, but one that paid off in spades as the greying 27-year-old battled, harried and bullied the Saints' change side and caused no little issues going forward. In midfield, Tyreeq Bakinson again gave an excellent account of himself and Dele-Bashiru caused untold headaches, offering a bustling performance that showed attributes that could surely grace the Premier League if good career decisions were made along the way. Up top alongside the tireless Lee Gregory, Windass, too, offered touches of quality that would have had the uninitiated wondering which team was from the top tier. He would develop a moreish hunger for the big stage as the season progressed.

It was an evening when Wednesday grew and grew with every tackle and every passage of play, rising from back-to-back draws against Lincoln City and Bristol City and the ire that came with them: they were growing taller, passing sharper. As expected, Southampton got a foothold, but the Owls gave as good as they got and plenty more. David Stockdale made a couple of classy saves and Michael Ihiekwe a couple of much-needed blocks. The match turned when Marvin Johnson was outfoxed by Malian international Moussa Djenepo to hand James Ward-Prowse the chance to equalise from the spot on the stroke of half-time, but the point had been made – Wednesday had set up to win and were going about the task with their chests out.

Back-to-back goal-line clearances to deny former Arsenal and England superstar Theo Walcott were pulled off by Ihiekwe and Scotland international Stuart Armstrong hit the bar in a second half that swung in Southampton's favour. But when the tie went to penalties, nobody could argue Wednesday hadn't deserved their shot at the spot kick lottery. When Dominic Iorfa, awesome on the night on the right of the back three, had his penalty saved by the feet of McCarthy, it felt cruel and undeserved. As Southampton's players celebrated and noise carried down from their fans, it felt as though the Owls had been the only real winners.

It was a defeat, but a performance that would breathe huge belief into not only the changing-room, but Sheffield Wednesday as a football club. There was something in the way they'd gone about it, not cowering or compromising, but looking to smash their way past a side weakened a touch, but full of internationals. For all the gritty wins over towns with no train station, they proved they could mix it with the big boys. It was a seismic evening in the season and a feeling they would revisit.

At the heart of it had been Ihiekwe again, growing into the totem around which Wednesday's defensive efforts were being built. Much had been spoken about the club's need for an aerial battering-ram in the heart of defence, a player capable of playing a little football while organising those around him. When the scale of Heneghan's injury had become clear, Ihiekwe was pushed in to perform the all-important central role. He did so with ease.

A product of the glittering Liverpool youth academy, Scouser Ihiekwe had dreamt of growing up to become Jamie Carragher. You can see a little Carragher in how he plays: committed, whole-hearted and calm at times when those around him may dip into a sense of panic. He tells tales of being turned inside out by a young Raheem Sterling in training, of enjoying the odd session with the seniors when making up the numbers during international breaks and how his release from the club he still watches when time allows, spurred him on even harder to make himself a career in the game.

Along with Smith, he'd arrived at Wednesday that summer in a whirlwind of controversy and confusion, both making the short trip from Rotherham United after helping them to automatic promotion only a month or so earlier. It's a switch that still rankles with the Millers' fanbase, a sense of "Anyone but Wednesday" stinging hard alongside the reality that even with a division freshly opened up between the two clubs, the pulling power of the Owls – both financial and in terms of size and heritage – was enough to steal away two key men. Smith had scored 19 goals in Rotherham's impressive promotion-winning effort and Ihiekwe had been named in the League One team of the year.

Their seismic double transfer had been confirmed on June 22, not long after Rotherham boss Paul Warne had sat in a *BBC Radio Sheffield* studio and expressed his growing confidence that both would be retained. The following day they were pictured smiling at the launch of Wednesday's new kit sponsor Host and Stay, a holiday rental company who had become the first external front-of-shirt sponsors signed in the Dejphon Chansiri era in exchange for what was described as "a large six-figure fee."

Rotherham fans took it as a deliberate Wednesday wind-up – in reality it was the first opportunity for players to be photographed in the new shirts – and senior Millers figures felt disappointed in what they felt was gloating. In response their media team posted a bizarre tweet based around an image of 36-year old former Wednesday centre-half Richard Wood: despite the growing rivalry between the two clubs, he had only a year or so earlier discussed his ongoing love for the Owls in an interview. In an age of zappy social media banter, the back-and-forth fell a little flat.

Technically under contract until the end of June, Rotherham refused to allow the pair to start training with the Owls, as is relatively normal practice in such circumstances, until July when their new deals at Hillsborough kicked in. Warne – who by the end of September had also dropped back to League One to take up the manager's position at Derby County – was left cold by the pair's decision and one player in particular, whom he felt had given soft word on signing a new deal. Warne is said to have been bitterly disappointed, but any initial frostiness has thawed – he was later seen chatting to the pair in jovial tones when Wednesday met his Derby side later that season.

"I came close to staying," Ihiekwe said in an open and honest interview with the *Rotherham Advertiser* in the days after his move to Wednesday had been confirmed. "There were points in the negotiations when I thought it might happen. I'm 29 and at this stage of my career I had to take my time with the decision and speak to everyone around me – my family and missus and all that stuff. It wasn't something I could just do in a couple of days. I appreciate Rotherham making me the offer they did, but ultimately I had to do what was best for my family.

"Listen, I'm a football fan myself. I'm a big Liverpool follower. I get where the Rotherham fans are coming from; I fully understand it. You can't control how people are going to think or feel about you. All I can say is that I didn't take my decision lightly. I had to have a long, long think about it. It was based on doing right by my family. The size of the club is huge. I know that from being around the area. The fanbase is massive. As I said earlier, it came down to me being 29 and doing the best for my family. That's it really."

Smith followed a similar line, tinged with a little sadness about how things had played out. "I'm a smart enough lad to know that my Rotherham reputation built up over four and a half years is going to be tainted now," he said. "I made the decision and I'm big enough to take everything that comes with it. I've given my all for the club. It's really sad that it's ended this way. Football is completely ruled by emotion and I get the response to what I've done. Hopefully once the dust has settled a bit, people might understand. They might not. That's just part and parcel of it."

Although a pint in Rotherham town centre probably isn't on the cards for the pair any time soon, they stuck together through the vitriol of a story that dominated South Yorkshire football for a few days before fizzling out. The Millers recruited well and went on to overcome the departure of Warne and his staff to finish well clear of safety in the Championship under another bright young manager, Matt Taylor. The families of Smith and Ihiekwe are close and the pair thick as thieves, perhaps brought closer together by the whirlwind that they were packaged in during those few weeks. It was a big win for Wednesday.

They both started in a gnarled 1-0 win at Accrington Stanley – a club Ihiekwe had spent time at in a loan stint just five years earlier – three days on from Southampton. Mighten was again on the scoresheet on an afternoon when more Wednesday fans entered the Wham Stadium than Stanley supporters. Stanley chairman Andy Holt later indicated that £24,000 had been taken over the bar from a travelling fanbase he described as "immense."

The mid-November trip to Accrington had been the first at which blue and white Santa hats had been pulled from the drawer and worn on the terraces – others can debate the appropriate wearing of Christmas garments outside December – as Yuletide began to draw in. And it transpired Wednesday supporters weren't the only ones who could throw a few quid behind a bar either. On November 19, after an unremarkable 1-0 home win over Shrewsbury Town that is quite possibly only really remembered by match-winner McGuinness, given it proved to be his only goal in Owls colours, Wednesday's squad rushed from the stadium, hopped on a train and travelled to the Big Smoke for their annual Christmas shindig.

While he understood the importance of social events within the squad and would come to embrace them, the suggestion is that Darren Moore wasn't a huge fan of the idea before being talked around by senior players. The previous season's Christmas escapades took the squad to Manchester days before a number of positive Covid-19 cases forced the postponement of games against Accrington Stanley and Burton Albion before sluggish defeats at Sunderland – Wednesday losing 5-0 in a chastening evening at the Stadium of Light – and at Shrewsbury.

A healthy dollop of hearsay and swirling rumour meant that fans joined the dots, but the speculative link was never confirmed and remained unsubstantiated. A back-and-forth between the Wednesday boss and a local reporter on the issue was about as fractious as a Moore press conference would get, his angry stare down the lens of a Zoom call fierce. No concrete answers were given as to whether the shindig had disrupted the Owls' season in any case – albeit no denials from Moore either – so an editorial decision was made not to publish or broadcast the exchange for fear of furthering what could have been an unsubstantiated rumour at a time when the side were stalling a touch. After all, Moore's men were not the only squad in the EFL to suffer a spate of postponements in late December 2020.

The following year, with Covid largely in the rear-view mirror and a gruelling early start to the season behind them, the "do" was granted fairly happily in the end. Two nights in London, a sojourn around Winter Wonderland, meals out and the chance to bond. It's one of the rare and momentary throwbacks to a bygone era enjoyed by the legendary drinking schools of old – of Messrs Sheridan, Palmer and Hirst. Given the ultra-professionalism of the modern-day footballer, you'd suspect the volume of refreshment has dipped a touch and that there are rather more gin and slimlines on display.

"They're always good value, the Christmas parties," Bannan later said. "You get to know different sides of your teammates. When you have a drink, people tend to open up a wee bit more about their life away from football and you end up making bonds that might not be as strong at the start of the season. You can end up sitting and talking to somebody you might not always speak to that often. It's brilliant.

"You come back and, because of whatever has happened, maybe somebody has made an arse of themselves on a night out, that feel-good factor rolls on and you're all talking and cracking up about stories that have happened on those nights out. It's always good for team bonding – as long as everybody stays out of trouble and behaves. The squad we had was brilliant because we were all good lads. We had loads of experienced lads who had been to a million Christmas parties, we knew what the boundaries were and that made us all easy to marshal. Not that the young lads would have caused any bother anyway. They were a really good group."

The hardcore kicked off as early as 11am and one senior player –

who may or may not be partial to the occasional somersault – was the life and soul of the party, packing two sets of fancy dress for a dramatic mid-session change at Winter Wonderland, a vast pop-up metropolis set up in Hyde Park that includes a number of bars designed for such frivolity. He even went as far as to jump on to the stage to sing and dance with the live performer, sparking a rapturous reception from the rest of his teammates. A draw held at Middlewood Road a couple of weeks earlier had players pulling letters out of a hat to determine what their fancy-dress options would be. Bannan drew C and dressed as Captain Jack Sparrow. Liam Palmer picked D and took on Doctor Doolittle.

The World Cup started on the Sunday evening with a 2-0 win for Ecuador over the hosts Qatar, although such was the entertainment on show that nobody really seemed to notice. Booked in for a meal at high-end French restaurant Bagatelle on Sunday evening, one heavily-refreshed player felt the pinch of a busy couple of days and momentarily fell asleep in the hotel bar, unable to rouse himself for the 9pm booking.

A good time was had by all, it seemed, and a tight-knit changing-room packed with characters such as Vaulks, Stockdale, Wilks, Adeniran and Paterson meant no shortage of jokers at Middlewood Road when the time was right. The ends of socks are cut out, youngsters are ribbed for music choices and the banter expected from a room full of 20-and-30-something lads is relentless. When Vaulks hung a Gucci jacket belonging to Wilks on the ceiling, it got a rise out of the former Hull City man, but it was always in good jest. Two senior players later nearly came to blows about some changing-room ribbing although that, too, fizzled out soon enough and cuddles were shared. Nobody apparently dares to wind up Akin Famewo. The vast majority of hijinx stays very much behind the safety of closed doors, of course, as it always has.

Wednesday's was a tight changing-room full of bubbly characters, not completely devoid of ire about niggly issues such as time-keeping – some of the squad's younger players had the odd issue with that, it seems – but bright and buoyant, together. There were pockets of the group that tended to sit together, as was their placing in the changing room at Middlewood Road; from the "dad corner" of Barry Bannan,

Jack Hunt and Lee Gregory to the younger lads and another centred on Josh Windass, Callum Paterson and Liam Palmer – who, as an elder statesman of the changing room, was in charge of the music.

What struck those on the fringes of the Sheffield Wednesday machine is that this was a conscientious and personable squad. The days of a young reporter politely asking for an interview and being met with a player silently putting on his headphones with a dead-eye smirk were over. That bygone individual will remain unnamed and it should be stressed that the vast majority of Wednesday players have always been warm and personable, but it wasn't a wholly isolated incident in previous squads containing an over-inflated ego or two. This lot were gentlemen to a man.

During the 2022/23 season there were vast individual charity efforts, nice-touch exchanges with supporters and a feeling that this group of players were genuinely warm, normal lads who just happened to be pretty good at knocking a football about. Few, if any, of the autograph-hunting supporters stationed at the edge of the players' car-park on a matchday would walk away disappointed. As Moore would mention a number of times during the campaign, here was a side embracing its role at the centre of a community that needed them. Away from the miserable glare of social media, it was clear a bond was being built back up between the changing-room and the terraces.

It helped, of course, that things were ticking along nicely on the pitch. The performance at Southampton had excited Wednesday fans and the feeling was that this was a side growing in stature. Were they so routinely blowing teams away as some fans would have preferred? No. But in achieving the goals set out at the start of the season, they were bearing down on the top two nicely – a nine-point chasm had been opened-up on fourth-placed Peterborough, while their win over Shrewsbury came as Ipswich drew at Burton. With a greater goal difference than Ipswich, the Owls were now a win off top spot and a solitary point behind them. Taking the Saints penalty defeat as a draw, they were unbeaten in 10.

To boost morale further, confirmation came beyond any reasonable doubt that Bannan would remain a Sheffield Wednesday player into the next season, regardless of their divisional status. The Scot confirmed that an extension clause in his contract would trigger automatically on hitting a certain number of games played – and that figure was close.

With the travails of Winter Wonderland well out of the system, Sheffield Wednesday's November would close out with an FA Cup tie at home to League Two Mansfield Town. It was a second-round clash that had failed to get Wednesday supporters salivating, but had certainly piqued the interest of Stags fans who made the trip to South Yorkshire in huge numbers – a touch less than 4,000 at a club that averaged home gates of 4,323 the season before.

That Mansfield were managed by former Sheffield United boss Nigel Clough, who also had a brief loan stint at Wednesday, added a morsel of narrative to which the local media clung. And the presence of Stags midfielder Stephen Quinn, another former Blades figure who, after scoring against the Owls in the Papa Johns Trophy the previous year, seemed keen to goad the blue and white support before Wednesday's late winner.

On the night the League Two outfit were the better side, particularly in the first half. After George Lapslie had given them a deserved lead by poking Kellan Gordon's cross past Owls goalkeeper Cameron Dawson, Quinn had the chance to double the lead, but snatched at it. Dawson made a couple of good saves and the second half brought more joy for Wednesday, Wilks having jinked his way into some good positions. But the arrival of Smith made the difference with his late double, both coming from excellent crosses by Marvin Johnson down the left.

"I back myself to score whenever I'm on a football pitch," Smith told reporters post-match after claiming his fifth and sixth goals of what had been something of a stop-start season. "So I was delighted to see the ball come across the six-yard box. As a striker, your eyes light up. I haven't found myself in those positions in the last few weeks, so I need to be consistent now and find myself there more regularly. Winning breeds winning and we've got that mentality in the changing-room – we want to win every game that we go into. It doesn't matter the competition, whether it's a five-a-side in training or here at Hillsborough."

That fierce competitiveness and will to win shone through in the final minutes of the clash as Wednesday were delivered yet another killer defensive blow. After injuries had decimated the contributions of Famewo and Heneghan, it was felt their share of bad luck had been doled out on that front already. Not so. Ihiekwe, so coolly impressive in the 23 appearances made to that point, twisted awkwardly and hobbled off in the 89th minute. It transpired that he'd damaged his cruciate ligaments, the first long-term injury of his career. An initial diagnosis suggested a comeback in the new year, but he didn't step back on to a football pitch until May.

It had come at a heavy price, there'd been huffing and puffing, luck was ridden at stages and it took a late show to down the plucky Stags, but Wednesday were into the third round of the FA Cup, where the possibility of another Premier League tie lay in wait. After the Southampton "oh-so-nearly," the feeling was that they'd have rather fancied that.

"Hopefully we can get somebody good in there," continued granite-jawed Geordie Smith in his post-match chinwag with the press. "Personally I'd like Newcastle away, but I'll take someone in the Premier League away; that'd be nice. I love the FA Cup because anything can happen."

Newcastle away? Smith would very nearly get his wish.

EIGHT

MOORE IN, MOORE OUT

ecember. The month of festivity and cheer, of goodwill and compassion... when forgiveness comes for all. That is, of course, unless you've just drawn 0-0 against Oxford United in League One. For some people that was cause for anger, social media outrage and a reason to want manager Darren Moore – currently on a 10-game unbeaten run – fired from his job. Merry Christmas, Sheffield Wednesday.

Christmas Day 2022 arrived for Wednesdayites with a running war of words taking place between fans again. One side, the *Moore Outers*, had decided that they'd had enough; others, the *Moore In-ers*, were pleased enough with a run in which their side had lost just three of their last 20 games in all competitions – including just one in the league – even if some of the football had been far from inspiring.

So the boos on December 17 were far from unexpected as they emanated from the stands at Hillsborough that night, but there was something far more positive at play as well. As David Stockdale made a beeline for his teammate between the sticks, chants of: "He's one of our own" started up. Cameron Dawson smiled as he walked towards the Kop and looked up to the seats he used to sit in. The result had not been ideal, but this night was his.

"Pragmatic" is probably the word best used to describe Wednesday's season until December. Moore had managed to fix so many problems from the previous year and now the Owls were holding on to those 1-0 leads, they were seeing games out under pressure and they were even coming from behind to win games. A lot of their victories, however, remained narrow. Wednesday were hardly blowing teams away and, going into their game against Derby County on December 3, had managed to score more than once in only one of their last five league games.

Not great, then, that they were heading to probably their biggest bogey ground of them all.

Ben Heneghan's season was over, George Byers was still out of action, Dennis Adeniran remained weeks away from a return, Josh Windass and Lee Gregory would both miss out and Michael Ihiekwe had a problem that would prove to be very, very serious. The defender had played 134 matches in just three seasons before joining the Owls, but the knee-ligament damage he sustained against Mansfield Town caused him to miss 22 consecutive League One games and put even greater strain on Moore's back line. Up front, in the absence of so many others, young loanee Alex Mighten was called upon and Moore was clutching at straws a little as he headed to his old stomping-ground.

For the handful who were present for the last game between the two sides, there was an air of PTSD about returning to the scene of Wednesday's relegation two years previously. But for those involved, it was a chance to banish some of those demons by taking advantage of results elsewhere and going top. In order to do so, they'd have to find their way past long-serving Owls goalkeeper Joe Wildsmith, who had opted against a new deal to go in search of regular game time in Derbyshire – a choice that was proving prudent under Paul Warne.

It had all the feeling of a big game; two sides playing at a level that they felt was below their station, a hefty crowd present and plenty on the line as both pushed for promotion back into the Championship. In reality, though, they cancelled each other out. Fans going back and forth with chants of: "We sent you down" and "You're staying down" proved to be the highlight of a drab affair and if the two sides had played until this very point, with you reading this book, there probably still wouldn't have been a winner.

Wildsmith, who had joined the Owls at just 13 years old before working his way through the ranks, received a very warm welcome when collecting a ball in front of the away end and found it all a bit surreal. "It's always nice to get a clean sheet in any game as a goalkeeper," he explained afterwards. "And with all the added things going on today it was a really nice touch for me personally, but I thought the team defended well and were very deserving of that clean sheet. It was very strange, a bit surreal, really because I was there for so long until last summer, I've never really known anything but that club and to see some familiar faces – ones I've known for years and years – was nice. But obviously then it was down to business and getting the job done on the pitch." Former Sheffield United man David McGoldrick, meanwhile, didn't get quite the same sort of reception.

After a game with plenty of huff and puff, but little quality stuff, Wednesday missed a big chance to go top and Warne admitted that he didn't feel either team "really did enough to win it," adding that "it felt a little bit like both sets of players had the mindset that a point was better than nothing." Fans left disappointed, but not too much so, given Wednesday's horrific Pride Park record, and the club was certainly in a better place than the last time they drew there.

A few thousand miles away England were preparing to face Senegal in the 2022 World Cup knockout stages and Wednesdayites who like their international football had already made a mental note that victory at Al-Bayt Stadium would mean a quarter-final the night of their game against Exeter City. It was a logistical nightmare made more difficult by the fact that Exeter wouldn't bring the kick-off forward to accommodate fans looking to get back to watch Gareth Southgate's Three Lions. Alternative arrangements would be required.

The trip from Sheffield to Exeter is long and arduous at the best of times, but, with concerns about the pitch amid almost freezing temperatures, it's safe to say that there wasn't a great deal of excitement to visit St. James' Park – a ground where Wednesday had lost four of their five league encounters and drawn the other. Moore had suggested that his side would be working on ways to be more effective going forward after seemingly managing to sort their previous issues at the back. But aside from a couple of half-chances for Windass – back alongside Gregory after injury – the Owls certainly didn't show much of a threat as their 1,300 or so away fans watched on, growing increasingly frustrated with the lack of chances against a team back in the third tier for the first time in a decade.

And frustration turned to worry with half-an-hour gone when Bannan chased back to make a tackle on the edge of the Wednesday box and stayed down. The Owls' captain doesn't really get injured. Alongside his incredible football brain and often breathtaking technical ability, he's also blessed with joints and ligaments that can take a bit of a kicking. So when he stays down, there's a problem. He did get up and try to carry on, as you'd expect, but after making one more pass, he dropped to the turf again, cutting a forlorn figure as his arms hunched over his knees. Having not missed a matchday squad in the league for three years, it would appear that the Wednesday talisman was human after all.

Just before the hour mark things got worse, as Jack Caprice's strike from range bounced awkwardly between bodies and nestled into the back of the net in front of the Big Bank. Exeter's support took great pleasure in taunting Stockdale with chants of: "Cameron Dawson, he's better than you" – a bit of support for the shot-stopper who had helped them to promotion the season before. "Sometimes you have to look at yourself and say it wasn't good enough personally," Stockdale said afterwards. "I will always do that and always be honest." Any other year recently that would've been that, but Moore's Owls never said die, and not many embodied that spirit like Callum Paterson.

There was increasing concern that he may be tempted away in January as his contract ran down and his former club Hearts went very public with their interest in bringing him home. Fifteen minutes remained on the clock when he was thrown into the mix to bosh people around in the cold Devon air and, with just 20 seconds remaining of four minutes added on, he highlighted his importance again. Gregory turned on the edge of the box and the ball rolled the way of Paterson, who, with laser-like precision, side-footed it past the outstretched arms of Jamal Blackman and into the back of net. Cue an eruption in the away end. They may not have played well and they may not have deserved anything, but the Owls would be leaving Exeter with another point to their tally. The downsides? Another chance to climb into the top two was missed and Wednesdayites' wait to see a win at St. James' Park continued – their only victory coming behind-closed-doors in the FA Cup during the Covid-19 pandemic. There was also that Bannan predicament.

Nobody from the terraces to the press box really wanted to stick around afterwards. There was a World Cup quarter-final to watch, frozen hands had long since lost the ability to type properly and the performance was hardly anything to rave about. Moore's comment about Stockdale having "lost sight" of the ball for Exeter's goal didn't feel like much at the time and Wednesday's latest come-from-behind victory had made it 13 league games without defeat. Pretty? Absolutely not. But the Owls train kept on rolling on as England fell to defeat against France in Qatar and in a pub in the market town of Bridgwater a handful of Sheffield folk finished their drinks at the final whistle and plodded back to the car. A few more years of hurt lay ahead of them.

For the first time since his arrival Moore would be without Bannan in a league game and with Byers and Adeniran also still out, he was forced into a bit of a reshuffle against Oxford United at Hillsborough. They weren't all enforced changes, though, and it would turn out that the manager's subtle criticism of Stockdale had led him to ask questions about his place in the side. So when Palmer led the team out at Hillsborough, Dawson was ready to take his·chance in his first league start of the campaign – a redemption story there for the taking after what was frankly some unfair criticism in the past.

Dawson had come back from Devon different – "more rounded," as he put it – and there wasn't a chance he was going to miss his opportunity to show what he could do. He might not get another opportunity to slide into Stockdale's spot and a couple of solid moments early on settled any minor nerves that may have been present in front of the Kop. The lad from Millhouses didn't put a foot wrong all night and his big moment came in stoppage time when Mark McGuinness bundled over Gatlin O'Donkor in the box, giving Oxford the perfect opportunity to puncture Wednesday's unbeaten run from 12 yards. But there was an air of confidence about Dawson, with all eyes on him, as Josh Murphy stepped up to the spot and the goalkeeper guessed the right way. Wednesday's two-month run continued, largely thanks to one man, and Moore's decision was more than vindicated.

A lifelong Wednesdayite, Dawson had had a rapid rise in professional football. Baby-faced, full-kit kickabouts with mates round Millhouses saw him pretending he was Glenn Whelan or Chris Brunt rather than David Lucas or Kevin Pressman. Playing outfield for Greenhill in the Sheffield and District Junior League, he didn't take up goalkeeping properly until he was 14 or 15. Within three seasons he was a Wednesday scholar playing in England youth sides with Dominic Iorfa, among others.

He may not have even chosen football. At the time he chose to take on a scholarship with his beloved Wednesday, he was also playing junior tennis for Yorkshire and was nationally ranked. He was a promising cricketer, too, stepping out for Norton Oakes as a hard-hitting middle-order bat who occasionally took the wicketkeeping gloves. It was something he enjoyed and in 2010 he scored 700 runs. His last first-team game came in August that season when his 16 not out steered them to a thrilling tie against Doncaster Town's second team.

After the game – the Oxford one, not Doncaster Town – Dawson spoke openly about how his spell away from home, out of his comfort zone, had improved him on and off the pitch. "I'm now someone who's much more laid back now in terms of how I feel," he said. "There are no ups and downs like there was. I was at a fantastic football club and you leave Exeter City normally being both a better player and a better person. In terms of my goalkeeping I think I've matured.

"There are times as a goalkeeper where you're going to make a mistake again – I'm not coming here and saying all is fine and dandy and that's it. There will be tough times because that's the life of a goalkeeper. It's just about staying level. So I think in terms of that, that's what last season gave me. I'm just miles more relaxed in terms of how I go about my business."

The goalkeepers' union is a special one; unique in the world of football, it could be said. No position on the field sees less space for error and no substitute is less likely to get on the field, yet the majority of the time you see the stoppers club together in a sense of: "We're in this as one." So when Dawson's penalty save in that 0-0 draw all but guaranteed another game warming the bench for Stockdale, there was no sulking. Instead he was the first one beating his teammate's chest, the ultimate hypeman that he said he'd be from day one.

"We've got a really good relationship," Dawson explained. "We're two very straightforward Yorkshiremen, so there are no airs and graces. We just are what we are and it works well together. There are no secrets; we just get on with it. Obviously one of us will play and one won't. It's not been me for the first half so that was tough, but I've been working away trying to get my chance." He'd certainly taken it.

Aside from Dawson's deserved praise, though, the mood was not good and a vocal group of Wednesdayites had had enough. Social media was littered with calls for Moore to be fired, his tactics and style heavily criticised. "We're not getting out of this division this season," said one. The manager understood the jeers, putting it down to a new-ly-found hope for more, and, as condensation followed his words on a frigid pitch side, he knew that Wednesday needed to start winning games again. Their run of 10 undefeated games wasn't much use when half of them were draws.

Dawson's penalty save also secured a second outing for a cheap polyester Christmas jumper with Homer Simpson's Mr. Plow plastered on the front, donned by Joe Crann – one of *The Star's* Wednesday reporters who had promised to wear it for as long as the Owls remained unbeaten. Had they lost at Exeter, it'd have never been worn again. It was exactly the sort of attire you wouldn't want to be wearing in the sunny month of May.

Come Boxing Day, a handful of Owls fans were still making their way to their seats at Fleetwood Town's Highbury stadium when the ball was nudged towards Shaun Rooney. He caught his strike beautifully from the edge of the Wednesday box, and the ball lasered past everybody and nestled in the net. Wednesday were one down and fans watching or listening elsewhere were more likely to be reaching for the Christmas spirit than feeling any. Bannan and Byers were back, though, and less than 10 minutes later Byers was standing in front of the away fans and saluting again, having turned home a wayward strike by Johnson for 1-1.

There was nothing wayward about Johnson's next effort of note. The sun had already set in the Lancashire sky and a bitter wind whipped along the Parkside Stand when the wide man struck true after setting the ball up for himself on the edge of the D. His lovely volley made it 2-1 and there were 73 minutes on the clock. Wednesday were on course for yet another come-from-behind victory, but the drama wasn't over yet.

Johnson, again involved, went down after a collision with Rooney, an incident that led to a second yellow for the Scot and left him incensed. After screaming at the referee, he stormed over to the touchline, remonstrating as he went, before going for the fourth official – finger sharply pointed – via the equally-hefty Owls boss. Moore, famously one of the few to intimidate the great Roy Keane in their playing days, looked almost perplexed as Rooney attempted to shove him to one side, but his composure never faltered. His next task was to hold back Stockdale, the Wednesday substitute not taking kindly to a slight against his manager.

Scott Brown, the Fleetwood boss, wasn't impressed. "Roons has let himself down," he said. "It's not the sending-off: it's the manner of what happened afterwards and that's not the way I want my players to react. If you get sent off, you take it on the chin. Sometimes you might clip somebody if they get in, that's fine, but you take it on the chin. You don't start World War Three in the middle of the park and then, with the fans chanting, start to go for everybody else. It's not for me, that."

Moore's take? As calm as always. "I'm standing in the dugout, trying to bark out orders, and he's pointing straight at me and he's decided to manhandle me. He was fired up for the game and he had a go at the fourth official... It is something that he can learn from, but that's my account in terms of what happened in the incident." With a wry smile he added: "I did keep my hands in my pockets when he did do it, just to make sure there was no malice on my side."

On the face of it a 2-1 win against Fleetwood wasn't that big a deal, but the nature of it felt big for the Owls. To come through that swirling wind on an uncomfortable surface and the early adversity on the back of the Oxford game showed strength and determination. More traits that could be attributed to a Wednesday side for the first time in years. It was far from a case of all being forgiven, but by the time that Smith had added a couple of goals to his tally with a brace – including an absolute pearler – against Port Vale, the Owls were level with second-placed Ipswich and there was a sense that one of those sliding-door moments may have arrived. It was time for Wednesday to turn up the heat on those above them and hope that they let things slip as 2022 became 2023. The big question was: How much could Bannan, down with a recurrence of the same hamstring issue, be a part of it?

For the first game of the year, against Cambridge United, they needn't have worried. Windass, used in his favoured No.10 role, ran riot with a hat-trick at Hillsborough and Smith got another brace as they continued their pursuit of 20-goal seasons. Byers, meanwhile, was back to his marauding best in the heart of midfield to make sure that the skipper wasn't missed too much and Rio Shipston, a couple of weeks after signing his first professional deal, got his league debut. Wednesday were racking up clean sheets as never before. McGuinness was settled, flying, and even talk of a possible recall couldn't dampen joy of a 5-0 rout.

The new year might be a fun one, it seemed. No doubt the Wednesday boss felt the same way as he got into his BMW on New Year's Eve, his foot hitting the accelerator in a trip destined for St. James' Park to catch a glimpse of the newly-anointed richest team in the world.

NINE

A WELL-MACHINED OIL

Tick followed tock followed tick followed tock. Time slowed down in the opposite direction to blue and white heart rates as Newcastle United just... kept... coming. A strained Callum Paterson header; a Mark McGuinness block. Wednesday's defensive unit crabbed from one side to the other as the Premier League superstars sought to pick their moment. A Cameron Dawson claim; a Marvin Johnson clearance. "How long, ref?"

Tick followed tock. George Byers and Josh Windass, heroes on the shoulders of heroes on an iconic night under the Hillsborough lights, trudged off the field exhausted, late substitutes leaving their stage to standing ovations. A Mallik Wilks dart at the opposition half-thwarted. Added time in added time, spectators standing in the stands of Hillsborough, waiting for their veins to be filled with the euphoria only a truly special win can offer a football fan. Not yet.

Sheffield Wednesday were seconds away from achieving something remarkable in the oldest competition of them all, desperately throwing themselves into every strained defensive effort, excitement having built up over 40 days, starting 70-odd miles away in a much more serene setting at one of the world's famous football stadia. On that day the cameras had pointed at an opaque bowl of ping-pong balls bearing the numbers of the teams remaining in the FA Cup third-round draw. In any normal season for any normal third-tier team, it is in that Anfield hospitality suite that the would-be highlight of the story begins.

Anfield, Liverpool. This was nothing new: Sheffield Wednesday's ball had always seemed to be drawn out of the hat late when it came to a cup draw – in recent years anyway. And as the balls were whittled down and the names left on the BBC graphic showed only eight names, Wednesdayites desperately did the maths and scratched their heads as to what would be the plum tie. It was November 28, 2023, and the draw was being broadcast live from the home of the FA Cup holders.

So, who? Rotherham would be fun, given the travails of the "Two Mikes" signings and a modern rivalry that had kicked up a touch in recent seasons. Everton? Sure, especially given the Owls' last trip to Goodison Park was played behind-closed-doors in the clutches of Covid. Manchester United was surely the best of the bunch, depending on your outlook, but there were no gimmes available to those who prefer a lighter touch when it comes to a cup draw – Reading, Watford and Ipswich making up the list alongside Newcastle United, the in-form and newly-crowned richest club in the world, against whom Wednesday had enjoyed relative success in Championship seasons not long past.

Former Liverpool and England defender Mark Wright drew the ball to seal a home tie for Wednesday and presenter Manish Bhasin, so polished and smooth in his delivery, rolled off a pre-prepared mini-statistic, as is tradition on these occasions: "Sixty is Sheffield Wednesday, doing well in League One, they're third." With interest in South Yorkshire piqued, thousands shuffling to the front of their seats just for a moment, it fell to Rachel Brown, herself a former England international goalkeeper, to pull out a fresh ball and confirm the Owls' visitors in early January.

"Twenty-seven is Newcastle, doing brilliantly under Eddie Howe," Bhasin delivered. "They're third in the Premier League – and will go to Bramall Lane." Once the collective gasps of Bhasin's slip of the tongue subsided, and once celebrations of a more-than-half-interesting draw were completed on social media, the narrative was directed at one Sheffield Wednesday man.

Michael Smith has a Geordie accent as thick as you can imagine within the realms of the understandable, deep in tone and characteristically tuneful. He pronounces the word "Shearer" with an extra syllable as people from that way so often do – they know best, to be fair – and talks about football as enthusiastically as anyone in the game. He is, of course, a proud Newcastle United fan, his love for the game fired up by treasured boyhood VHS videos of Kevin Keegan's entertainers; Les Ferdinand, David Ginola and of course the man himself; the man whose first name is obsolete where Smith comes from, reduced to one word much like Madonna, Pelé or God himself. Without the Toon career of "Shearer" – he arrived for a record-breaking fee the season after Keegan's side had famously finished second in the 1995/96 Premier League – Smith's life would likely have been very different indeed.

"Wor family are all big black-and-whiters. all my friends go to all the home and away games," he said. "It's a bit of a goldfish bowl up there; there doesn't ever seem to be much going on outside of football. You're black and white or you don't follow football. The club meant everything to me growing up, I've managed to get to a few games when I haven't been playing and stuff. When Shearer signed that really kick-started my love for football.

"The city in general love a proper No.9. They love someone who battles for goals; they become the hero for the whole city. With him being from the area I grew up in as well, he's like a god up there and he was to me. He was the one player who everyone wanted to be and who everyone looked up to. A goal against Newcastle would mean more than you might think."

You might have expected Smith to have later regaled images of the family crowded round a television set, unable to catch Bhasin's stadium error for the madness of excitable celebrations. The fact is, though, that he missed the draw altogether. He'd forgotten it was even on. Flying in the whirlwind that envelopes the arrival of a new baby just a couple of days before, the six-foot-three targetman was in that moment a dad, a husband and a brother first and foremost, FaceTiming his sister to update her on how mum and daughter were getting on. When his phone started buzzing relentlessly in the background with WhatsApp messages, texts and calls, he realised what had happened.

Wednesday had reached the third round in no small part down to Smith himself. A confident and routine 2-0 first-round win at home to Morecambe in front of 8,558 barely-interested diehards left the lasting memory only of a classy Windass opener curled in wide from outside the box. Alex Mighten sealed the deal. In the second round things got a little complicated when League Two Mansfield Town arrived with a big away following and took a deserved lead before, in what was becoming a habit for the Owls, they found a way to "win ugly," Smith poking home twice in five minutes from a combined distance of about seven yards. Another comeback win chalked-up; Howay the proper No.9. The third round beckoned.

With the draw undertaken at the end of November and ties to be played, as the third round always is, in January, it was quickly decreed that the Hillsborough one would be televised on the *BBC* – Gary Lineker, tweaked kick-off time, under the lights. Full mashings. Sunday, January 7, 2023. Six o'clock.

Newcastle United were a far reach from the Championship-slaying Rafa Benitez outfit against whom Wednesday had achieved a home-and-away double six years earlier. A club of kindred spirits as far as Wednesday were concerned, they are a monster football club of working-class fanbase, iconic shirts, under-achievement and slow-motion images of Chris Waddle dropping shoulders. Halcyon days in the rearview mirror, both clubs had spent years seemingly trudging through their respective motions – the Magpies twice relegated to the second tier in the previous few years, Wednesday now in the third tier for the third time since a Premier League relegation season that featured an 8-0 defeat at Newcastle's St. James' Park.

While green shoots of a hard-fought Wednesday rebirth were there to be drawn on, being clawed for desperately with every win at places such as Port Vale and Accrington Stanley, Newcastle's had been more instant, more glamorous. Controversial, too. Saudi owners drifted in with widely-reported assistance from the UK Government to accelerate a "sports-washing" programme that had already changed the landscapes of other leagues and other sports. Newcastle won the lottery and had elbowed their way ahead in the transfer window queue in rapid terms. Bright young manager Eddie Howe had taken over from Steve Bruce, who had walked out on Wednesday a few weeks before the start of the 2019/20 season to take the poisoned black and white chalice, and steered them away from relegation headaches to find themselves in the Champions League conversation.

They were pushing on well ahead of schedule and, to the soundtrack of Sam Fender tunes, the Newcastle fanbase arrived in South Yorkshire as upbeat as might have been expected of any set of football supporters. Despite the clouded nature of the circumstances that had afforded it to them, only those doubled over with jealousy would begrudge the supporters themselves the success that would surely follow.

The match would be Wednesday's 34th competitive outing of the campaign, 161 days on from the opening day goalfest against Portsmouth and with miles of water already having flowed beneath the south stand bridge. By that point 95 days unbeaten inside 90 minutes – a decision to discount the Southampton penalty defeat in the League Cup was silently, but unanimously agreed upon – they had built up a head of steam, they were third in the League One table and were bearing down on Plymouth and Ipswich with the full weight of their vast support behind them. Albeit in a very different way from Newcastle, another football giant was stretching and yawning.

That theme informed the *BBC* narrative of the evening. A pre-match montage featuring music by famous fans of the club coursed viewers not especially well-versed in all things "Modern Wednesday" and provided an all-too-evocative reminder of the club's highs and mainly lows for those that were. It was a "little introduction to the state of things," but it showed a club on the up, cautiously daring to dream of a return to good times. A night such as this, it suggested, was a step towards the ultimate goal.

That notion had been screen tested six-and-a-half years earlier when Arsenal had arrived at Hillsborough for a League Cup clash to face a club growing rapidly in the early stages of Dejphon Chansiri investment and Carlos Carvalhal carnival. A 3-0 win set to the backdrop of phone lights and bewilderment set optimism ablaze ahead of back-to-back, play-off involvements and near misses at that holy grail of a return to the top flight. For clubs such as Sheffield Wednesday cup matches don't matter, apart of course from when they really, really do. A win against Newcastle, unbeaten in matches that didn't involve Champions League runners-up Liverpool to that point, would surely provide a further upturn in belief so cruelly sapped from the terraces in a morbid generation of under-achievement.

***

For whatever reason Michael Smith had never quite got the chance to make his boyhood club his playground. The closest he'd get were long school holidays – and perhaps the odd day playing truant – when he and his mates would cycle at double speed to the Newcastle training ground, rest their bikes against the fencing and crane their necks for a glimpse of their heroes. In a lighter moment he revealed to the *Sheffield Star* that his dream dinner party guest list comprises three sadly-deceased grandparents, Bobby Robson and "Shearer," providing an insight into the pedestal on which Toon legends of old are placed in his psyche. A seat is saved for Leonardo Di Caprio, too. It's not really explained why.

Smith grew up playing at the Wallsend Boys Club, perhaps the most feted junior amateur side in the country. The social club is now blessed with top-of-the-range facilities, but when Smith came through, there was a gym with a wooden floor and netting taken from nearby ship-yards to prevent precious footballs from disappearing. Peter Beardsley, Lee Clark, Steve Bruce, Michael Carrick, Steven Taylor, Fraser Forster, Shearer himself are all alumni. And while a handful of his teammates were picked up by Newcastle and – whisper it quietly – Sunderland, Smith would instead jet-set his way through the professional ranks of junior football, having been spotted from afar. From the ages of 14 to 16 Michael Smith travelled by plane from Newcastle to London and was picked up in a club car to represent West Ham, flying home later on the Saturday. He'd often train above his age group in the youth team alongside the likes of Mark Noble.

"It was an unbelievable experience as a young lad," he said, reflecting warmly on a couple of years that turned him from boy to, well, slightly bigger boy. "I'd barely even been into Newcastle as a lad and then I was thrust into the big smoke. It was definitely an eye-opener. Me and an-other lad would go down from Newcastle airport and I felt like the bee's knees, honestly. I really enjoyed it. I used to get the train down every now and then, too, but being left at the airport by my dad and getting picked up at the other end in a car was class. They let me go obviously, but gave me this confidence and belief."

That boyish enthusiasm was apparent throughout a pre-match in-terview recorded in the Hillsborough dugout where Smith was awk-wardly thrust into the company of his hero. The pair hadn't met before, but there was something in the 31-year-old's inability to barely look at Alan Shearer that reduced him from a man-mountain centre-forward who was playing chest-out, four goals in two matches, to that school-boy resting his bike up against a fence. In many ways, his dream had come true before the evening's match had even kicked off.

Owls fans shuffled into the ground to take their seats full of opti-mism, but not expectant, even given the competition's penchant for the unthinkable. Eddie Howe had made a raft of changes, but selected a team including £59m Sweden striker Alexander Isak, £40m Brazilian midfielder Joelinton and £35m centre-half Sven Botman, a shoo-in for future Holland squads. Elliott Anderson, a rumoured Wednesday loan target in the summer months, had been hailed as one of the bright young things in British football and was one of the changes.

Jacob Murphy, who regards his season on loan with Wednesday under Garry Monk as the period that changed the direction of his career and took him kicking and screaming towards the Champions League, would also start. Bruno Guimarães, Miguel Almirón and England superstar Kieran Tripper – who had played alongside Darren Moore on his professional debut on loan at Barnsley 13 years earlier – were all named to provide an intimidating cavalry from the bench. To win the tie was a big ask for Wednesday; against Palace, Chelsea, Bournemouth, Leicester, Leeds and Arsenal, Newcastle hadn't conceded a goal for more than a month.

The preamble was over: Jeff Beck belted, Hillsborough tingled. There was a heightened sense of occasion in the night's sky, a feeling that Wednesday were indeed rousing themselves from the doldrums and that this, this was the night to remind the nation about the power of Sheffield Wednesday Football Club. Gaps in the crowd were visible and drew scorn from the typical quarters, but a 25,884-strong crowd not tempted by the warmth of a free *BBC* ticket were there to play their part and then some. A press box more crowded than your run-of-the-mill Wednesday match had opposition analysis staff swollen from one or two to double figures and a photographer covering the match slipped into conversation that he was not there on club or agency duty, but was being paid by Brazilian superstar Guimarães to snap him on an exclusive basis. It wasn't even guaranteed he'd get on the pitch. How the other half live.

The players responded appropriately and from the start it soon became clear that Wednesday – so cautious, so cagey in recent cup outings against Manchester City, Everton and Chelsea – would go for it. Moore had spent time watching, plotting their attack on the millionaire Magpies and their approach seemed to take the visitors by surprise. Reece James thundered into a tackle on Matt Ritchie in front of the always-raucous T1 Block to send a message after just a few seconds. The backroom staff had impressed on their players that they wanted to see a fast start, one designed to push supporter involvement and let Newcastle know they were in a game. When a sloppy Jamal Lewis throw set Liam Palmer through on goal, only for the lifelong Wednesdayite to drag it wide, they'd ticked all boxes in a few minutes.

The first chance went to the Owls but there was soon a reminder, if it were needed, that the Magpies were chasing down European dreams for a reason. Former Real Madrid youth prospect and Liverpool wingback Javier Manquillo found some space on the overlap and in front of an away end packed with the travelling Toon Army, Isak found space in the air to force a classy, close-range save from a pumped-up Cameron Dawson. At both ends Wednesday would have to be on their mettle and the early signs were promising.

In the busy Leppings Lane End a separate narrative to the evening would take place. A stand marred in unthinkable tragedy after a 1989 crush needlessly and preventably killed 97 Liverpool supporters in an FA Cup semi-final against Nottingham Forest, a tweet posted by a national journalist at half-time suggested issues coming from the footfall of the stand's central tunnel. *That* stand, *that* tunnel. It was an image that for some triggered images of that fateful April day and witness accounts published in national newspapers in the days following painted a regrettable picture.

In a 224-word statement released two days after the match Wednesday made it clear that they had complied with, and in places exceeded, the terms of their safety certificate and that no reports of injuries or medical assistance were logged with their first-aid operations manager. Later national media accusations of a "scandalous cover-up," claiming the Newcastle Supporters' Trust had had to uncover news of a SAG-enforced reduction in capacity at that end of the stadium via a Freedom of Information request, were clarified by a Sheffield City Council statement that showed the information had been passed over freely and promptly on request.

It transpired that Wednesday had in fact been notified of the 1,000-strong capacity reduction 24 hours after the information had been made clear to Newcastle, having initially offered to do so amid what was described as a "robust review" of the situation. Fifteen recommendations had been made and acted upon. The council statement ended: "It should be made clear that Hillsborough Stadium never breached its capacity or its safety certificate at any time."

On the pitch the opening stages came and went and Wednesday had more than done their job. Half-chances had been hard to come by and, while television pundits and many in the ground expected the Owls' approach to become cagier and Newcastle to shake themselves and grow more assertive, the League One journeymen seemed to grow taller. Windass broke on to a misplaced Anderson backpass to belt through on goal and poke his weaker left leg at the ball to deflect it past Martin Dubravka. It bobbled just wide. Within a few minutes a bending, searching Will Vaulks pass forced Botman to outstretch £35m worth of boot to prod the ball wide and out of Windass' sprawling reach. With every passing minute, the crowd believed.

All the while Smith thundered about alongside main man Windass with the fire of someone for whom a goal would indeed mean more than you think. It had been a long road to playing against the Toon, in front of Shearer, for the man who had spent much of the previous decade jumping from League One to League Two and back. Once his own Portsmouth supporters celebrated as if they'd scored a goal when he was callously substituted, as a 24-year-old in a defeat to Exeter City. Smith was wilting under the pressure of playing for a big club, they would say down south. The big stage was too big for Big Michael.

There was another smart Dawson save, a half-time break that offered United a change of ends and further opportunity to get their stuff together. Newcastle's central threat Isak was replaced by Chris Wood – a mere snip at £20m a year earlier – at the break and Dennis Adeniran came on for Fisayo Dele-Bashiru in midfield. Dele-Bashiru had been unable to make his mark on the night, not long after Moore had admitted that those drawn-out contract talks had, he felt, chipped away at the youngster's sense of focus. Energy was the order of the Sunday and Adeniran was a player roused by cup outings earlier that season and able to provide it in bags.

And then the moment. George Byers, battling Premier League players in midfield with every sinew of his not-long-past, top-tier potential, felt an opening on his shoulder with Anderson and Sean Langstaff bearing down either side. His Cruyff-esque turn, both deft and brutal in the same instant, opened up space, left the Newcastle pair in scrambling awe and the Wednesday crowd even more so. Three touches into space, cutting diagonally across the Toon defence, a first-time nudge from Palmer into the feet of Adeniran and a first-time cross. A heartbeat, a flicked instep, a ball trickling towards goal. And then chaos.

"And in! Windass scores for Sheffield Wednesday! It's a dream of a goal. Wonderful, wonderful goal for Wednesday!"

Scarcely believable at the start of the night, it was a lead Wednesday had deserved. So too Windass, the star of a show building towards box-office proportions. Where a supporting cast had graduated through the acting schools of Ajax, Arsenal, Manchester United and Real Madrid in years gone by, the man with a short-lived career in bricklaying was setting himself up for a starring role. Offside? Yes. A care in the celebrating Wednesday crowd? Not a single one.

Mark McGuinness, a youngster surely set for more regular tussles with Premier League sides, threw himself into tackles and blocks with the vigour of a man who had long since grown to love what Sheffield Wednesday was about. The news out that he would be leaving the club after this grandstand fixture and recalled to Cardiff City's seemingly flailing Championship survival attempt, he gave a performance of little concern as to injury-prompting change of Welsh thought. Indeed every suggestion was that the former Arsenal youngster would have preferred to stay in any case. Later that night one senior Wednesday player was introduced to McGuinness' father as he entered the car-park to leave the ground. Such was the impact Sheffield Wednesday had had on his son, 56-year-old John McGuinness was close to tears. He wanted his son to stay and finish the job.

Anderson, never far out of the match for good and bad, had another shot saved. Wood saw one blocked. With the belligerent Palmer, Dawson gave the display of a man well-versed in what a win would mean to the people sitting nervously in the seats behind him.

Smith may well have dreamed it differently, but not by much. While the stat columns would come to show a typically whole-hearted and bustling effort, it is in goal contributions that these evenings are so often measured. As the two midfields wrestled for ascendency and the blue and white cohort won out, his opportunity came some 13 breathless minutes on from Windass' opener and only five minutes after Howe had turned to his bench to throw on £83m worth of midfield talent – £30m Joe Willock, £33m Bruno Guimarães and £20m Miguel Almiron. Adeniran made a nuisance of himself to cause confusion between Brazilians Guimarães and Joelinton, prompting a misplaced touch from Joelinton. From nowhere Smith was met with the sort of split-second decision that can win an FA Cup tie or send 25,000 home with a sinking feeling of: "What if…?"

It's difficult to know what really went through his head at that momentary flash of opportunity. Perhaps the flash of his first black and white jersey or the waiting lounge at Newcastle airport. Maybe it was strewn bicycles, VHS Keegan memories or a first experience of live football, a 1998 FA Cup win over Shrewsbury Town in which you-know-who scored a double. Maybe it was dinner with Leonardo Di Caprio.

More probably it was nothing more than whatever thoughts run through the mind of a professional footballer when these moments arise. With the Newcastle defence bounding in, a half-glance showed Windass curving his run between Botman and Jamaal Lascelles. It needed an inch-perfect ball. Smith delivered an inch-perfect ball in one inch-perfect touch. The crowd roused once more, locked in a slow-motion sense of anticipation and disbelief. They watched white-knuckled, clenching at the garments of those close to them as Windass followed Smith's lead by releasing an inch-perfect finish. Firmly struck with the confidence of a man bang in form, he curled the ball round Dubravka's sprawling hand and joyously inside the post to send Hillsborough into pandemonium. No question of offside this time, Windass was the only Wednesday figure in the stadium too cool to celebrate, including even his usually icy-veined manager. It was Windass' fifth goal in his last 141 minutes of pitch time. Perhaps he was simply getting bored with it.

This felt as if it were a new Sheffield Wednesday. But Sheffield Wednesday they remained and four minutes after a two-goal lead was opened up, Guimarães poked the ball into the Kop end net from an offside position after the Owls had failed to deal with a corner by Trippier. In the half-an-hour of remaining football the hat-trick chasing Windass crashed the crossbar with a free-kick that would have provided a little Wednesday sparkle to FA Cup montage packages for years to come. And for all their glamour, for every long ball into the Owls' box and for every attempted space-finding pass, Newcastle failed to create another clear opportunity in the face of a defence renewed in strength and belief. Tick followed tock and during seven-and-a-half minutes of desperate devotion to the cause, Wednesday became the first team not managed by Jürgen Klopp to beat Newcastle in a season that ultimately ended with qualification for the Champions League.

"You get through the smaller ties for nights like this," a glowing Dawson told media post-match with one professional eye on what was yet to come in the day job – a brutal League One promotion race. "It was fantastic to play in it from my point of view and I was desperate to play. When you get a win like this, you cherish those moments because Hillsborough was rocking. Look, it is nice for everyone, not just for me, Palms and the other local lads. It is for everyone to see what this football club could be like – it is a gentle reminder to everyone. If we keep on tanking in the right direction, we can have nights like this more often – so it is good for everyone to see what we can give the fans and what we could give the football club as players.

"Any footballer will tell you they don't want to ply their trade in League One or League Two," he continued. "We are professionals and we want to get higher up in the pyramid, but it doesn't come easy and we are here for a reason. We have to show hard work, dedication and commitment to this club and try to get it moving in the right direction. We have had a good first half of the season, but this is the business end now, the second half, and we will try to keep winning games of football."

Smith waved to friends and family in both ends of the ground while Wednesday supporters drifted into the Sheffield night to celebrate a win unthinkable just a couple of hours before. Now 19 unbeaten, something was growing and the unlikely potential of a cup upset against the world's richest club had been realised as conversations flowered towards what was possible with a home tie to Fleetwood Town waiting in the fourth round. Images of McGuinness seemingly saying goodbye to a fanbase still desperately clinging to hope of a sensational U-turn did little to dampen dreams on what was surely the best Hillsborough evening since a play-off win over Brighton nearly seven long years earlier. The message was to savour the moment. That level of drama and that level of emotion doesn't come around very often and it would be years until S6 saw anything as captivating and as pulsating as that. Wouldn't it?

During the evening's coverage, co-commentator and former England international Martin Keown had glowingly described Sheffield Wednesday as "a well-machined oil." An hour or so later, while scrumming his way through media from all over the world, Moore spoke of pride in the result and a need to enjoy the moment, but above all the need to let go of an emotional evening and quickly re-focus for a chalk-to-cheese trip to Wycombe Wanderers six days on.

The mood described from within the Owls inner sanctum in the coming days was exactly that; focused, well-drilled and buoyed by a famous win. It was the sort of win that can propel a side to great things and wrestle the focus of a fanbase, from years of disappointment to one of optimism and excitement. The bars were bouncing and Sheffield Wednesday were ticking.

A well-machined oil, indeed.

TEN

(AHA)

Will Vaulks doesn't score too many goals but when he does, they're usually pretty memorable. And as he wheeled away at Adams Park and prepared for his trademark cartwheel and front flip, the away end had descended into pandemonium. He had scored Sheffield Wednesday's first goal away at Wycombe Wanderers for over a decade, and it looked like the Owls were going four points clear of Ipswich Town in third. Fourteen games unbeaten, four wins on the bounce. Wednesday had clicked into gear.

Vaulks didn't have the easiest of starts to his professional career. After starring as captain in the youth ranks at his childhood club, Tranmere Rovers, the young lad from the Wirral was released at the age of 19. They said it was by mutual consent, but in reality he was about to be let go anyway – it wasn't working out under Ronnie Moore, who happened to be giving Liam Palmer his first full season of senior involvement whilst on loan, and it was decided that Vaulks, then a defender, would be best moving on.

After a short spell of loans with Workington, Vaulks was forced to make a decision that could change the entire trajectory of his career: Stay in England and earn enough to survive whilst playing on a part-time basis, or take a leap of faith north of the border where an opportunity had presented itself at Falkirk – the catch being that they had no money to pay him. Backing himself, teenage Vaulks went with the latter and earning £4.33 per month, in his paid-for apartment, he set about getting back on track in an industry that has no qualms chewing up and spitting out those deemed unworthy.

"The lowest point of my life was sitting in that flat in Stirling," he told *the Daily Record* as he recounted the days when Wembley finals and trophy wins seemed worlds away. "No money, nothing to do, didn't know anyone, couldn't afford to go out, five hours from home... I was sitting in that flat from maybe two o'clock for the rest of the day. Not many of the other players lived there, and the ones who did were so young they still stayed with their parents.

"I played my Xbox, walked to Tesco, occasionally went to the cinema – I remember going to see *The Hobbit* on my own! That was the closest I came to feeling it was the end. For 10 years I'd never worried about anything because I'd always been assured I'd be a pro – and a good one."

It was with the Bairns that he perfected his post-goal acrobatics, a celebration he'd become known for, but eagle-eyed fans may have noted that the backflip was missing at Wycombe – Vaulks' cartwheel wasn't up to his usual standards so he cut it short. Not that anybody in the away end that day was bothered as supporters – including Akin Famewo's dad – lapped up a thoroughly enjoyable away day that cemented the mood that something special was happening. But the story of that day had started days in advance, while fans revelled in the aftermath of that famous victory over Newcastle United.

With Mark McGuinness having played his final game for the Owls on that famous night under the lights, Wednesday were short at the back and still hadn't made a single January signing. For all the talk of finishing the window stronger than they started it, the midway point was approaching and Darren Moore's side were actually worse off than before. Alex Mighten's loan had been terminated after Wednesday decided that his relative lack of minutes was not worth paying a significant portion of his Nottingham Forest wage. Forest boss Steve Cooper was far from happy, telling the media at the time: "We chose carefully over where he went and the staff he went with, thinking that would be a good fit for coming back and trying to push to get into our team. For me, you give that trust to a club and they commit to it."

Hearts were still pushing to sign Callum Paterson, too, and it was about this time that Palmer – in the form of his life – started to feel some issues with his groin. Though he fought through, he couldn't really seem to shake them. But behind the scenes there were also reasons to be cheerful. Dominic Iorfa was back, the injury list was shrinking somewhat, and Famewo's return to contention had a feel of the old cliché that he'd be like a new signing. Fans were starting to believe and in the mind of one, a famous ABBA track bounced around. A new song idea, *aha.*

"The Famewo song was a drunken stab at youth by me and my 40-something mates," laughed Gaz Robinson, a stalwart supporter with a penchant for causing mischief on Twitter. "We'd watched Akin at MK Dons away and were gutted when he got injured, as he looked a player. I thought up these words to an Abba song, and genuinely thought that I'd get a barrage of abuse from the X-Block WhatsApp group!

"But the night before Wycombe away, and after three too many Babychams, it started flying around the chat group. I walloped it on Twitter hoping to make people laugh, which is my favourite pastime in all honesty. It absolutely flew out the blocks, and was getting retweeted more than a crocodile handler getting his arm bitten off at the zoo! We were howling, but never ever thought it'd actually take off on the terraces. Fast forward 12 hours and there were people singing it on the train, in the pubs...We all found it equally mental and funny!"

To the tune of Voulez-Vous: Famewooooo (aha) ... Reece James at the back (aha) ... Windass in attack (aha) ... Wednesday's gonna win the league ...

By the time the team walked out at Wycombe the earworm that so many had found themselves singing to themselves through the week was in full flow, and the main character was blown away – especially knowing that, as he looked over, his old man was in the midst of it, chanting away. "It was special, a special moment," the former Norwich City man reminisced. "Because I've never had a song before – especially not one that's been sung so loud... It was a proud moment – away from home on my first game back, and also because my dad was there in the crowd that day, and my name is his name. So it was a heartwarming moment – hopefully it made him feel as proud as I did. He was singing along to the chant, and he's taken the mick out of me about it."

Very few teams go to Adams Park and breeze it and as the Buckinghamshire wind howled that afternoon, even early doors it felt like it was going to take something a bit special to get things rolling. A scrappy affair saw Cameron Dawson forced into an early save and there was far too much head tennis going on for some. Something a bit special, you ask? Over to Vaulks.

Paterson held up the ball well and slotted it calmly to Wednesday's No.4. His first touch set it, shouts of "SHOOOOOT" emanated from the stand behind him and his second touch rifled through the very centre of the ball, as he rocketed it towards Max Stryjek's goal. He was never getting anywhere near it. The Owls hadn't scored away at Wycombe since 2011, but now they had something to hang onto – and nowadays they had the capability to do so. The joy couldn't last too long, though, with George Byers stretchered off just before the break with blood gushing from his foot after a collision. He wanted to try and carry on but Wednesday's medical team were having none of it and with Barry Bannan still out, the second half could have proven tough.

But there would be no resting on a one-goal lead here. Josh Windass twice went close, Vaulks fizzed another effort wide and there was a feeling that if there was to be another goal, it would be the visitors that got it. Old scars meant that supporters were almost forced to feel nervous, glancing at the clock every other second as it drew closer and closer to the 90-minute mark. The Owls were holding on.

Five minutes to go; no change. Down to three; almost done. But then came another slice of that bad luck that fans have become so accustomed to. Reece James, performing valiantly at left wing-back, went down in a heap, writhing in pain as he grasped at his ankle. On came the stretcher again and Moore's already dwindling backline looked set for another hit. The makeshift Owls saw out the game, earning a humongous three points, but once more it felt tainted – two unavoidable contact injuries leaving them further depleted for the visit of Fleetwood Town a few days later.

Gaz enjoyed it, at least. "The following week I got a direct message from the club," he explained. "My content is varied so I'll admit I got a bit of a cold chill opening it, wondering if I'd said something that was a bit too much. But they were reaching out because Akin had been so touched by the gesture on his first start back after injury that it had spurred him on and with his family being there, they'd loved it too... He sent us the match shirt from that game, and we were really humbled. We're just middle-aged lunatics who love our club – and this showed that they love the fans back, too."

Oh, and boy was the love mutual. Not too long after the final whistle Vaulks could be seen bouncing along with a group of Wednesdayites at the train station and eating their crisps as they chanted his name. Iorfa chuckled alongside him – it may have been a long trip home.

It was less than a month since the Owls last faced the Cod Army in that feisty affair at Highbury and by mid-January, anyone associated with the two clubs would have grown weary of the other as they faced off a further three times in the league and FA Cup, including back-to-back matches just a week apart as the month came to a close. A Wednesday victory on January 21 in their second league meeting would make it six wins on the bounce, and potentially take them seven points ahead of Ipswich Town if all went well.

It seemed like nothing could derail Wednesday. But late on Friday night, as fans began to settle into their sofas and sip away at their big cup of tea, South Yorkshire Fire and Rescue get a concerned phone call from somebody in S6 reporting that Hillsborough looked like it was on fire. One local journalist, who thought his work day had ended when Windass' press conference had been written up hours before, burst out of his chair and grabbed his car keys. Hillsborough on fire, the night before a game? It didn't sound good. Social media was abuzz with concern, images appearing to show what looked like plumes of smoke rising into the night air by the Owls' club shop. *The Star's* roving reporter would get to the bottom of it but, as he drove down Penistone Road, he feared the worst, even though there were no signs of any issues. No flashing lights, no sirens. No anything really. And with good reason.

Because it wasn't even a case of there being no smoke without fire. There wasn't any smoke to begin with. Sheffield was just really, really cold. Those plumes at S6 happened to be water vapour from the boiler room for the pitch's undersoil heating, and the fire engines came and went quickly when they realised as much. Panic over, it was full steam ahead for the visit of Scott Brown's boys.

There is an argument that the "fire" drama had been more eventful than the following afternoon's game, as the Owls kept a clean sheet and won 1-0. Marvin Johnson scored the winner, Lee Gregory missed a late penalty and boss Moore likened the game to a "dog's dinner." But it didn't matter. Three more points to the Wednesday boys, and their almost machine-like run would continue – even with five potential start-ers all sidelined by injury.

Moore rang the changes for their third meeting between Wednes-day and Fleetwood, in the FA Cup fourth round, and by the time the Owls had come back from a goal down to draw 1-1, there was a sense that maybe things were going to come together after all. Bannan and Byers had both featured after their respective injuries, Mallik Wilks had been involved in the goal, and Wednesday had shown once again that they wouldn't roll over when the going got tough. There had also been a late cameo for Aden Flint, who had joined the day before on loan from Stoke City. It'd taken them 27 days, but the Owls finally had their first winter signing, and in Flint they'd picked up a man mountain that would add to an already ginormous defence. His height and physi-cal prowess would certainly come in handy.

Like a number of his new teammates, the former Bristol City de-fender had done this football thing the hard way. There was no acad-emy structure for him and if it hadn't been for an exhibition game in 2008, to mark the opening of Pinxton Town's new floodlights, then who knows where he'd have been. Thankfully, Nicky Law's Alfreton Town were there that day and after inviting him for a short trial, paid just £1,000 to get him on board. From there his status just rose and rose, going from balancing his part-time football with shifts tarmack-ing roads to scoring a 'rabona' to round off a hat-trick in a famous pro-motion campaign for the Robins.

"I never had a trial or a sniff of an academy or anything when I was at school," he explained with a smile. "I played as much as I could for any local team that would have me... When I left school I wasn't particularly tall. I had a growth spurt when I was 15 or 16 and started to play men's football straight from there. I didn't think a thing of playing professionally really. I just loved playing four times a week; Saturday morning, Saturday afternoon then the same again on a Sunday.

"I was playing as a striker for ages then and was playing for my vil-lage when my manager one day pulled me and said I'd be better as a de-fender, which came as a bit of a surprise. But it worked out in the end. I know what it's like to have that proper job and I think it makes me even more grateful for the position I'm in now. I've done the hard graft and gone through non-league to get where I am now. It definitely gave me an appreciation of what a week's pay packet looks like."

He was exactly the sort of gnarled and grizzled centre-back that could be vital in League One, and the expectation was that the defender's arrival would be the first piece of the puzzle, Moore having been very clear about the fact that he wanted to strengthen his side before the window closed. In Flint Wednesday had replaced McGuinness but with more injuries inevitable, Moore wanted to make sure that he was covered elsewhere. A game against table-topping Plymouth Argyle was coming up, and still the Owls were in a weaker position squad-wise than they had been a month earlier.

"We're trying and we are looking to do some work," Moore said after the Fleetwood draw, no doubt growing increasingly bored of the constant questions that the modern-day transfer windows bring with them. "I'll get back on the phone and now that one or two of the targets' teams have had their fixtures, they'll hopefully have had no injuries which will give us a chance to get them on board... I'm prepared to go all the way until Tuesday at 11pm if needs be. But hopefully with the targets we've spotted and seen, if they are available then hopefully we'll get the work done. We've identified certain players to give us the right balance... The targets that I've looked at, if we get them on board they'll make us better."

It did go to 11pm, and then past it. Wednesday knocked back approaches for Paterson and Jack Hunt – who would both go on to be quite important – while Michael Hector, who'd spent time on trial with his former club having been out of employment for a while, signed for Charlton Athletic. Moore said that the Owls opted against signing Hector in the end, and Wednesday would face Plymouth without a single new face coming in after Flint's arrival. It later became clear that Huddersfield Town had come in with an attempt to take David Stockdale, but they too were knocked back. The Owls boss put on a brave face and looked at the positives of returning players, but behind closed doors there would have been a frustration that their only aim – to end the window stronger than they started – had quite literally not been achieved.

Not one to complain, Moore put his head down and got on with it. No new attacking players was a concern, but with the squad starting to look stronger there was hope that Wednesday would at least be able to ride it through and keep up the fine form that had got them to where they found themselves as they approached the crunch game against the Pilgrims. Their opponents' form wasn't quite as strong as their own, but Steven Schumacher's side had kept ploughing on, ignoring any talk of their bubble bursting from anyone outside their circle. Unbeaten in 10 in all competitions, thousands of their impressive fans were making the almost 600-mile round trip and a bumper crowd was expected for what would be one of the biggest attendances of the day across all of England's divisions.

February felt season-defining. After Plymouth and the Fleetwood replay stood fellow promotion-challengers Ipswich Town and the general feeling was that if Wednesday could get through this month with their unbeaten run still intact, then they'd be well on their way to achieving the top-two finish that they so craved. Moore, though, wouldn't be swayed from his "just another game" approach. Keep looking forwards. "It's just about playing the game, and not the occasion," he said in the build-up. "Yes, it's first against second, but it's just the next game – and that would have been the same irrespective of who was playing. We know we'll have to be at our level best, but we train for that every week. They're a good team, we're a good team... Hopefully it lives up to being a spectacular game."

In the week of the tie it was confirmed that it was heading for a sell-out. Around 3,700 Plymouth fans would be doing their thing in the away end and with 30,000 Wednesdayites descending on S6, there were huge expectations of the occasion. Wednesday had lost just two league games in the past year on home soil, and this one gave them the chance to take their place at the top of the table. "It's going to be loud," admitted Schumacher. And as much as Moore was telling his players it was "just another game," the tens of thousands filling up those seats knew that it was more than that. His comment to anyone not making noise the following day – "I will personally see you myself!" – suggested that he knew it, too.

By the time Moore spoke in the changing room at 2.15pm, anyone present could feel the atmosphere start to build. The fan zone was busy, the beers were flowing, and a huge whiff of 'what if' filled the air. Wednesday's players had all done their rounds outside, the manager had been cheered by those waiting for autographs and selfies outside, and a young girl got a "You all right, sweetheart?" as his big frame made its way from the car park to the bowels of S6.

"Is Baz starting?" asked a member of the stadium's staff, anxious to hear whether captain Bannan would be fit to return to the XI after injury. Even then Moore wouldn't give anything away. "I'll tell you what," he replied with a wink, clapping his hands. "He's in the squad."

Questions had been raised about Paterson starting at right wing-back, but with a midfield of Bannan, Vaulks and Byers there was a confidence that Wednesday could get the job done. Moore broke his steely focus while clapping along to a raucous *Hi Ho Silver Lining* to fistbump a delighted young fan, and his gaze swiftly shifted to the ball as Tyreik Wright got things underway in front of the 33,442 that had made the trip from near and far. Wednesday wanted to start fast, and wasted no time doing so.

Nothing of note had even happened by the time Vaulks had won a throw-in halfway into the visitors' half, both sides still feeling each other out in what was all set to be a cagey affair at S6. But when many thought the midfielder would lob it into the box, he went short, finding Byers in front of the north stand before making his way down the line. His fellow midfielder gave it back, and his ball into the box was perfect – Paterson taking a step backwards to evade his man, and then volleying it home past arguably the best goalkeeper in the league, Michael Cooper. Cue pandemonium. The goalscorer was mobbed before offering a salute of sorts to legendary club photographer Steve Ellis, and Palmer punched the air towards the T1ers losing their minds. As things stood, the Owls were top.

Wednesday of the past would've sat back, tried to hold on, but not this Wednesday. A couple of tricks and flicks from the returning captain got the crowd going even more, while Michael Smith, Byers and Windass pressed the life out of the visitors who, by 34 minutes, not only found themselves a goal down, but suffered the loss of Cooper and key defender Dan Scarr to injury.

Dawson saved from a Wright free-kick in Plymouth's only chance of the half, and the hosts remained in the driving seat going into the second. But, in a moment tragically in keeping with so many aspects of the season, it couldn't all be good news for the Owls. With just under an

Above: Despair for goalkeeper Keiren Westwood after the Owls' relegation to League One was confirmed following a 3-3 draw at Derby County *(Steve Ellis)*

Left: Wednesday's players wore T-shirts in support of boss Darren Moore before their home draw with Bristol City, after he fell ill with the effects of Covid-19 *(Harriet Massey)*

Above: The Owls' hopes of making an instant return to the Championship were dashed by a 93rd-minute Patrick Roberts goal to knock them out of the play-offs at the semi-final stage against Sunderland

Right: Joy for Cameron Dawson and Co. as the Owls upset the odds in the FA Cup against megabucks Newcastle United (*Harriet Massey*)

Below right: All aboard Windass Taxis as Josh celebrates his goal at Portsmouth, after doing so much to ensure his teammates could make the long journey south in the first place (*Barry Zee*)

Above: Boyhood Owl Liam Palmer celebrates his 98th-minute goal to help overturn a 4-0 first-leg deficit against Peterborough and reach the play-off final (*Harriet Massey*) Below: Michael Smith is chaired from the pitch after one of the most remarkable games in Hillsborough history (*Steve Ellis*)

Left: Wednesday supporters took over Covent Garden on the eve of the play-off final, with this young Owl loving every moment (*Sarah Poole*)

Below: A fan in a Darren Moore mask was the centre of attention as supporters drank in the pre-match atmosphere, left, before a blue-and-white invasion of Wembley, right (*Ben Leonard and Mark Newton*)

Above: Fat chance of that! *(Pete McKee)*

Right: There's only one Darren Moore... right?
(Ben Leonard)

Below: Joe Crann's famous Mr. Plow jumper graced
the biggest stage in English football *(Alex Miller)*

Adam Hadfield

Pete McKee

Dan Garcia

Scott Cropper

Cameron Dawson, left, and Darren Moore celebrate promotion on the Wembley balcony - with the play-off final turning out to be the manager's final game in charge of Wednesday *(Jon Wakefield)*

Above: Limbs in the Wednesday end after Josh Windass' winner to send the Owls back into the Championship

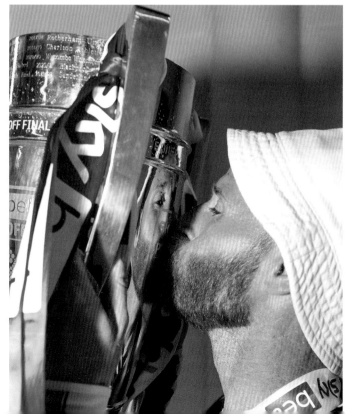

Right: Barry Bannan plants a kiss on the play-off trophy, the skipper helping to exercise the demons of relegation two years earlier on a day never to be forgotten at Wembley
(*Harriet Massey*)

hour on the clock, Wednesday's goalscorer tracked back to chase down an attacker and the concern was immediate as he grasped his hamstring, collapsing to the floor while the ball went past him. His latest blood and guts performance would end on a sour note, and worse, there were tell-tale signs of a lengthy injury. It would be the last time that the Scot would pull on a Wednesday shirt for more than four months.

Moore's side were good value for their lead but Wednesday fans had seen this all before, the capitulations and late goals against their side, and sat gnawing at their fingernails and wishing away the minutes, urging their team to get a second and finish the job. Wilks and Gregory were thrown into the mix, and both would have a role to play in the drama that followed.

With 77 minutes on the clock Vaulks found Bannan, who slotted Wilks into space and watched Wednesday's storied summer signing drive towards the byline. Out of the corner of his eye Wilks spotted a Byers-shaped figure ghosting into the box and cleverly cut it back. Inch perfect. With his left foot the midfielder caressed it goalwards, under Gregory and beyond the reach of substitute goalkeeper Callum Burton. Two-nil. The Kop erupted, daring to dream, as their increasingly well-known ballboy threw his arm around Bannan in celebration. Byers, his stature at Hillsborough growing with every passing month, saluted once more; this time with the vigour of a man who knew that he'd sleep well that night, his side sitting pretty on top of the table.

Thirty seconds went by, then 40. The stadium announcer called out Byers' name and the crowd cheered again. But then, down by the bottom corner of the Kop, an offside flag was raised – 48 seconds after the ball had hit the back of the net, and moments after the replay had been shown on the big screen. In a league with no VAR, the officials couldn't have. Could they?

"The referee said Lee was obscuring the goalkeeper," a somewhat perplexed – but still magnanimous – Moore explained afterwards. "After a long, really lengthy discussion, it turns out they picked that up from the video replay instead of coming to the decision themselves. For 30 or 40 seconds it appeared it was a perfectly good goal. Obviously having seen the video, I think it is the right decision. But it came through after everyone had finished celebrating what we thought was a second goal."

It didn't matter in the end, Wednesday seeing out the game to make sure that they did indeed finish the night in first place, but the decision certainly got tongues wagging. Even legendary Sheffield official Keith Hackett, the former referees' chief, was left bemused. "The terms of the competition are quite clear," he told *The Star*. "There's no VAR operating at Championship, League One or League Two level and that would be akin to using VAR. It is a complete and utter no-no. They have to make any decision or judgement at the time. The law on offside is not an easy one, especially when it comes to aspects of interfering with play. In awarding the goal initially, the referee has clearly determined that there is no offside in his own mind. To refer to the big screen – if indeed that is what has happened – is a major and complete no-no. It's bizarre."

What really mattered was that Wednesday were top. After a season where they'd been accused of bottling the big games, where Moore had been criticised for a perceived inability to see off the teams around his own, the Owls had come up trumps. And not even an FA Cup exit on a cold Fleetwood evening could put a downer on that. A 1-0 defeat at Highbury meant full focus on the league, but Wednesday had already had their scalp for the season – and everybody knew their priority. With Ipswich on the horizon, there were bigger fish to fry.

ELEVEN

WINDASS TAXIS

On February 11 2023, somewhere in an alternate universe, Michael Smith wheeled away at Portman Road having just made it 3-0 to Sheffield Wednesday and opened up a seemingly unsurpassable nine-point gap over Ipswich Town. Town boss Kieran McKenna, under increasing pressure, is turned on by the fans and eventually loses his job. Their promotion push gets derailed and the Owls kick on as champions of League One. There's no need for play-off comebacks or Wembley heroics. Darren Moore's men are cruising.

But that universe wasn't ours. And as the excellent Smith bore down on Christian Walton's goal, latching onto a hospital pass from Harry Clarke, he takes a touch. It's heavy, it sends him too far wide, and Wednesday will be left to rue the chance to put the game to bed. Smith, who would go on to become the club's first 20+ goal striker in over a decade, would more than make up for that mistake in the months that followed – but we'll never know what would have happened if Walton had been beaten. Sliding doors, and all that.

You'd be hard-pressed to find a time in recent years when the feeling around Wednesday was as good as it was leading into the game against Ipswich. The 1-0 win over Plymouth Argyle had equalled the club's record for clean sheets in a season – matching 1978/79, 2014/15 and 2015/16 – despite it still being February, and there was real hope that they could lift their first league title since way back in 1959. Wednesday headed to Suffolk on a 16-game unbeaten run in League One, knowing that a victory would put serious breathing space between themselves and their opponents.

There was the added bit of spice beforehand given that not-so-popular former Owl and son of David, George Hirst, had spoken about trying to knock his boyhood club off their perch and two vastly different January transfer window approaches had seen a fair bit of back and forth between the two fanbases. Ipswich had gone moneybags, while Wednesday had taken out a loan.

But before the long trip to Ipswich, there was something Moore needed to do first. On January 2 it was announced that long-serving 'Mrs. Sheffield Wednesday', Elaine Murphy, had sadly passed away. Rarely will you see the sort of loyalty shown that she offered over the course of four decades of service to the Owls and according to her son, Darren, there was never any talk of retirement. The much-loved Wednesdayite, who passed on at the age of 77, gave so much to the club – and the incumbent manager wanted to do his bit to make sure her family and friends knew how much she'd be missed.

So as his team began the journey over to Suffolk, Moore stood alongside chairman Dejphon Chansiri, head bowed at Hillsborough, as her coffin drove past. It was his tribute to a bonafide club legend, who he referred to as a "special lady." Members of the Wednesday family past and present attended her funeral, and the following month – on what would've been her 78th birthday – the club dedicated a game to her. "Sadly missed and never forgotten."

Only afterwards did Moore and Jimmy Shan turn their attentions to Portman Road. They knew once again that Wednesday would need to start strong, get out of the blocks, and try to turn up the heat on a side that – despite their league position – was really struggling for form. What they definitely didn't want to do was concede an early goal and so when ref Geoff Eltringham pointed to the spot before the game had even reached the 20-minute mark, Owls fans feared the worst. Wes Burns had been fouled, apparently, but nobody really seemed to know what had happened or who'd done it. But a penalty was given, no card was shown and with half the ground still in confusion over what had just gone on, Conor Chaplin stepped up to the spot.

But beating Cameron Dawson from 12 yards out isn't for everyone and as he stood tall in the centre of his goal, bright pink kit glinting in front of a huge crowd, Wednesdayites knew that he had it in him to be the hero once again. His penalty record is one that many of the best in the world would envy and when a goalkeeper develops a habit of saving penalties, then the battle becomes as much a mental one as technical. "For me it's all about timing," he'd said before. "It's about going at the right time, picking your spot and then executing it... I've obviously saved a few so I'd say it's a skill rather than just luck."

Once again Dawson delivered, stopping Chaplin's effort with his legs to execute the sixth penalty save of his Wednesday career – a remarkable feat considering that he'd only faced 12, and 80 per cent of spot-kicks are scored on average. Marvin Johnson, as it would turn out, was the aggressor, and was a lucky man – or so they thought, until a few days later.

For now, Wednesday were in the ascendancy and, buoyed by Dawson's heroics, found an extra gear. Within 15 minutes they were 2-0 up; first a peach of a cross from Windass was expertly headed home by Smith, and before George Byers was on hand to rifle past Walton and double their lead a few minutes later. The winds of discontent began to roll in to Portman Road. Wednesday were cruising and there was a growing sense amongst Ipswich fans that something did need to change if they were to keep up their promotion push. So when Smith bore down on goal in the 36th minute, you could almost feel the collective intake of breath. The chance was missed, but the home fans' ire was audible – many were getting to the end of their tether.

That was until Nathan Broadhead, a £1.5m signing from Everton, began his run-up for a free-kick about 25-yards out from Dawson's goal just before half-time. It was perfect, there was no denying that. The Owls 'keeper had no chance as it clipped the bottom of the bar and hit the back of the net. It was 2-1, and the momentum changed. The atmosphere changed. Wednesday had fought back from 2-0 down at Hillsborough just a few months again in the reverse fixture and now, it felt like this game could go the opposite way.

Many in football speak of critical phases, key parts of games where concentration levels need to be extra high. Two of those critical phases are the five minutes or so before half-time, and the five or so minutes after the restart. So after conceding in the 43rd minute Wednesday would want to make sure that they used the break to reset and come out strong in the second half. To regain control.

But an early foul from Byers gave the hosts a free-kick on their right-hand side, and Leif Davis – another seven-figure signing – placed it down. His left foot had caused, and would continue to cause, problems throughout League One that season, and his whipped delivery took a devastating touch off Byers' head to beat Dawson once again. Any chance of regaining control seemed gone; the pendulum had swung, and now it was the Owls hanging on. A lashed strike from Aden Flint was their best chance as they rode the storm and by the time the 90 minutes were up, it was probably Moore who was the most pleased to hear the whistle blow. The game was done, but over on Twitter the battle would rage on.

Home fans had footage of the incident that had led to the penalty, Johnson appearing to elbow Burns off the ball. It spread like wildfire and as supporters went at each other, Eltringham and his assistant, Ian Cooper, were in discussions about what had played out. Their conclusion? The Owls man would have been sent off if they'd been able to identify him, which is why he was charged and ultimately suspended for three matches. Burns himself had submitted a letter stating that he was "deliberately elbowed."

To lose Johnson wouldn't have been like losing some of the others. While so many were in and out of the team due to fitness or form, the man affectionately known as "Neymarv" had become almost ever-present. Since his arrival at S6 he'd played left back, left wing, left wing-back and even slotted in at left centre-back when times really got tough. In his career as a manager, Moore has only used Bannan and Palmer more often.

It's a regular line when recalling the tales of this squad, but Johnson's route to chants to the tune of *Waka Waka* from the Hillsborough stands was not the simplest. You don't have to go far back to a 20-year-old Johnson giving defenders whiplash in non-league football for Romulus in the Northern Premier League First Division South. He bided his time and ended up at Wednesday via Kidderminster Harriers, and Motherwell, and Oxford United. Even a short spell down the road that we won't speak of.

So the wide man knows the slog, and will never take what he's got for granted. Once a year, the chairman of Romulus, in his home county of the Midlands, receives notice of a payment into their bank account to help fund their season. Johnson never misses a payment.

Throughout his time at Wednesday just Bannan has provided more assists than Johnson and there was no doubt that he would be missed

– to the extent that the merit of an appeal was hotly debated in-house before being decided upon. Despite the rumours going round about fan footage being used, that was never actually the case. The EFL used their own film to find Johnson guilty of improper or violent conduct, and he would miss the three games that followed Morecambe and MK Dons. With a host of defensive injuries already leaving Wednesday light at the back, another absentee was the last thing they needed. To make matters worse, Wilks had limped out of training with what was described as a "little bit of a calf injury" – which ended up keeping him out until the end of March.

But 10 points from 12 in a run featuring Wycombe, Plymouth and Ipswich was more than acceptable and such was a shift in the mood that the point at Ipswich was still seen as one gained rather than two dropped despite the throwing away of another lead. By this stage Wednesday were 17 unbeaten in League One and drawing ever closer to the club's all-time high of 23 league games without defeat. Normal service resumed against Morecambe as Barry Bannan opened the scoring in the first minute and Josh Windass bagged a brace. Dawson's latest clean sheet – his seventh in nine games – meant 18 for the season, breaking the record first set in 1979. It was only mid-February.

Notably, the replay of Wednesday's first goal was delayed on the big screen and the second and third weren't shown at all. Can't take any chances with those officials...

MK Dons had joined Wednesday in the play-offs the season previous but a host of key departures, a managerial firing and a torrid run of form saw them make the trip to Hillsborough as relegation battlers rather than pushing for promotion. Wednesday fell behind twice but still came out on top, winning 5-2 thanks to Smith's brace and goals from Windass, Lee Gregory and Byers. Being 2-1 down at the break would have worried fans 12 months prior, but no longer... Voices around the ground spoke of a confidence, of the faith that Wednesday come back. Moore didn't even change his team, letting his half-time chat do the talking and reaping the rewards within 10 minutes. Those team talks had proven vital, and it was often no more than a dressing down.

High up in the south stand, analysis gurus Richard Stirrup and Liam Bracken cut clips in real-time, making sure they're ready to be gone through at the break. Cut out that run, exploit that gap. Moore referred to it as a "learning perspective." It was only at 2-2 that he changed it, and both new arrivals – Gregory and Adeniran – had a hand in helping them take the lead. Despite their injuries, the Owls were still able to call the cavalry and turn games around. Sometimes they also just had to trust the process.

The end of the MK Dons game brought to an end their last three-game week for over a month, giving Moore and his team some of the time on the training ground that he so desperately craved. It'd give Wednesday time to work, time to prepare, and – given their injuries – time to recover. That time had been a rarity in a busy season, with League One bereft of international breaks and midweekers popping up all over the place. As the club took aim at a remarkable club record, Jaden Brown was pulled to one side.

Wednesday's boss had always preached that football was a squad game. That every player would need to play their part if they were to be successful. Brown had made one league start all season as February came to an end, but a setback with James' return from injury – coupled with Johnson's suspension – meant that the former Huddersfield Town man would come in at Charlton Athletic. At least it wasn't a pressure game. It wasn't like they could go top of the league, or set a new club record of 20 games without defeat if they won. Oh wait...

Any concern about Brown's ability to play that role was diminished within 10 minutes. Bannan, booed by Addicks fans because of a #Karma tweet when they got relegated in 2016, spotted the young wide man on the overlap, and he took a touch before expertly finding Palmer in the middle of the box with the freedom of the Valley to slot home. One-nil to the Wednesday. Ten minutes later, Plymouth found themselves 2-0 down to Peterborough United and all the Owls had to do was hang on. Though they weren't able to add to their tally, they remained largely in control.

Wednesday had gone from a team where 1-0 was rarely enough, to one about to set a new record for most 1-0 victories in a single campaign. In the away end it was party time. Plymouth had lost 5-2, Wednesday were top of the league, and for the first time in the club's long, storied history they'd gone 20 league games without a single loss in the results column. Moore's side were ticking along nicely, and the scenes afterwards showed just how much the player/fan relationship had grown under the manager's watch. They roared together, celebrated together, and even in the changing room after the game, the players were talking amongst themselves about what they'd seen and heard from their supporters in the Jimmy Seed Stand.

"That doesn't happen by chance," Palmer would explain months later. "You look at past teams, the great Premier League teams, they'd pick up 1-0 after 1-0. There is a real art to it. It's dangerous, but so many of ours felt comfortable at the time – you can still be convincing at 1-0, and we felt that in our minds. We had this long unbeaten run, and we knew that people coming to play us would be looking at that. Psychologically, we knew that if we got to 1-0 then for some it would be an: 'Oh, here we go again' type thing. Building that up was key."

Brown was all smiles as he spoke to the media afterwards. He'd been taken off after an hour, self-admittedly because he ran out of gas, but after being called upon at the 11th hour the defender had held up his end of the bargain – and he couldn't have done any more than that. "I don't play that much," he said in a frank conversation with reporters. "But I do a lot on and off the pitch to make sure my mentality is right, and that I'm fit enough. I was struggling towards the end today, but training is never the same as games... It was quite tough, but I stuck at it until the gaffer saw me struggling and I'm really happy with the day in general. I'm a footballer, everyone wants to play matches, but it is what it is. When the team is winning and we're doing well then you have to wait for your chance. Today I waited for my chance, and I like to think I took it as well."

He'd get another. Peterborough were up next a week later, fresh on the back of demolishing the Pilgrims, and the Owls had a chance to solidify their spot on top of the table. Wednesday's steam train was rolling on, having picked up 28 points from the last 30 available, and in blue and white-leaning homes, fans were allowing themselves the pleasure of getting carried away. But at Middlewood Road, there was no talk of titles. "Don't get too high with the highs, or too low with the lows" was another of Moore's mantras and unlike the season before, the consensus was that Wednesday needed to speak less about promotion, and rather focus on actually achieving it.

"We are likening it to the British rowing team," Moore said in the build-up to facing the Posh, an analogy that felt incredibly befitting given the smooth way his side were manoeuvring through the division. "Their backs face the finishing line, and every single stroke matters in terms of what they are doing until that finishing line comes into their vision. By that time, they have given every stroke to get across that line. It's the same analogy with us as a group in making sure we put all our energy into each and every single game and making sure we give the best account of ourselves. If you look at the rowing team, if you turn your head and try to look at the finishing line, it means your stroke goes out of sync, which can disrupt things and lead to complacency."

One-nil to the Wednesday? You betcha. Brown was again involved in the goal, his ball into the box being diverted past the goalkeeper by Nathan Thompson to give the hosts the lead. But while that was celebrated most by the fans, it was at the other end where he received his biggest plaudits – quite literally. Moments later, Kwame Poku broke free of the Owls backline. Aden Flint has plenty of attributes, but speed isn't one of them. Akin Famewo was also too far away to catch Poku. But hurtling back on a sprint that had started in the other half, Brown somehow managed to do just enough to see the ball end up in Dawson's safe hands, rather than the back of his net. Fans rose to their feet to applaud, and Flint shoved him not once, but twice in celebration. High praise indeed. "It was as good as a goal for me," the big defender said. "He'd scored the goal and then, at the opposite end, did his actual job defending. It was brilliant." Wednesday had needed Brown to step up, and his standing ovation as he was substituted with 78 minutes gone was a testament to his efforts.

In the directors' box after the game, chairman Dejphon Chansiri could be seen waving an Owls shirt on a stick in celebration. He'd sunk millions into the club, taken his share of criticism over the years, and continued to prop things up when times got tough, none more so than during the Covid-19 pandemic. So he was going to enjoy this, a broad smile spread across his face. His side were 21 unbeaten, three points clear, and had no new injuries to worry about. If you can't wave a shirt on a stick in that situation, when can you?

You'd think that Wednesday's ridiculous return of 15 points from five games would see them go well clear of the Plymouth and Ipswich-shaped shadows in the background, but that wasn't the case. The Pilgrims had dropped points but remained well within touching distance, refusing to conform to the idea that their bubble would burst. Meanwhile, McKenna's side were doing a madness of their own. They'd not conceded a single goal since facing the Owls and on the same day that Wednesday had beaten the Posh, they'd stuck four past Burton Albion to make it nine goals in three games. They remained hot on the Owls' heels.

***

March 10, 2023, and Sheffielders woke up to a winter wonderland outside their doors. Heavy snow overnight had seen depths of upwards of 30 centimetres recorded for the first time in over a decade, and on a day that Wednesday were meant to be making the long trip down to Portsmouth Josh Windass hopped into his BMW X7. That four-wheel drive was going to come in handy for this one.

The snow had caused all-sorts of issues for Wednesday. As they prepared for another important game they'd had to deflate their Middlewood Road dome for safety reasons, amid fears that a build-up on top of it would be a serious hazard. So, shovels in hand, Moore and his staff joined the grounds team to clear a sizeable area of the snow-covered turf that they could use for training on the Thursday. By Friday, though, not even elbow grease and determination would be of any help. Wednesday had decided to bring forward their departure time so as to avoid any delays, but a few of their players had some snow-related issues getting to work.

Over to Windass Taxis Ltd. "He's got a big seven-seater and he's gone round picking up six or seven lads," Moore grinned as he spoke of Windass' efforts that morning. "He's done great, he's gone on a big loop picking everybody up." The Owls striker had made sure that teammates with less-suitable vehicles were not going to miss the trip. Moore and club doctor Richard Higgins drove out to Chesterfield to get another player, and others had to make their way in by train.

A few were even more proactive, staying the night before in hotels in the city so that they wouldn't have to brave Snowmageddon the following morning. It felt almost gloriously Sunday League, everyone doing their bit for the cause, and you could sense Moore's pride at the collective effort. "The whole group is only together now because the whole group has made small sacrifices to be here today and ensure we can travel south," he said, sincerely. He'd moved his press conference forward as well; now they could just get on the coach and go.

Well, they could've done, if the coach had been there. Wednesday, of course, weren't the only ones affected by the weather and somewhere in the north of England, the driver of the Owls' transport was stuck. They waited, for hours. As boredom and frustration set in, somebody suggested that a bit of grub might lift the mood – and not long afterwards, a large order of Nando's arrived at Middlewood Road, so at least they weren't bored and hungry. Still, they waited. Usually Wednesday's players met at the training ground and left but hours passed by as they sat, twiddling their thumbs. Moore spoke to them about controlling the controllables – the weather and transport not among them – but safe to say he was not a happy man when they finally arrived at their hotel in Portsmouth more than five hours later than planned.

Fratton Park can be a venomous place and there was a hostility in the air as things got underway at Pompey's famous old ground – notably the only professional English football stadium not found on the mainland of Great Britain. It didn't take long for that atmosphere to transfer to the pitch, either. These were two former top-flight clubs, two big fanbases, two teams who genuinely felt that they were playing below their station, but only one looked likely to get out of the third tier as the business end of the season drew ever closer. And amongst all that, some hotel wares became the flashpoint.

Will Vaulks and his towel were a regular feature for the Owls, the former Miller wiping away any moisture or dirt before lofting the ball as far as he could towards a teammate. That service resumed once more against Portsmouth, until a word in the ear of one of those pitchside saw a member of staff take a lap around the ground, picking up any strategically-placed towels in sight before running back to the bench looking like a cleaner's trolley in a Holiday Inn. "Towelgate," it became known as, and Moore's opposite number John Mousinho claimed later that month that the Owls had actually commandeered the items in question from the Marriott hotel that they were staying at. "Where's your towel gone?" came the chant from the Pompey faithful.

They weren't chanting it for long, though. A lofted ball from Dawson, an inch-perfect knockdown from Smith, and Windass – of all people – found himself in space inside the box, albeit with a tough angle to work with. Superbly, he drilled it home, the ball nestling into the side netting by the far post as the away end was sent into raptures. As his teammates sprinted towards him he sat down, arms outstretched as if holding a steering wheel. Palmer, Smith, Vaulks and Brown all got aboard Windass Taxis once more on that chilly afternoon in March. Over on the Wednesday bench, a certain substitute goalkeeper swung a towel around his head in celebration.

But with only 11 minutes on the clock there was a long way to go and even though Wednesday had shown time and time again that they had the grit to see things through, they'd have a job on keeping these hosts at bay. That task would become even tougher when Byers, a genuine tone-setter in the heart of midfield, had to be taken off with what looked like a hamstring injury – and as he left the field there was a very definite sense of sadness. The midfielder, through his passion and genuine love for the club, had well and truly found a place in the hearts of the Wednesday faithful, and justified it almost every time he played.

Often, when he was at his best, picking him up for free from Swansea City felt akin to a Dick Turpin robbery. The lad from Essex has a bit of everything – technical, physical and mental. The sort of player that makes those around him better, that gives them the freedom to do their thing. But above all, and most importantly for the supporters, you can tell he genuinely bloody loved Sheffield Wednesday Football Club. "This club has got a place in my heart," he said at one point. "I've been here a couple of years now, and this fanbase, everyone involved with the club, has just sucked me in. There's nowhere that I'd rather be. This place means so much to me, the fans mean so much to me. I can't even put into words how much it means to me. I've seen players like Palms and Baz that have been here for years, and the way they talk about the club is how I feel now."

Like so many in this group, his route hadn't been an easy one. Having worked his way up the youth ranks at Watford from the age of seven, Byers would have thought he was en route to first team football after Gianfranco Zola plucked him out of the youth team for a pre-season camp in Italy. He was up with the big boys, at just 17, and was getting his chance to mix it up with the likes of Troy Deeney and Fernando

Forestieri whilst a Chelsea legend ran the show. But just two years later he was on the move, and – as with so much that he does – he took it in his stride.

"I'd been at Watford a long time," he explained. "And in all honesty it was one of the best things that happened to me, in terms of needing a change of environment. I wasn't surprised that they released me. I'd had a feeling building up that I needed something else and an opportunity to go and prove myself somewhere else. Those opportunities at Watford weren't happening, the club were promoted to the Premier League and there was lots of stuff that came with that. It was a sad time, I'd come through the academy from seven years old and it was a big change but in a weird way it was probably the best thing that could have happened to me."

Byers had come from a football-mad family. Rangers. His grandad had worked for the Scottish giants, his dad had a season ticket, and if you delve far enough back there's a picture or two of the midfielder donning that famous blue shirt as well. He'd played for Scotland as a youngster, turning out for their U16s and U17s despite an accent that leaves no mistake as to his place of birth, and his parents, Alan and Jenny, made sure he was fully aware of their Renfrewshire roots. But in Sheffield he had found a home, settled his family, and had slide tackled and headed his way into the hearts of the locals.

And that injury played a large part in why, instead of seeing out a comfortable 1-0 win, the Owls would have to fight tooth and nail for three points. Wednesday's 1,600 travelling fans did their bit to support them, cheering every challenge, every block, getting to their feet as Gregory cleared a goal-bound header off the line. Where teams of the past would have crumbled, Wednesday stood firm, and could've doubled their lead when James' brilliant cross picked out Windass, whose diving header went just wide. Still the hosts pushed, Fratton Park a cauldron of intimidation as they sought an equaliser, and they were offered a helping hand as Dominic Iorfa was sent off for two debatable yellow cards.

Knuckles white with determination, Owls fans punched the sky as the final whistle was finally blown. It hadn't been pretty, far from it. Wednesday had ridden their luck, dealt with another injury blow, weathered the storm both on and off the pitch – and come out of the other side still top. Still flying. They'd won almost double the amount of aerial duels, twice the number of tackles, made three times more clearances than their opponents, and showed a solidity that Darren Moore the player would have been ever so proud of. Five months had passed by since they'd last lost a league game and Wednesday wouldn't let something like struggles with transport be an excuse to let things slip. "I got five stars on my Uber rating," joked Windass.

The image of him on the grass at Fratton Park, with a beaming grin across his face, felt destined for the history books at Wednesday. That day was a show of intent, proof that they could fight dirty when they needed, a result that made the rest of the division sit up and really see Moore's Owls as potential champions-in-waiting. Josh Windass on the turf, and things couldn't be going much better.

TWELVE

DON'T COME KNOCKING

Josh Windass was on the turf, his mud-covered, baselayered fore-arms over his face, and all around Hillsborough thousands turned to the fan next to them. "Not Josh, please." Before too long he was sat up, his arms on his knees, and a despondent look fell over his face as physio Antonio Quintela checked him out. Wednesday were locked at 1-1 with Bolton Wanderers, they were top of the league and with 18 league goals and assists, their No.11 had been a key part of it.

Reece James had gone off earlier in the game, Lee Gregory would go off after, and in the end Wednesday did just enough to hold on at 1-1. Their long unbeaten run was now at 23 games but that night it felt like it really had come at a cost. Windass left the ground in a moonboot, de-scribed by the official party line at the time as "only precautionary." He went from maybe being back for the next game to missing six weeks of action. They were six weeks in which Wednesday's season very nearly fell apart completely.

Unfortunately the week would be tinged by sadness off the field, too, as the Owls family was rocked the day before by the news that Don Megson, one of those truly worthy of the "legend" tag, had passed away. Very nearly a one-club man, Megson spent the best part of two decades at Hillsborough, racking up an incredible 442 appearances and writing his name in folklore as one of the greatest left-backs the club has ever seen. In 1966 he famously became the first losing captain to lead his side on a lap of honour at Wembley and news of his passing was one that hit supporters hard. He was remembered at Hillsborough before the Bolton game, to immaculate effect, as fans bade farewell to one of their favourite sons.

For the current crop injuries were taking their toll and Palmer's groin injury had reached the point where post-season surgery was already being discussed. It might have been bad, so bad that on some days he struggled to get out of bed, but it was manageable. "There was never any point where I thought: 'I shouldn't be playing this game'," he explained once said surgery had been completed. "But I may have been a bit deluded in my thinking, to be honest. You have to be, because it's easy to just chuck it in if things aren't going well. That never once crossed my mind. In my head I wanted to play every minute of every game, and nothing was going to stop me."

As they headed to Barnsley just four days after Bolton, Wednesday were depleted, battered and bruised, and amongst Owls fans there did feel almost an inevitability that their neighbours would be the ones to bring their record-breaking unbeaten run to an end. The game had meant to have taken place in January, two months prior, but FA Cup progression for the Owls saw it knocked on the head for a while – and if it had taken place on the original date, Wednesday would have found Michael Duff's side with two wins in six. Instead, they were on an 11-game streak without defeat that had well and truly put them in the promotion argument. They'd won nine of them, too.

In the return leg at Hillsborough the Reds had been superior, one of the few times all season that Wednesday had been genuinely outclassed, and a large part of that came down to the way they started the game. Wednesday couldn't afford to let the Reds burst out of the blocks just over the border; they needed to be robust and tough to break down, in front of one of the biggest Barnsley crowds in recent years. Keep it tight at the back, and then start to turn the screw.

Within 10 minutes Wednesday were 1-0 down. Just 18 seconds after the restart, it was two.

Devante Cole got the first, slotting through Cameron Dawson's legs after nobody checked his run, and James Norwood doubled Barnsley's lead. Both goals were avoidable and for Wednesdayites, it all felt a bit like Groundhog Day. But instead of rolling over, Moore's side bit back and with just over half an hour gone, Will Vaulks whipped a fantastic ball over the top into the path of the onrushing Michael Smith. A quick glance to his left saw Gregory making a beeline for the penalty spot and the usual goalscorer turned provider with an excellent driven cross. Gregory made no mistake from that range, and it was game on.

Dawson saved brilliantly from a Norwood header but it was at the other end where most of the drama was happening. A jeer turned nervous as Marvin Johnson managed to centre a Bannan ball over the top, Barnsley bodies were on the line to block Gregory's strike, then Dennis Adeniran's, and then Harry Isted's outstretched right arm somehow kept out a bullet header from Smith. The *Sky* cameras caught the Geordie's colourful language just afterwards, and thousands of others in the away end would've agreed with his sentiment. Wednesday went in down at half-time, but most certainly in the ascendancy. They weren't unbeaten since October by accident.

And when Johnson's fantastic cross found more tremendous movement from Gregory in the middle in the 74th minute, the equaliser was absolutely warranted. Wednesday had rallied, and deserved something out of it. Their pressure continued, Palmer struck wide, defender Aden Flint – who on another day could've had a hat-trick – did the same. And then came the sucker punch. Akin Famewo's clearing header should've been enough, but instead it bounced unfavourably off Flint and right into the path of Max Watters. His finish was excellent, but the goal itself felt unjust. Chasing the game once again, gaps opened up, and in the 96th minute Liam Kitching finished the job, landing the final blow in front of a raucous Ponty End. It had been 168 days since it had last happened, but Darren Moore's Owls had been beaten in League One.

Having spoken to the players to describe his pride at how they'd gone about piecing together such a historic unbeaten run, he sidled up to reporters for his post-match debrief, taking cover from the conditions beneath the roof of the west stand, brushing rain from his forehead.

"I said to them in there that I was super proud," said Moore, in a typically-relaxed manner. "I got them to look at me, focus on me, so I could tell them how proud I was. I went around every single one of them, and my staff, and congratulated them on the run of games – because that run takes focus, takes mentality, commitment, drive and togetherness. We've seen that, and now we have to move on to the weekend. There's still football to be played, and another quick turnaround, and we have to be ready for it. I'm proud because they're a good group, and honest group, and we'll get back to it."

As the press conference wound down, Owls chairman Dejphon Chansiri stood on the other side of the stadium, smoking and bemoaning an unlucky evening with senior staff members at the club. Within a couple of days, social media rumours began to bubble that he'd entered the changing room after the final whistle, with stories ranging from him delivering a miffed team talk to leaving the door swinging from its frame, with the gun-slinging veracity of a John Wayne-style entrance.

It never happened. Chansiri is believed to have briefly spent time with players in the changing room long before the match, wishing them well as he had so often done before. But after the final whistle he had left them to it. The whispering confusion may have arisen in that the Thai businessman is believed to have held a private meeting with the players in the days after the defeat, something he had done on a hand-ful of occasions in his premiership – including earlier in the season, via Zoom, after defeat at Plymouth – in an effort to gauge the mood of the camp and offer a pep talk of his own. On this occasion, one of those present remembers topics including the idea that, while Wednesday had achieved something remarkable, they still hadn't quite hit their full potential as a side. It's something that, in the cold light of day, may not have been argued by some Wednesday fans. It's stressed that not many of the players disagreed with the sentiment either. Chansiri would speak to Moore and his staff later.

And while the Oakwell defeat was disappointing, of course it was, even the biggest cynic would struggle to be overly critical after going 23 games unbeaten for the first time in the club's history. Wednesday had still fought, they'd not laid down and died, even after the early blows, but it just hadn't been their night. Luckily, they had the division's whip-ping boys up next. Forest Green hadn't won since December and were on a 17-game winless streak that saw them almost guaranteed to drop to League Two. Wednesday, second in the league with one defeat in their last 24 league matches, simply couldn't drop the bag at The New Lawn. Surely.

But it never felt right. Wednesday still had their injuries, a bit of a Barnsley hangover remained, and while fans tucked into a vegan pie in the meat-free stadium, it was oddly quiet in the away end. It was a mid-day kick-off, on the day the daylight saving method had robbed them of an hour's shuteye, but Wednesday were still there in numbers for an-other sell-out affair. In terms of decibels, however, there was little. The game got underway with a whimper and from the offset, it was obvious that the Owls were going to struggle. Cumbersome, sluggish, without urgency. With short passes back and forth, often not even trying to probe the worst defence in the league, Wednesday looked out of ideas.

Dawson made a tremendous save early doors to make up for a sloppy pass that handed Rovers the chance in the first place, but he could do nothing about Jordan Garrick's opener in the 35th minute as Duncan Ferguson's side took a shock – but not undeserved – lead. It would have been two in the second half had it not been for another fine Dawson stop, while at the other end Ross Doohan was left largely untroubled. "Not at the races" was the phrase that sprung to mind.

"It was a nightmare from start to finish that day," Bannan said, recalling a period where his normal football stresses were compounded by his wife Chloe being on the brink of giving birth to their second child. "I remember walking out onto the pitch to line up and it was quiet. I just thought: 'This is not normal'. It's not usually like that from Wednesday fans, especially in small grounds like that. I think a lot of the younger fans who make the noise couldn't get tickets, so it was quiet. It was weird in that sense, and the game hardly got them on the edge of their seats. I think we got caught off guard, not because we underestimated them, but sometimes the other team just looks like they want it more.

"You get games like that, where too many don't turn up, and there can be lots of reasons for that – my missus was about to give birth so I wasn't 100 per cent, there were others who hadn't had a run of games, and there are loads of factors. There weren't many matches that season where we could be questioned about how much we wanted it, but that was probably one of them."

Palmer remembered of the altogether forgettable occasion: "I think what had happened, looking back, was that the manager tried to change a few things with personnel who had not really played for a little while, thinking that because it was Forest Green and there was another game midweek it could be managed... But we tipped up to somewhere we've never been, with a different stadium, and nothing went well at all. We could've been still playing today and we still wouldn't have scored."

It was inadequate on so many levels, and afterwards there was a frustration that some of those who had been banging Moore's door down because of a lack of game-time had not pitched up when they'd been given their chance. The squad was being tested by key injuries, and those being called upon weren't stepping up. Words were shared in the changing room from the manager, but there was also a sense of shock among the players. Former Premier League midfielder Robbie Savage, sat in the stands to watch his son Charlie in action, told those around him that he could not believe this Wednesday team were pushing for the title. You couldn't blame him. In the changing room the players were told in no uncertain terms that none of them should come knocking on the manager's door this time if they missed out the following game, because they simply hadn't turned up.

Moore was forthright with the media afterwards, saying how it hadn't been good enough, how they'd got what they deserved, and few would disagree. The goodwill built up over months unbeaten was drifting away in the wind, and with back-to-back league defeats for the first time in over a year came the latest calls for change. Moore had taken them far enough, said some. The players didn't have it in them, others would state. In-fighting on social media was rampant and below the Owls, Ipswich Town were smelling blood.

As always Moore spoke of moving on, never one to throw any of his players under any sort of bus, and he knew that in games against Cheltenham Town (away), Lincoln City (home) and Oxford United (away) his side had more than enough to get themselves back on track. Wednesday had only gone three league games without a win once all season, and – despite this setback – had shown levels of bounceback-ability that suggested they wouldn't let it get away from them.

***

An hour had passed by in Cheltenham and both sets of players were soaked to the bone. The heavens above Whaddon Road had opened up, and decided not to close again. Waterproofs dripped in the stands and kids shivered, wondering why they ever let their parents talk them into this stuff. In the Wednesday goal stood David Stockdale, surprisingly recalled to the XI by Moore after a 16-game spell on the sidelines. He was already on his second shirt in the game, after a very busy first half display left him caked in mud, and he'd certainly been the busier of the two goalkeepers in a game that the Owls once more struggled to get into. The decision to drop Dawson felt an odd one but had so far been more than justified and as the second half got underway, Wednesday had started to find their feet a little bit more.

But then a mistake. Dominic Iorfa's clearance was mistimed and fell straight to Aidan Keena, who bent it around Stockdale from close range. Once more Wednesday found themselves behind and the collective sigh from the away end was audible as frustrated breath left the mouths of those present. Seven minutes later it happened again, Alfie May on hand this time to poke home after Stockdale parried Taylor Perry's long-range effort into his path. "HMS Piss The League" had hit a big red iceberg, and the weather suggested there may be a need for a rubber dinghy or two as well.

The Owls weren't abandoning ship yet, though, and this time were able to rally. Flint and Mallik Wilks came on and things started to happen. Within moments of the second change it was 2-1, the former heading home what would end up being the second and final goal from any Wednesday centre-back all season. After that it was all Wednesday.

Gregory struck over the bar, Wilks headed one wide, and as fans started to sense that something was coming the ball landed at the feet of Smith out wide. His whipped cross was excellent, once again he found Gregory, and it was 2-2. Those shivering kids weren't shivering any longer, and the Owls weren't done just yet. Bannan got Gregory in a headlock as they sprinted back to the centre circle, rubbing his head in delight, and with just three minutes of normal time remaining they felt like they could complete the turnaround.

Adeniran, on in stoppage time, could've sealed it but he blazed over the close-range, and then Vaulks' effort left the post rattling in the night air after a rasping shot that proved to be the last kick of the game. Wednesday had fought back once more, but again it wasn't enough to reclaim top spot. Praise would come, for their character and spirit, but elsewhere Ipswich were licking their lips. It was two more points dropped, and those previously unbeatable Owls were on shaky ground.

Speaking to reporters with fine rain crashing against his face, Wednesday's veteran 'keeper went through the standard whys and wherefores of a traditional post-match interview before his eyes reddened with emotion. He'd made an emotional return to the side, thinking at one stage that Dawson would see out the final months of what would prove to be his final campaign in league football. The pair had only been told two hours before the game, as Moore rolled his decision over in his mind.

"I might not get another chance," Stockdale said with vibrating chin, gulping down tears. "It meant a lot to come back in. It shows the gaffer has faith in me. Both Cam and I were surprised when it happened to me after Exeter and I was surprised now. We had a hug, we dealt with it and at the start of the season we made a pact that whoever was picked, we'd support and have total trust in. This might be my last chance to win a promotion. I have my heart set on winning one more promotion.

"I want it badly. I'm in my 20th year in football. As you get older, I'll be 38 soon, you start to realise you might not get another chance. I have a son, he texts me before and after every game, and they're in it with you. For my kids to be able to have these memories it leaves a lot on me. I'll tell them I played at Old Trafford or I was in the same England squad as Steven Gerrard or Wayne Rooney, but I have to pull up a picture because they weren't there. I'm emotional because this is being lived with by the people I love as much as it is by me."

A blip had been expected, but having overcome such difficult runs throughout the course of the season it was genuinely thought that Wednesday had managed to navigate the banana skins that could stop them achieving their end goal. The problem was that Plymouth and Ipswich were proving relentless, remaining in first and third respectively, and Wednesday's games in hand had fizzled away. Ipswich, on a six-game winning run, were now just four points behind the Owls, having played a game fewer. March was not meant to have caused as many problems as it did and heading into the penultimate month of the season, they desperately needed to get back on track. Draw specialists Lincoln were next, and the Owls were back at fortress Hillsborough. Surely this was where their longest winless run all season would come to an end?

But six first team players were still out injured – including two, in Windass and Byers, who had contributed 27 goals and assists prior to their absence – and fans were now officially concerned. The players had got back at 2am from Cheltenham, trained that day and the next in preparation for the Imps, and when Smith opened the scoring with a trademark header it looked like it might pay off.

But their joy didn't last long, and less than 20 minutes later they were back to square one, Daniel Mandroiu tapping into an open goal after Stockdale palmed another effort from range into his path. It was a familiar story once again and fans of expected goals will have noted once more that – on paper – it should have been three points for the Owls. In reality though, it was just another one. Wednesday were back top, but it came with little pleasure given that the draw took automatic promotion out of their own hands. Now they needed favours.

Moore, a stickler for work on the training ground, went as far as to grant an extra day off following the Lincoln draw in an attempt to revitalise his side after what he called a "relentless surge" of games. Oxford were next, with no wins in 12, and it was another encounter that Wednesday really should have been winning. Three points from 15 would have been unthinkable just a few weeks earlier.

Fans wanted an answer, they wanted something to blame. Background interference, a change in attitudes, differing training ground work. Something. Anything. There had to be a reason why their title-chasing side were now on the brink of ending up in the play-offs. But behind the scenes it was as methodical as ever. Nothing had changed. Moore is a big believer in consistency, both on the pitch and on the training ground. So as results fanned the flames of fan frustration, the work remained the same. Complacency hadn't been invited in, nothing had slackened off, Wednesday were just enduring a blip that happened to coincide with a ridiculous run of form for their rivals.

"Other than Forest Green, I think we did enough in all of those games to win them," Palmer would say months later from a hotel lobby in Spain. "If you'd spread those results over the course of a season, nobody would have spoken about it. But for us it happened in five or six games and became a big thing. We remained calm, and we knew that the automatic places were still available – the points tally we ended up getting proved that. The other two teams managed to sustain a run that was incredible, though, and you have to say fair play to them. We kept thinking they would tail off."

And while Plymouth and Ipswich bounced around the grounds with the confidence and swagger that Wednesday had had for so long, Moore's Owls found themselves on the ropes. They needed a voice driving them on, a growling North Lanarkshire accent barking at them not to throw in the towel.

***

Barry Bannan knows how to upset the odds; he'd been doing it for 33 years by that point. On December 1, 1989, up in Scotland, the newborn lad from Airdrie had to undergo major surgery. In his own words it was "touch and go" whether he made it or not. By the time he was eight, he'd had to undergo four different operations. He'd always been a fighter.

He was too small to make it as a footballer, many would say. But spurred on by the faith of his parents, Kate and Jimmy, Bannan was having none of that. As a youngster he could be found striking balls through a gap in two trees close to his childhood home, or below his flat's window as his dad dropped balls to test his touch. Watching him in full flow, you can see how that repetition has paid off.

Starting out at Lenzie Youth Club, a young Bannan continued honing his trade, desperate to make a go of things. His technical ability was clearly good enough, but numerous coaches – including one from Manchester United – expressed concern about his physique. In 1999 he shot to prominence locally, aged just nine and an Albion Rovers ballboy, when he started doing kick-ups on the sideline and proceeded to flick the ball over an opposition player's head as he ran towards him.

North of the border they refer to those raised like Bannan as a "tanner baw" player, someone brought up playing on the streets, a reference to the cheap football – if a ball at all – that they often had to play with. His efforts served him well and by the time he was 14 he'd get his chance down south, at Aston Villa. Despite his frame, the young midfield technician was playing above his age group before too long and in 2008 he played a huge role in helping Villa win a Premier League academy title. A few months later he was turning out in the UEFA Cup, coming on for his debut in Hamburg to take his first steps in senior football.

It was in the Midlands that Bannan started to grow up; where he would realise that his ability alone wouldn't be enough. He'd need to be aggressive, tenacious, disciplined, and had all of those attributes already in his locker. After cutting his teeth in loan spells with Derby County, Blackpool and Leeds United, winning a bit of silverware along the way, the youngster got his first real shot at the big time. Between 2011 and 2013 he became somewhat of a Premier League regular with Villa, playing 52 games in two seasons, but it became apparent as the 2012/13 season came to an end that he'd need to move on in order to kick on. A transfer to Crystal Palace didn't quite work out and after a loan at Bolton Wanderers came to an end, he became a free agent.

Given his pedigree, Bannan wasn't short of options. But up in Yorkshire there was a club under new ownership that had shown an interest; a club that tickled his fancy. "There is something about this one," he said after signing and to say it has been a journey since then would be an understatement. In his first season Bannan was on the brink of helping the Owls return to the promised land of the Premier League before an agonising play-off final defeat. The following season he helped spearhead the club's most successful league finish in two decades before more play-off pain. In 2020 he was made captain and in 2021 he lay on the grass at Pride Park after Wednesday's devastating relegation to League One.

"It was such a dark day in our house," his wife Chloe wrote in an emotional letter to her husband, published in 2023 by *The Star*. "Watching you from home, seeing you crying on the pitch – it was the most devastated that I had seen you. I was heartbroken for you. After a few days we spoke at length about next moves, and what you wanted to do. Your phone didn't stop ringing all summer. You had options, you had other clubs wanting to sign you and put you back into the Championship. But I could just tell that wasn't what you wanted. You had a job to do, a mission to accomplish, and it seemed the only right thing was to stay. You made it your mission to take Wednesday back to where they belong."

Mission was the correct term. Numerous times he could have left, numerous times the opportunity arose to jump ship, but he stayed put – even signing a new deal with the club whilst on the brink of dropping into the third tier. He could have left again after defeat to Sunderland in the play-offs. But no; he still had work to do in the city that had so gladly taken him into their arms.

Speaking in the aftermath of that Sunderland disappointment, Bannan was adamant. "I've got unfinished business," he said. "I wanted to get promoted this season, it hasn't happened, so I see myself staying here to get promoted next season and giving it another go. I wanted to lift a trophy as captain of this club. That's what I'll continue to do. We've come up short, we were a game away from Wembley and that chance to lift that trophy, but it's unfinished business and hopefully I'm back here to do it again next season."

So as Bannan saw automatic promotion slipping away as the 2022/23 season reached its final straight, the Owls skipper took matters into his own hands. He held team meetings, he stepped up his work with psychologist Tom Bates, he tried his best to keep the mood up, and his assist at Cheltenham would be the first of seven goals and assists in eight games. Managers and players alike knew that he was too good for League One, they spoke about it all the time. But knowing you should stop him, and knowing how to stop him, are two different things.

And as he bent one around Simon Eastwood in the 35th minute at the Kassam Stadium there was a sense of relief as much as anything else. Bannan doing Bannan things. Wednesday were desperate to get back to winning ways and with the wee Scottish man wheeling away in the Oxfordshire sunshine, it felt as though today was the day.

But after Eastwood somehow kept out a Wilks header, and Gregory fired inches past the post, doubts began to creep in among the travelling supporters and eyes rolled back as referee Rebecca Welch gave an Oxford penalty with 20 minutes left to go. It seemed as clear as day to most that it was Akin Famewo who was clambered all over, but Cameron Brannagan would get his chance from the spot. "I'm on the floor!" shouted Famewo on his knees, but no amount of remonstration would change Welch's mind. Stockdale went the right way, but there was no keeping it out.

Another draw, six without defeat, and all of the traits that Wednesday had prided themselves on seemed to have disappeared. All of those comfortable one-nils felt a long time ago and to make it worse Wednesday had now officially fallen out of the top two as well. Just like after their home draw with the U's, some were baying for blood. "He'll never win us promotion," they cried. "Absolute bottlejobs," said others. "I should never have got my hopes up," many thought.

In the stands post-match, a lone, slurring voice screamed into the afternoon, launching a tirade of abuse towards the players undertaking their warm-down. A lone voice it may have been, but an albeit extreme example of the fractious feeling on the terraces it certainly was.

There had also been a flashpoint in the game that saw Bannan and Palmer separated by Stockdale and Adeniran following a heated exchange of words. A petulant push, a couple of snarling faces, that sort of thing. And it carried on into half-time as well. Having known each other for the best part of a decade the pair had become close, Palmer believing that his captain had matured from being a "great player" to also being a "well-rounded individual" over the years. They holiday together, their families are close, and they both want what's best for a club very close to their heart. But that doesn't mean they don't fall out from time to time.

"We've looked, and we've both played alongside the other more than any other player in our careers," a smiling Palmer said later down the line. "I've been here since he walked through the door, and we know how to push each other's buttons. He's fiery and wants the best out of you, out of the moment, and in that scenario I was doing something that I'd been asked to do in a team meeting.

"He thought it was wrong, and we said we'd get it up on a screen at half-time and then we were shouting at each other. But we went in at half-time and got it up, then it was diffused and nothing more got said. We both knew it was from a place of just wanting to win. We know what each other is about, and when we do disagree we move on." Palmer has seen his friend grow into the captaincy and become a brilliant dad and husband – and they share the desire to succeed for Sheffield Wednesday.

Bannan agreed. "You need that fire," he said. "You wouldn't be successful in a football changing room where nobody speaks their mind – you need altercations, you need opinions. At the end of the day we all want the same thing, and that's to win games." They were sat next to each other on the bus on the way home, that flash in the pan forgotten.

But while their momentary feud was done, it didn't change the result – or halt the anger emanating from a decisively baffled fanbase. Ipswich and Plymouth had won again – convincingly – and the Owls were down to third. The two teams above them both had a game in hand, and had collectively picked up 27 points from the last 30 available to them. While Wednesday faltered, their rivals had hit steamroll mode.

There would be no time to sulk about it. Things weren't over for Moore's side and three days later they welcomed Accrington Stanley to Hillsborough. Games had long since become must-win for Wednesday but back on home soil, against a team destined for the drop, there was a feeling that it really was now or never. The top two faced Cheltenham and Lincoln City, and were expected to pick up three points again. All the Owls could do was try to hold up their end of the bargain by getting back on track after an absurd three-week spell.

After 11 minutes Adeniran – shining at right wing-back – made it 1-0, giving Wednesday just the sort of start they needed. They'd burst out of the blocks and could've had a couple, but Stanley weren't folding and Sean McConville rattled the crossbar – and a few nerves. The players probably didn't know it yet but as Reece James was down receiving treatment before another injury setback, Lincoln had taken the lead at Plymouth and Ipswich had been pegged back by Cheltenham. As things stood, Wednesday were going top again.

James had to go off, unfortunately, and wouldn't be seen for a few weeks – Moore said afterwards that he might not make it back at all before the season ended. Mallik Wilks was also forced off, with an injury that would end his campaign, and Callum Paterson made his long-awaited return. He'd rushed back, a quick healer apparently, and Wednesday were now very much in a needs-must situation. He'd still have quite the role to play.

But despite the injury setbacks, Wednesday weren't swayed and the start of the second half couldn't have gone any better as Adeniran grabbed his second. Over in Plymouth, the Imps had doubled their lead and Cheltenham were holding on. In control and heading back to League One's summit, fans were breathing that bit more easily as Gregory knocked the ball back to Bannan about 40 yards from goal.

He clipped it over the top first time, with the nonchalance that Wednesdayites have become so accustomed to, and right into the path of an on-rushing Palmer, who took one touch to set himself and finished expertly with his second. He'd got more goals this season than in his entire career combined, and few doubted his ability in front of goal these days. Bannan, his creator, rushed over to the corner flag and together they faked a punch, Palmer falling to the ground in a jokey nod to their previous bust-up. There would be no row this afternoon.

The 3-0 scoreline didn't flatter the Owls, and Dawson got a clean sheet on his return to the XI, but more importantly things had gone for them elsewhere. The victory saw Wednesday become the first team to officially qualify for the play-offs, but vitally a rare home defeat for the Pilgrims and a shock draw for Ipswich meant that the Owls' hopes of automatic promotion were back on again. All they had to do was win every game that they had left, and hope for a bit of luck…

THIRTEEN

96 POINTS

The final whistle goes at the Pirelli Stadium, and in the away end a smorgasbord of emotions are on show as the blue and white masses turn mainly blue. Anger, frustration, bewilderment, and just downright sadness. Many can't believe the position they find themselves in, just over a month after what had felt like a season-affirming win at Portsmouth. Sheffield Wednesday are out of the top two, and with four games left to play their fate is now well and truly out of their own hands. They may well set a new club record points tally in 2022/23, but it's looking increasingly likely that that simply won't be enough.

Wednesday's win over Accrington Stanley had sent them to the summit once again after a torrid run, but they knew that they'd need a 100 per cent record from then on if they were to stand any chance of stopping Ipswich Town and Plymouth Argyle – two teams who, frankly, looked unflinching in their pursuit of promotion until they both dropped points on the same day the Owls beat Accy. The chances were that lightning wouldn't strike again, but Darren Moore's side needed to keep up their side of the bargain and hope for the best.

So when former Sheffield United man – of course – John Brayford put Burton Albion 1-0 up with barely 20 minutes on the clock, it felt like a huge punch to the gut. Wednesday fought back through Callum Paterson in his first start since being rushed back from injury ahead of schedule, but less than 10 minutes later they were 3-1 down. A failed Paterson backheel, a Tyreeq Bakinson slip, a quickfire second for Mark Helm shortly after bagging his first. Those fans that had dared to dream before felt like they were in the midst of a nightmare. Maybe it wasn't going to be their year after all.

Behind Cameron Dawson's goal one man leant on the advertising board in front of him, half his body draped over it and his head in his other hand. It wasn't meant to be this way. Wednesday hadn't started badly against Burton, and on another day could've won it still, but Michael Smith's penalty wasn't going to be enough and they went on to lose 3-2. The first two goals conceded felt all too familiar, both the result of balls into the box and a failure to deal with the aerial threat of their opponents. These were the issues that were supposed to have been ironed out. For others it had come sooner, but it was this day that Wednesdayites knew that the once-unstoppable Owls train had been derailed. No talk of going again, or focusing on the next game, would suffice. This side, it would seem, had managed to grasp defeat from the jaws of victory, and the thought of another trip to Fleetwood Town next season was enough to drain even the most optimistic of fans. Had that soft underbelly been exposed again?

Wednesday had gone into the game with six senior players unavailable. Reece James and Mallik Wilks were back on the injury list after short-lived returns to fitness, and the continued absence of Josh Windass and George Byers was leaving a monumental gap in Darren Moore's side. Pessimism crept around the fanbase like a Grim Reaper, tapping more and more on the shoulder as the days went by.

And it wasn't just in the stands that the feeling was shifting. After a season where Wednesday felt destined for a top-two finish, there was a sense of doubt creeping through the ranks. Panic even. Would it all have been for nothing? Would the unbeaten record mean nought? It needed a steadying hand; or voice, as the case may be.

Sensing the worry, captain Barry Bannan called a meeting after the Burton game. "It was one just for the players, because I could see that people were starting to panic," he said. "We'd lost our way from going up automatically, but I made sure that we nipped it in the bud there and then. We had games to play and I told them that if we could win them, then we'd got two chances. Either somebody slipped up and we'd go up, or we'd have strong momentum going into the play-offs. I felt like nipping it. There was a level of leadership I needed to show, and it seemed to work because we did manage to kick on from there. It was something that I'd thought about at night, and felt I had to do."

He was right, of course, and the meeting was required. Between themselves Wednesday's players talked things through, making a vow to finish as strongly as they possibly could. The final blow hadn't been struck yet, and they were going to try and do their best to avoid it coming at all. Four more games, 12 more points, a club record of 96 to aim for. All or nothing, now. As they began the long trip to Bristol Rovers, Owls fans were not so optimistic. For them, it was just a matter of time.

The Memorial Stadium was Don Megson's only other home as a professional footballer and it was decided that his life would be commemorated beforehand, with almost 9,000 putting their hands together to pay tribute to him. Around the centre circle, both sets of players joined in and the moment was exceptionally observed by all of those present. It would be the final nicety of the evening.

It didn't take long for things to get heated, unsurprisingly given the pugnacious opposition manager Joey Barton, and there were already a few rough tackles being ridden by the time Smith's excellent header bounced off the crossbar. Adeniran had an effort saved, and home fans jeered Smith as he kicked the ball in frustration at not quite having the legs to get to it after knocking it around James Belshaw. But a moment of magic was on the horizon…

Bannan, having been found by Gregory, took one touch to steady himself, looked up, and drove his trusty left boot through the ball to angle it past the Rovers goalkeeper and into the back of the net. Wednesday had deserved it, even if things hadn't been pretty, and the Owls' wee Scottish man cupped his ears and slid on his knees in front of the home support. It was the fourth game in a row that he'd directly contributed to a Wednesday goal, and another clip to add to his already impressive highlight reel in the club's colours. Though it had gone unreported, it later transpired that Barton had suggested, in his pre-match press engagement, that a Wednesday side with Bannan in it was easier dealt with. That strike would suggest otherwise.

Wednesday kept pushing and just before the break, it was two. An almighty scramble in the box, with shirts being ragged all over and players being shoved to the floor, ended with the ball at Akin Famewo's feet. Composed, he used his left foot to shift the ball to his unfavoured right before smashing it into the back of the net from close-range. The unbridled joy of a man who had been through the ringer was palpable as he roared, running towards the halfway line. The moment was perfectly captured by club photographer Steve Ellis and in Famewo's eyes, you could see that all the hard work had been worth it after scoring his first goal for the Owls.

Half-time arrived, and out came the phones. Wednesdayites inside the ground, journalists up in the press box, probably a few in the away changing room too. They all couldn't help themselves. Their chances had been written off, often quite publicly, but that fat lady hadn't sung, and the Owls weren't done just yet. Plymouth were being held by Shrewsbury Town, and somehow Ipswich had found themselves 1-0 down at home to Port Vale. The old meme from the film *Dumb and Dumber* started doing the rounds once more. "So, you're telling me there's a chance?"

A phone buzzed. A notification. Shrewsbury had scored. Surely not? They couldn't, could they? The phone buzzed again. Ipswich were level, but still dropping points. Wednesday had been comfortable in the opening stanza, but within 35 seconds of the restart Aaron Collins, later to be named League One's player of the year, cut the deficit in half after latching onto a long ball that was somewhat misjudged by Dominic Iorfa. A glance shared between those of a Wednesday persuasion acknowledged that it could be a long 45 minutes. The challenge was made even more difficult when Famewo, in such a cruel twist of fate, was forced off with what looked like a worrying injury. Tyreeq Bakinson replaced him, Liam Palmer undergoing his almost weekly positional change into central defence. Another setback.

But with 60 minutes gone Wednesday were closing the gap, they had a chance, and they were holding up their end of the bargain – often by the skin of their teeth – in Bristol. The atmosphere was bubbling, yet the Owls were keeping their cool. Aden Flint, booed at every possible opportunity as a former Bristol City player, was on a mission to make sure the home crowd didn't get the satisfaction of celebrating an equaliser. His towering frame headed clear time and time again while Iorfa, rather than dwell on the goal, seemed to get stronger. Wednesday were resilient, they were steadfast. They were everything they'd not been at Burton, and their strapping centre-back was showing the sort of mental strength of a man who'd known struggle in recent years.

***

Dominic Iorfa comes from a strong footballing family. His dad, of the same name, had a lengthy career that took him from his birthplace of Gboko in Nigeria's Benue State through stints at Queens Park Rangers, Galatasaray, Guangzhou Apollo and more before retiring in the early 2000s. Unlike his son, though, Iorfa Sr. was a striker.

Before you even see Iorfa play you know he was born to be an athlete of some sort. Tall and athletic, he wouldn't look out of place on a track or basketball court and on first impressions you get the feeling he could turn his hand to either. They wouldn't be wrong. In his youth he ran both the 100m and 200m for his school and his best times, of 12.7 seconds and 22.4 seconds, saw him set records at his school in Southend and go on to represent the County of Essex in national championships. He didn't play but is a big fan of the NBA, too.

Football won out in the end, though, and by 2017 he'd represented England at U18, U20 and U21 levels while coming through the ranks at Wolverhampton Wanderers. In 2015 he'd even had the chance to train with Roy Hodgson's senior ranks at St George's Park and his journey brought him to Wednesday in 2019 as Steve Bruce's first signing. A fee of £200,000 seemed a snip, given his pedigree. Brought in as a right back, he moved more centrally as time went on and won the club's player of the season award in his first year.

The seasons that followed would not be kind to the man who Wednesdayites fondly call "the fastest man in Yorkshire," with an Achilles rupture in 2020 ruling him out for what he referred to as "the most frustrating six months of my career" and hip surgery meaning another season stunted in Owls' colours. "The worst bit for me is when you're just sat at home on crutches, and you can't move," he said as 2021/22 came to an end. "They're the really dark days when you're down and thinking: 'Oh, so it's another injury. Will I bounce back from this?'

The 2022/23 season gave him a chance to do exactly that. He played 43 games in total, and had to work hard for them. Putting in the hours, waiting patiently, doing extra in the gym. And as he kept Rovers at bay that night there was a growing feeling that, after some had questioned his quality and form post-injuries, Big Dom was getting back to his best.

It was shaping up to be the perfect night, with results going Wednesday's way elsewhere, but tempers were fraying closer to the action. Barton was unhappy with decisions in the game, and would later be so furious at a disallowed goal that he'd end up getting sent off. One fan right by the media box – who had grown increasingly enraged – screamed "You lemon tit!" at the ref. It may have been linked to Wednesday's yellow kit, but nobody really knew. A short while earlier, after Paterson had headed over the bar, he stood up and simply shouted: "You dick!" He was not a happy man.

By this point phones were not leaving the hands of their owners as the scores were constantly refreshed at Portman Road and the New Meadow. By 70 minutes Plymouth had got it back to 1-1, though Wednesday were still making up ground as things stood. WhatsApps were disregarded as fans prayed for a Shrewsbury goal to pop up on their phone, but it wasn't to come. After 84 minutes, the buzz – GOAL! IPSWICH TOWN. Nathan Broadhead had scored from the spot, the Tractor Boys were ahead. After 90 minutes, plus five of injury time: GOAL! PLYMOUTH ARGYLE. They'd found a way through Callum Wright. Trevor Braithwait, the club's director of communications and a long-time Wednesdayite himself, gave the media an all-too-familiar look. "Well, nearly."

The final whistle went and Flint, after receiving dog's abuse for 90 minutes, celebrated vociferously right in front of Rovers' hardcores. No holding back, he'd won his battle that night. Wednesday were victorious, and congratulated each other on a very good away victory, but those watching knew just how close they'd come to being top once again. Late goals from Ipswich and Plymouth had become par for the course but didn't numb the disappointment. It began to dawn on Wednesdayites that they were, in all likelihood, going to see their team achieve the highest-ever points tally in English Football League history that didn't secure automatic promotion.

Barton had described Wednesday as "archaic" in a post-match rant that saw him forecast relegation if the Owls did go up, comments that Moore predictably took in his giant stride. "I'd just like to say: 'Thank you Joey for your kind words'," was Moore's dignified response, with a mischievous smile stretched across his face. Privately, Moore will have been grimacing at the continued injury absences of Josh Windass and George Byers, with games rapidly running out, and both were again absent from the squad to face Exeter City in the Owls' penultimate home game of the regular season.

And boy could they have done with either. The first half was so dull that the game's official highlights on YouTube featured only two minutes and 40 seconds from the first 45 minutes, including a long throw-in from Will Vaulks caught by Exeter goalkeeper Jamal Blackman. What didn't make the cut was referee Declan Bourne going down with injury and being replaced by fourth official Andy Haines. That period may have been the most interesting part.

Ipswich were only 1-0 up at half-time and Plymouth were drawing, so Wednesday were missing a trick with their lacklustre start at Hillsborough. In the dressing room they were met by an incredulous Moore, bemused given the occasion that they'd not pitched up in front of the 26,000 in attendance. The Owls boss wasn't a ranter and raver, but his sheer size gives him the ability to hold the attention of his squad. Jamie Smith would often be bad cop when required, but on this occasion the manager needed a word. With Moore's touchline manner so calm and collected, an idea had built up amongst fans that he was too nice. In reality, it was more about picking his moments.

"Sometimes you need that to wake you up," recalled one player. "Some managers shout all the time and in the end it doesn't really register because it's like: 'Oh, he's shouting again'. And then there are managers that do it at the right time... The gaffer had the odd occasion when he'd dig people out, and with the size of the man... He had an element of surprise as well. Because when a man that big goes from being nice all the time to raising his voice, it makes you sit back and listen."

Two minutes into the second half, Wednesday were 1-0 down.

Exeter had seven starters out of action for this game – a squad depletion that Wednesday could relate to – and had a right wing-back playing up front. They weren't even able to name a full bench but that right wing-back, Josh Key, was the one who opened the scoring. Moore had wanted to see a reaction from his side and hadn't got one, so it was time for the changes. Dennis Adeniran was introduced to inject some energy down the right, and he did just that – a couple of minutes later it was him bounding towards goal before being hacked down by Archie Collins. Bannan stood over it, whipped it in, and Lee Gregory's glancing header beat Blackman at the far post. The Owls were level and their No.9 was in double figures once more.

A draw wasn't ever going to be enough though. With an hour gone the Tractor Boys and Pilgrims were both winning – obviously – and the Owls needed another to keep their already-fading hopes alive. On came Michael Ihiekwe, for his first game in almost five months, and moments later he was on the ball, feeding it out to Iorfa. Adeniran was once again causing all sorts of trouble down the right and although his cross from the byline was scrambled away, Marvin Johnson got a shot away. It was wayward but Paterson – not for the last time in the right place at the right time in front of the Leppings Lane end – was on hand to poke it home. The Owls led, and the dream lived on that little bit longer.

It'd been a tough time for the versatile Scot. Relegation to League One had in no small part cost him a place in his beloved national team and a chance of playing at the 2021 European Championships, Scotland's first major tournament in 23 years. Promotion could help remedy that, it was felt, and bring him back into the fold. Interestingly he had a choice of three nations to represent due to his family heritage, the others being South Africa and Zimbabwe, but to meet Paterson is to know that there was never a choice to be made there – even if he does have Africa's Big Five game animals tattooed on his leg. Rhino, buffalo, leopard, elephant and lion. The latter sums him up the best.

A fiercely intelligent man with a love of fishing he says melts away the stresses of life as a footballer, youth coaches at Tynecastle Boys Club that guided his formative steps in football remember a player who had no idea of his talent and ability to make it in the game. He was, it was described, something of a tearaway that lacked a little focus. At 13 he was a solid performer but not the best on the team – in fairness they did go on to become national champions – but a chat at 15 seemed to focus him. He beefed up and focused. At 17, he was lining up for Hearts in a Europa Cup tie at Anfield against Steven Gerrard and Luis Suarez.

Brave, burly and ferociously strong, Paterson had built up a cult following pretty much everywhere he'd played and it was no different at Hillsborough, for those that appreciated what he brought to the side. He'd scored at Burton, his first since that cruel injury against Plymouth, but this one was the first winner since then – having worked so hard to return from his injury ahead of schedule, he was ready for the run-in. He'd certainly have a role to play.

Wednesday were still third, their competitors both going on to score three, but once more they'd managed to show the inner strength need-ed to fight back. It was now 32 points earned from losing positions over the past two seasons – nine more than they'd managed in the previous four combined – and the Owls remained on track for that record points total as well. Moore made sure to point out afterwards, however, how displeased he'd been by their start. "I think the first 45 minutes was non-existent from us," he said. "They looked tired, and jaded, and at half-time we came together and said that we needed to give more to the cause and take the game to them… The goal almost sparked us into life, and they were better after that. You raise your voice, but it's all in context of the game. There's no point shouting at them as they have got to see the plan and vision within the game in the second half and the players have to remain calm and composed."

With two games to play, Wednesday had already beaten the previous year's tally by five points and the following night, a Wednesday con-tingent made their way down to London for the EFL Awards. Bannan was, of course, nominated for player of the season, Moore was up for the manager gong and Windass was heading south in the knowledge that he'd made the 2022/23 team of the season. Windass was in training again and "buzzing" to get back on the pitch and although neither Ban-nan nor Moore won, the awards going to Collins and Steven Schum-acher, the admiration for both was clear for all to see. Wednesday's boss isn't known as one of the nicest guys in football for no reason, and the amount of people who wanted – and subsequently received – his time was testament to that.

Unlike Leyton Orient's Richie Wellens, who admitted he'd "had a few" as the only champion in the room at that time, there'd be no big shindig for Moore and his Owls. The next game against Shrewsbury Town was six days later and though it would in all likelihood be the game that saw them condemned to the play-offs, Bannan is not the type to give anything up. So after an unboozy awards night, at the Grosve-nor House Hotel on Park Lane, he was back in the car and heading back north.

Wednesday didn't have a midweek game to play but would certainly be watching out for the ones that did. Plymouth faced Bristol Rovers and Ipswich travelled to Barnsley and on the face of it, neither was an easy task. But their respective steam trains had no intention of slow-ing down and comfortable wins sent them five and four points clear of Moore's outfit, who now really did need a miracle. For context, the Pilgrims' 2-0 win over Rovers made it 19 wins out of 22 at home and Ipswich, 3-0 winners at Barnsley, had dropped just four points out of 42 since that 2-2 draw with the Owls in February. You had to give them their due.

So preparations for Wednesday's trip to Shrewsbury continued with the knowledge that even a victory would probably be in vain in terms of a top two spot. But as per their post-Burton meeting, they still wanted to finish the season strongly; to make sure they'd take momentum into the play-offs if, as expected, that's where they ended up. Moore had ended all talk of injuries, insisting that he was focusing forwards, on who was available rather than who wasn't. Chairman Dejphon Chansiri, desperate for his club to return to where he found them, wanted to have his say as well and the day before Shrewsbury, on June 29, he issued his rallying cry.

"There are two games to go and while we have a mathematical chance of the top two, everyone must give everything for the team," he said. "The odds are not in our favour but while we still have a fighting chance, our fans have a huge part to play. Please give everything you have at Shrewsbury on Saturday and, if it goes to the last day, the same against Derby. If we go to the play-offs, the same again."

To his credit he took responsibility, urged fans to take their frustrations out on him rather than the manager or the players. "Now is not the time for inquests," he declared. "I ask all our fans, if you want to come to anyone now, come to me, I will take that as the leader of our club. I can take that on my shoulders but please, I ask to move any negative direction away from the football department for the games we have left. Until we know our destiny for next season, we must have one big positive push. Whether that is for automatic promotion or the play-offs, it is the same. It may be a small chance of automatic now, but it is still a chance. Now is not the time for inquests on the football, that can come at the end of the season, which is fine. Until this season is finished we must be totally positive and give everything we can for Sheffield Wednesday."

Moore said his piece too. In his press briefing he not only echoed Chansiri's thoughts but also suggested that maybe, just maybe, some had been living in the past way too much. "Probably the thing is that we've always been looking backwards here," he said. "Let's start looking forward. Let's all come together and look forwards. Everyone has their part to play, and we can do two things – we can either say that the cup is half empty, look backwards and that's where you stay, or we can come together – which we have done over the course of the season – and still formulate something."

There was no doubt over Wednesdayites selling out their allocation of 1,642 tickets for Shrewsbury, but less certain was the reception they'd hand out to those that, in the eyes of many, had let them down. As the Owls players ran out, in the pink kit from the season prior due to Salop's yellow and blue strip, it became clear that they needn't have worried. The fans, at their self-deprecating best, chanted: "Top of the league, and we fucked it up." They were buoyed by the sight of Windass' name finally back on the teamsheet – with four more games left to play after this one, the attacker was seen as a vital piece of the puzzle.

But as one hand giveth, the other taketh away. On the same day as the chairman's statement George Byers had confirmed on Instagram that, unlike Windass, he wouldn't be back before the end of the season. Like Chansiri though, he called for togetherness. "I thought there might be a chance, but the hamstring injury was worse than first thought," he said. "It's been a frustrating time, and it's not how I wanted the season to end. The lads still have a lot to play for, so everyone stick together and get behind the team like you always do."

It took just eight minutes for the Owls to take control. Starting at the back, including Dawson and the returning Michael Ihiekwe, Wednesday moved the ball forward one pass at a time, before Iorfa slipped through a killer ball to Smith. He found Gregory, and the No.9's back-heel was right into the path of the Owls' top scorer, who couldn't have finished much better as he placed it into the top corner to grab his 17th of the season in all competitions.

Three minutes after the break it was two, the striker adding another in the most Smith-like fashion, rising highest in the box to head home a lovely dink into the box from Johnson. It wouldn't matter, not really, because elsewhere Ipswich were already 6-0 up as they tore Exeter to pieces, and Plymouth were leading at home to Burton. But Wednesday were running a different race now. They just wanted to finish as strongly as they could – regardless of what happened elsewhere.

For his third, to complete a first hat-trick since 2016, the former Rotherham man was slipped though by Bannan and shrugged off Tom Flanagan like a rag doll before slotting calmly into the back of the net. The Wednesdayites behind the net already knew their fate, but celebrations were far from muted. As one they surged forward, cheering in unison after Smith had bagged his 19th of the season in the 81st minute. They cared that automatic promotion was off the cards, of course they did, but they cared more that on that day, in that moment, their team were getting the job done. And with style, too.

The final whistle went, and tentatively Wednesday's players glanced over at the away end – briefly. They'd failed in their mission to win the league, failed in their mission to finish top two, and that was now official. How would the fans respond if they headed over to see them? They'd soon find out.

It started as a rumble, then gathered a few decibels, and by the time the bulk of Wednesday's men had reached the north stand it had built into a cacophony. The noise itself was impressive, and was noted by the watching media immediately. But what was most extraordinary was what it signified. Title or not, automatics or not, those 1,642 were absolutely and unequivocally behind their team. Move on, move forwards. Somehow, 93 points wasn't going to get them into the top two, but it was still a phenomenal achievement. The fact that the fans recognised that gave the men in pink more of a boost than they could've known.

"We were talking about it on the bench in the 90th minute with the fans singing their heads off," Smith went on to say afterwards. "Obviously going over at the end, they're well within their rights to give us a bit of stick, but they were all with us and that's going to be massive going into the play-offs. We're going to need them in the home leg, the away leg, and hopefully if all goes well at Wembley as well. I think it is one of the most pivotal moments all season. To hear that at the end will give the lads a real boost, knowing that the fans are with us."

It wasn't just on the bench they were talking about it, either. On the two-hour trip home on the team bus it was a major topic of conversation as Wednesday's players waxed lyrical about what they'd seen and what they'd felt. When he'd arrived at Hillsborough Moore had spoken about reconnecting the fans with the club and that "real surge of energy," as he'd described it, was proof that they'd done that. To quote another Mooreism, they were all together. "Together as one."

Victory at Shrewsbury made it 12 on the road for the season, another club record, and Windass had returned to the field for the first time in six weeks. Dawson had one more clean sheet as the club's new record extended to 24 for the season and where pessimism had grown in the previous weeks, long shoots of optimism were bursting through. Play-offs it was, then.

But amongst the noise in Shropshire, while Wednesdayites' gallows humour emanated from the away end, there was a worrying sign. Palmer, an almost ever-present, limped off in the 89th minute, trudging his way around the outside of the pitch after another fine shift. It had been the 49th game that he'd played that season, and he'd given everything that he had to the cause. The man they called the "Worksop Cafu" had been playing through the pain for months, though, and there was no way he was going to miss what was to come.

Few know the man better than his captain, Bannan, the pair going through thick and thin over their years together at Hillsborough. The Scot found him at S6 when he arrived in 2015, and they'll be mates long after they've hung up their boots – whenever that time may come. "I looked up to Palms even though I'm the older of us, because he had kids before me, and I always wanted what he had off the pitch," Bannan said. "I used to look up to him as a family man then, and I still do now because it's one of the biggest things that stands out about him. He's an unbelievable husband and father to his wife and kids."

And his 2022/23 form hadn't gone unnoticed, either. It wasn't just the games or the goals, but the whole package. Despite being 31, the Wednesday academy graduate looked fitter and sharper than he'd ever been and as the season went on, even his biggest critics had to hold their hands up. In a club with an injury record like this one, he was almost always there – under Moore alone he'd notched up more than 100 appearances. When the time to vote for the club's awards came around, there was never really any doubt.

They've had their rows, Palmer and Bannan. They've kissed and made up more than once, and as a friend as much as a teammate, nobody was more pleased than Bannan to see the lifelong Owl get his flowers as he made his way up to the stage to collect his player of the season, players' player of the season and lifetime achievement gongs.

"It was the season that people started to get to see the Liam Palmer that we knew was there," his skipper would explain. "The real Liam Palmer I suppose. And there's not one bit of me that doesn't think he can keep it going – he's a top, top player. And on top of that he's a local boy, he's been here his whole career, so there will have been loads of pressure on him. Like me, 2022/23 could've been his last chance, so I'm just delighted for him. I became a fan, but he grew up one, so to actually lead your own team the way he did ... it must've been ten-fold what I felt. He'll be remembered for the rest of his life at this club, and nobody deserves it more. He's one of the nicest guys you'll come across in football.

"He's played loads of games, and been here a long time, but I think he should've played more because of the potential he's had. For him to perform to the way that he did on the way to promotion was no surprise to me – I've seen him day in and day out for years. I recall watching him for Scotland and thinking: 'That's the Palms we want' because he'd be brilliant for them. We saw more of him in 2022/23, with the goals and stuff, and he really grabbed the season by the scruff of the neck. I knew that he had it in him, that he could fly up the pitch and get goals. It's why we had arguments sometimes, because I knew there was so much more to him."

They didn't know at the time that more celebrations were on the horizon for Hillsborough's 1867 Lounge, but none were as important as that one on April 30, the day after Shrewsbury. Palmer was at the heart of it, as it should be given the rise of the defender that had joined Wednesday's academy at the age of seven, but he wouldn't be making it about himself. As his name was called to collect his lifetime achievement award, he looked around for John Murray.

One of the longest-serving people at the club, Murray had done it all. He's been the kitman, the bus driver, the in-house comedian, and dedicated decades of his life to the cause. For Palmer, he's the sort of person that should be getting the recognition. People like Johnny, like club stalwart Debbie Walker and jack-of-all-trades Rob Cox, are the ones that make football clubs what they are. Wednesday's No.2 has met enough of them to know. The Scottish international has worked his way through the ranks at S6, he's put in the yards. In 2005 he was at Cardiff, cheering on Paul Sturrock and his boys in the play-off final. In 2012 he was a 20-year-old watching on as Wycombe Wanderers were beaten at Hillsborough to seal Wednesday's promotion. For 2016 he was a squad member but missed out on the team for Wembley. In 2022/23 he played over 4,500 minutes, often with the help of pain-killers, before finally heading to visit the same groin specialist, Ulrike Muschaweck, who has treated the likes of Xabi Alonso, Michael Owen, and Ander Herrera. Not yet, though. The job was not yet done.

The disappointment of needing the play-offs remained but in that room, to the left of Hillsborough's reception, it was about celebrating what had been achieved. Smith's golden boot, Vaulks' incredible community work and goal of the season strike against Port Vale. The players, the manager, and his staff spent the night conversing with Wednesday-supporting corporate guests and sponsors, doing their best to refill their optimism gauges. It worked.

"It was a very good night, and it ran perfectly too," said Cobi Stokes, one of the fans lucky enough to be there for a night of David Stockdale compering, Vaulks singing Robbie Williams and general wholesomeness. "As a fan it was nice to hear the players so optimistic, and speaking so highly of the atmosphere in the club going into the play-offs. Personally, I don't need encouragement to be positive, but even some of the more negative people in the group came away so optimistic before the Derby game. Darren was his usual class self, he seemingly had endless time for everyone there. It was something that really stood out – after having a photo with us he thanked our whole table for our support throughout the season. I've been lucky enough to be in the corporate boxes quite a few times, so you sometimes hear the odd man-of-the-match come out and say that kind of stuff, but that night you could really feel the energy in all of the players."

It was an evening that Moore himself spoke of afterwards, reiterating its importance and how it was another example of the bond between fan and club being strengthened. Local crooner and Wednesdayite Paul Pashley sang into the night and those present at S6 had a renewed sense of hope. But it wasn't just a big moment for them.

"Having had the disappointment of not going up automatically," the big winner Palmer explained, "I think it was important to have that night. We'd won at Shrewsbury so things were more positive, but it would've been easy for the club to pull it because the season didn't end how we'd thought. It felt important for the fans in the room, for the players and staff, to be able to be proud of what we had achieved. It'd been a real effort, and we'd had to pick ourselves up. In hindsight I think it made us more determined."

Almost a decade had passed by since his first player of the season award, an achievement in itself, but this one will have felt different. Only once in his storied Wednesday career did he come close to leaving – under Jos Luhukay, when youngsters were getting selected ahead of him – but even though he stayed, Palmer had dealt with a lot. At times it would feel like he was given less slack because of being 'one of our own' rather than more – but 2022/23 made it all worth it. He'd come a long way since his days sat on that uncovered corner between the Kop and north stand.

His parents, Allison and Terry, had been there for all of it. He'd known his wife, Beth, since school. They knew the sacrifice, they'd seen the growth. "I know they're proud of me regardless," he'd say. "They've been there all the way through the ups and downs, but for me to hear that my dad is going to work and his mates are on about me, and that he can say: 'Yeah, that's my son' – it's nice. For my mum it's the same. Beth allows me to sacrifice a lot as well, allows me to be the man that I am. I think the whole of Worksop was at Wembley, and people keep saying how we've given them the best days of their lives. It's amazing."

It was the best possible way to prepare for Derby County a week later. The game wouldn't affect their league position, but it did offer a chance to write their name into Wednesday history. No Owls side in history had ever achieved 96 points, but against Paul Warne's Rams they had a chance to do just that. Derby – who had relegated Wednesday two years earlier – needed things to go their way to get into the play-offs themselves, and a sell-out crowd was expected. Palmer would be making his 394th Wednesday appearance.

The sun beat down on Hillsborough in what would be the first of four games in May, and former Blade David McGoldrick seemed eager to spoil the party. He rolled back the years on a number of occasions and very nearly gave the visitors the lead when his excellent effort was bettered only by the save from Dawson to keep it out. With half-time approaching there was nothing to separate the two sides.

But then a chance. Curtis Davies' backpass left ex-Owl Joe Wild-smith with a lot to do and after he'd foiled Paterson, it broke to John-son. Derby's skipper, desperate to make up for his error, barrelled back and clipped Johnson's heels. Penalty for Wednesday, and for Derby it got worse. Davies, in what would prove to be his final game for the club, was shown a straight red card and the hosts had a chance to take the lead.

It had been over a decade since the last time a Wednesday striker scored 20 goals in a season for the club. Neil Mellor managed it in 2010/11, but since then many have tried and failed to do so again. Smith had his opportunity now, but Derby weren't going to make it easy for him. Wildsmith had him re-spot the ball having complained to the referee, Haydon Roberts was yellow-carded for throwing a water bottle into the penalty area and another former Blade, Conor Houri-hane, had taken his sweet time when instructed to leave the box. Did it bother the Owls striker? Not even a bit. Calmly he sent Wildsmith the wrong way, slotting it to his right and sending the Kop into euphoria. Twenty goals. "About time," Mellor tweeted afterwards.

Palmer nearly made it two in first half injury time, but saw his strike saved onto the post by his old teammate, and moments later it was Dawson to the rescue again as he once more thwarted McGoldrick's audacious attempt. The second half brought more chances. Vaulks hit the crossbar with a fine effort early doors, Aden Flint cleared off the Wednesday line following a Derby break, and then Palmer came close a second time as he crashed a strike against the upright. Windass contin-ued his comeback as he entered the field on 65 minutes and very nearly set up Paterson as he caused problems for Derby's defence.

As Warne's side saw their play-off hopes slipping away they threw the kitchen sink at Wednesday. Iorfa's big block showed the commit-ment to victory, to exorcising some of those Derby demons from 2021. Dawson saved another, and another, and Warne looked to the heav-ens just before the final whistle went. From the stands came chants of: "You're staying down, we're going up." A penalty had relegated the Owls two years prior and this time, a penalty had condemned Derby to another year in the third-tier.

Hillsborough rocked once more and as the players and their families circled to the field for a lap of appreciation, the play-offs no longer looked so daunting. James had made it back into the matchday squad, Windass was looking sharper, Wednesday finally had a 20-goal striker, and they'd just kept their 25th clean sheet. Gregory, conspicuous in his absence, was out in Derbyshire somewhere having a mask fitted after a collision with one of the Owls' six-foot-plusers – later revealed to be Flint – had left him with a fractured cheekbone. The usual Zorro jokes made the rounds, but it was all good because he was going to be fine for the play-offs.

Results elsewhere meant that it would be Peterborough United in the semi-finals, over two legs. Plymouth had won the league and Ipswich had finished second, both deservedly so in the end, while the Owls would face a team who had finished 19 points – but only three places – below them. It was safe to say they were the favourites. What could possibly go wrong?

FOURTEEN

THE NIGHTMARE OF LONDON ROAD

Nightmare; noun
UK /ˈnaɪt.meər/ US /ˈnaɪt.mer/
- *A very upsetting or frightening dream / An extremely unpleasant event or experience or possible event or experience: "Being trapped underwater is my worst nightmare."*

Science tells us that nightmares are caused by an overly-active "sympathetic nervous system," a network of nerves tangled together that, when conscious, helps your body to react to moments of high stress of danger, a reflex commonly known as a person's "fight-or-flight" response. When sleeping, that tangle of nerves can dip into overdrive, prompting vivid, well-remembered and dysphoric dreams that in turn deliver symptoms of increased heart rate, excessive sweating, shortness of breath and, in extreme cases, loss of bowel control. This technicolour dream content is typically scary and vivid, with negative themes that usually involve efforts to avoid threats to survival, security, or invoke feelings of extreme humiliation. The activity of the sympathetic nervous system increases when you're stressed, in danger or physically active.

On May 12, 2023, as Jonson Clarke-Harris nodded into an open goal to extend Peterborough United's play-off lead to four, it was clear. Metaphorically, Sheffield Wednesday Football Club's sympathetic nervous system was bouncing off the walls. They were experiencing what one player later described as "a living fucking nightmare."

Wednesday had entered the play-offs in fine form, of course, buoyed by Shrewsbury roars, a breaking of Derby hearts and safe in the knowledge that, with a tally of 96 points, they were surely the best team of the four scheduled to battle it out in rabid, televised post-season chaos. The goldfish bowl of play-off campaigns can do ridiculous things to even the most experienced of squads, but the signs were good and the feeling one of optimism. Five wins in six had them higher than Barnsley, Bolton Wanderers and Peterborough United in the form table; they were a remarkable 252 days unbeaten at Hillsborough and in recent outings they had cautiously, momentarily recaptured a sense of swagger that had drained from their faces in March and early April. They had Josh Windass back alongside Michael Ihiekwe, Reece James and Jack Hunt. The tank had seemingly been pulled back in the right direction.

A finally fleshed-out squad posed questions of Darren Moore. Ihiekwe had provided the Owls defence with an air of authority before his injury, a dependability that perhaps had not been so evident in the latter stages of his absence as things went south. But where to fit him in? Aden Flint had matched up the physicality of Clarke-Harris – the division's top scorer – in Wednesday's 1-0 win over Peterborough back in March. It had been seen as a key factor in a characteristically hard-fought Hillsborough victory. With James not quite ready to step back into the cut and thrust, Ihiekwe started on the left of a back three.

There were talking points elsewhere, too. Callum Paterson was deployed behind a front two of Michael Smith and Windass, who would make his first start in a nose under two months as history repeated the events of the season before. Though a foot injury, not a season-exploding hamstring issue, Windass had failed to battle through the rustiness of a stint on the sidelines against Sunderland and hoped to recapture form quicker against a Posh outfit that would look to play from the back from the likes of Ronnie Edwards – an England under-20 international regarded as one of the best young prospects in the EFL – and through midfield man Jack Taylor, a prospect held in equal regard.

A whopping 19 points had separated the two sides in the final league table and while that blew confidence through the Wednesday sails, it mattered not in what was a double-header shootout. Peterborough were one of the teams Wednesday were seen as susceptible to; daring, dynamic and with pace and trickery in wide positions either side of Clarke-Harris through Kwame Poku and Ephron Mason-Clark. Exposing the Owls' preferred 3-5-2 system by finding space in the spaces around the wing-backs and running at a defence more comfortable with the ball in the air was a task that would suit them; arriving at London Road – otherwise known as the Weston Homes Stadium thanks to sponsorship opportunity – Wednesday hubris staring into the points gap was minimal from changing room to turnstile.

The mood in the stadium was one chest-out, almost intimidating. Peterborough's support is not one famed in the annals of football history quite like that of Sheffield Wednesday, their stadium smaller and their heritage shorter by comparison. But their fans arrived and arrived early, a drum playing to lift the sense of occasion earlier even than by the time the players had skipped out for warm-ups. The Posh had snuck in with a generous helping hand from their evening's opponents on the last day and a feeling of optimism swept across the ground pre-match. Wednesday, big, powerful Wednesday, looked just a little smaller than usual in their bright yellow shirts. Ominous? More intriguing, a fascinating contrast in profiles with the home side clearly there to impress their own efforts on the clash. But Wednesday were favourites.

It's perhaps the most irritating football cliché of them all; that the first goal of the tie would be key. And with play commenced, after a niggly opening few minutes in which neither side produced much in the way of quality, life played its little tricks once more on Smith. The Owls' top scorer, a vision of confidence bathing in the warm water of four goals in his last two outings, found himself the beneficiary of a nervous Oliver Norburn touch in the home midfield. One on one again, 12,965 eyes piercing into him, he was back at Portman Road once more. One touch, two, Edwards arriving from the right and goalkeeper Will Norris on the approach, it was a chance the fans at the other end of the ground expected him to take, killing the Ipswich demon with the fire of a play-off game-changer. His open-body effort to curl the ball into the far corner was too slow, too telegraphed, and Norris saved.

What would be quickly – and understandably – forgotten in the "Nightmare of London Road" aftermath was that the visitors were the better team for the first 20 minutes, passing the ball confidently and setting off on their mission to quieten a crowd well-versed in play-off glory. With Barry Bannan at the heart of proceedings, the Owls were bright if not blinding, quietly building another example of their collective know-how on a difficult away day. And then came a passage of play that left the tie spinning.

A missed tackle by Windass out wide, a failure to recover. A mis-judged lunge in attempting to clear by Will Vaulks. Paterson hadn't tracked back effectively, Bannan was wrong-footed, stationed too deep, and Taylor's magnetic touch gave him room that frankly shouldn't have been made available in an 18-yard box. His shot was well-struck, but should have been easily collected by Cameron Dawson. But it wasn't. Dawson had awkwardly got his body into the wrong position and with his hands unable to atone, the ball trickled inside the post to the shriek of a Wednesday supporter in pain. One-nil Peterborough, 20 minutes.

There's a feeling you get at football grounds at big games. No matter the personnel on the pitch, no matter form guides and 19-point defi-cits, it's a powerful thing and Peterborough sensed it. Taylor would a few months later be sold in a lucrative move to big-spending Ipswich Town and the 24-year-old struck as the sort of player who delighted under pressure, the *Sky Sports* cameras searing into the No.8 on the back of his shirt only a source of inspiration. "When we play like that, no team in the league can stop us," he later said while collecting the man-of-the-match award. On the night, he was peerless.

That's not to say Wednesday folded completely after that gut-punch opener but on 36 minutes, just as the yellows had regained some sort of foothold in midfield, Joe Ward pushed Norburn's turn-and-pass out of his feet to open up more space in front of the Owls defence. Rac-ing out to close the space, Moore's Mr. Dependable Marvin Johnson hesitated and jumped to block, turning his body in doing so. The ball spun devilishly off the wide man's squad number and hung in the air for what felt like an eternity before dipping beneath Dawson's bar. Bannan screamed in anguish at the goalkeeper, unable or unwilling to hide his desperation at the situation his team had found themselves in, deliver-ing the image of a grown man coursing with pain, powerless to stop himself from lashing out at whatever or whoever was in front of him. There was little more Dawson could have done beyond the scraped fingertips that had kissed the ball en route. Ward was awarded the goal but in truth, it had been going wide.

That in itself was a microcosm of the first half for Wednesday. They'd been okay – not devastating, not robust or water-tight or 10-foot-tall, but okay. They'd had chances, and not inconsiderable chances at that. With the final moments of the first half trickling down, Windass had seen a left-foot shot deflected wide and it was the visitors who could probably have claimed they had enjoyed the bigger, better first half opportunities. A scoreline of 2-0 felt harsh.

As nightmares go, this was a bizarre one. The sort of nightmare that starts off uncomfortable rather than terrifying; more a panicked anxiety. There's a breathless scene at the outset of Steven Spielberg's 1998 Second World War classic *Saving Private Ryan* that encapsulated Wednesday efforts on the night; bullets whistling past their heads as they navigated the Normandy of London Road, clamouring onto the beach in a breathless, lonely cacophony of chaos, limbs and quiet panic. The viewer knows that the odds are against them, but it's assumed they'd be okay. That they'd find a way to grab a goal back and take the tie back to South Yorkshire wounded, but alive and well. That was before Kwame Poku shot Sheffield Wednesday in the head on 50 minutes.

Poku finished off a counter attack that felt far quicker live than it actually was. The half-time message from Moore had been one of keeping things shored-up, the next goal vital. Wednesday were anything but. Careless in possession, the Owls players passed up several chances to clear. When Flint stretched out one of his Frankenlegs to prevent Taylor's through ball finding Clarke-Harris, it looked as if he felt a job was done. It wasn't. Mason-Clark set free wide left, five-foot-eight Poku was allowed to wander freely into the back post to head past Dawson, Flint tracking back with all the urgency of a rum cocktail. All that had been discussed about Posh's ability to break and break hard, that they were everything Wednesday didn't like to play against? Played out and laid bare in front of the watching football public. The Owls all of a sudden looked ancient, slow and second-best; drowning underwater.

What hurt that little bit more from a Wednesday point of view is that 100 miles up the road, the red and white half of the city were lost in celebration. Sheffield United had steamrolled any need for a play-off extension to their season, securing automatic promotion to the Premier League 16 days earlier and with three games to spare. It was the third time the Blades would jump into the top tier in Wednesday's 23 years of hurt. It stung.

Just the day before Wednesday's London Road clash they'd held a day of celebration, an open top bus tour through the city that ended with a civic reception at the Town Hall. Triumphant players were called out two-by-two to accept the adoration of the crowd below, offering an opportunity 23-year-old striker Rhian Brewster couldn't pass up. Before leaving the stage when his time was up, he grabbed the microphone from MC Paul Walker and brayed into the crowd in call-and-response stylee.

"What do you think of Wednesday?" "Shit!"
"What do you think are shit?" "Wednesday!"

It was a moment that set social media ablaze and angered a few within the Owls camp, a further example if it were needed that no matter the occasion, it is the passionate rivalry between the city's two clubs that so often burns at the forefront of minds. Or perhaps it was just a bit of over-excited braying. Either way, it was another reminder that it would be a long summer for those of a blue and white persuasion if they couldn't play their part in what hadn't been done since 1984 – the last time both Sheffield clubs enjoyed promotion in the same season.

Back at London Road, a penalty shout that would surely have seen Posh head boy Edwards sent off went against Wednesday and anything on the night that could go wrong looked as if it would indeed come to pass. But still they drove on, the masked Lee Gregory replacing Paterson on the hour before Smith was hauled off for Dennis Adeniran. Wrapped-up and pocketed on the night by Edwards, a prospect over a decade his younger and slighter in appearance, the ignominy of Smith's substitution, as Wednesday's top goalscorer at 3-0 down, was toe-curling. At the time of writing Edwards is the subject of multi-million pound interest from a raft of Premier League sides and Moore would later say that Smith had endured "one of those nights," privately praising the towering Posh youngster for one of the great play-off performances.

As the minutes ticked down, as Norris in the Peterborough goal claimed crosses, as Frankie Kent hooked Ihiekwe's shot off the line and as half-chances fizzled and disappeared, journalists in the press box went about searching for the greatest play-off comebacks of all-time. One remembered a 3-0 win for Bradford City at Blackpool in 1996, a Google search or two found that Northampton Town had leapfrogged Cheltenham by the same scorelines. Then there was Moore's Torquay, the plastic pitch and Paul Raynor. But no sign of a comeback from three goals. The play-off format had been introduced to the EFL in 1987 and there was no sign Wednesday's current task had ever been achieved before; 36 long years of no chance.

So what of four? If Poku had shot Wednesday's in the head at the back post on 50 minutes, Clarke-Harris took things to Tarantino levels of bodily harm with eight minutes to play. A smart Dawson save from Taylor rebounded from the post and with Wednesday's defence watching on with mouths open, his dinked cross left an opportunity to reach a tally of 27 goals for the season few could mess up. Clarke-Harris nodded into an empty goal, Wednesday were 4-0 down and their season had ended. Peterborough United, 19 points back and who only qualified on the very final day of the season proper, would go to Wembley. When the pressure was on, Wednesday had wilted. They'd had more shots, more shots on target, but had been lower on quality, desperate in defence and slow to mop up their sorry, sorry mess.

The final whistle acted as an alarm clock on the nightmare, Wednesday collectively waking up in a pool of their own sweat only to realise they hadn't been sleeping. The tentative nature of their slow trudge to the away end at Shrewsbury felt like a holiday wander through the park in comparison to what lay ahead of them at London Road and the crowd weren't at all in the mood to throw back the sunshine and roses of a couple of weeks prior. Hurting, tired of two decades of heartbreak, everything had come rushing back and the pain boiled over; the records, the points total, Newcastle. In a few cold summer months, the season would mean nothing to them. It would amount to failure. "You're not fit to wear the shirt," rained down the feedback and as the Wednesday playing unit trudged down the tunnel with an air of forlorn resignation, the Wednesday support fluctuated between foamy-mouthed anger and teary resignation.

The internal reaction of the players who had almost reluctantly applauded the furious travelling fans ranged from the humiliated to the ashamed to the angrily defiant. Barry Bannan would later reveal that the angry response had fired him up and that it delivered a sense of belief rather than despondency. A fire was lit. As a passionate football fan himself, he understood it on many levels. But after all the Owls had achieved, he thought, how can they say we're not fit to wear the shirt?

Waiting for Moore to emerge from the tunnel at a cold, empty London Road, while being quite strangely mocked by the local mascots in their fluffy suits and club scarves, patient visiting journalists chewed over the idea that it could be the Owls boss' last stand. Would Dejphon Chansiri swing the axe in order to bring the sort of knee-jerk reaction that could inspire the comeback of all comebacks? In the latter stages of the clash, it was said, Moore's body language had looked beaten, his shoulders pressed inwards and his eyes seemingly unable to flicker towards the away end as the Wednesday fans turned to irony and gallows humour to ease their suffering. A mid-play-off sacking? It seemed a ridiculous notion but, at the same time, not all that ridiculous at all.

Moore emerged with his customary paper cup of coffee. At each question he folded another piece inside on itself from the lip down, a physical manifestation of his careful consideration on each answer, perhaps an outlet for the pain he was feeling but couldn't express. Tearing away at the cup as he spoke, he blamed elementary mistakes, he reported a quiet post-match dressing room and he accepted questions over his players' body language and stomach for the fight when things were on the turn. He was polite, erudite and calm. So calm.

Asked if he had felt let down by the players, a pregnant pause said more than words could have. "All we can do is next week make sure we give a better account of ourselves," he eventually said; folding, folding and folding. "That was unacceptable, really. I told the boys they've got to regroup because we've got another game at S6 and our supporters, our club, want a better performance than that. It's an uphill task but we have to regroup and keep our focus and determination. If you go into next week and believe there is no hope, there is no hope."

"No hope indeed" was the theme of the post-match debrief as reporters made their way back into the stands to write up the season's obituaries. The *Yorkshire Post* went with "unsalvageable," the *Sheffield Star* rated Wednesday's hopes as "a thing of the past, fanciful," following it up with player ratings that were among the lowest ever awarded as emotion clouded the science of completing the most unpopular job in the industry. It had been that kind of evening.

On the streets outside, Wednesday fans dragged themselves to cars and coaches, to hotels and to train stations, some with tears in their eyes. Others bore only the feeling that this was what it meant to be

Wednesday. Outside one nearby car park, a small huddle of Wednesday fans fought between themselves, drunk on disappointment. Rushing over to end the fisticuffs, the Cambridgeshire Constabulary didn't even have the heart to lock them up, perhaps in hope of preventing further trouble. Or perhaps surmising that on a human level, the Nightmare of London Road had been punishment enough.

***

Inside the bowels of London Road's west stand, music blared. Clarke-Harris and Taylor completed their post-match media duties with the expected corner-smile platitudes; that "this wasn't over" and that "they had a job to do" at Hillsborough. But their eyes told a different story and one senior Posh figure was later heard whistling "Wemberley, Wemberley..." as he left the ground. Wednesday's players rolled up their towels and packed up their washbags in quiet disbelief, in anguish untold. They pulled hoods to their foreheads in search of sleep as the coach set its way north for home in pained, shell-shock silence.

As the coach wound its way up the A1, darkness was permeated only by the glow of a few iPhones and the hurt of miserable Instagram scrolls. One or two senior players said their piece, but otherwise silence. Those trawling social media may have stumbled across images of a poster a Sheffield Wednesday supporter had circulated in her local pub in the days leading into the first leg. Lisa Butterworth had asked an IT-savvy friend to design a message advertising a coach to Wembley should their beloved Owls make it. It hung proud on the walls of The Fox pub in Beighton for days, with no issue. The problem was, it didn't make clear the invitation was prospective. It read simply: "SWFC – Play-off final Wembley – Coach from The Fox – Call Lisa to book a seat."

The pub was due for a refurb and on the first morning, an eagle-eyed Sheffield United-supporting builder took a snap of the poster and mischievously plastered it all over social media, amused at what he thought to be another act of hubris from "them up the road." Within an hour or two it had made its way onto football banter pages all over the country and Lisa woke up to crank calls. A season ticket holder of 30 years, she was used to football fans. All good banter, she felt.

But as the goals flowed at London Road, as two goals flipped to three and as Wednesday's dreams of promotion crashed and burned, her phone blew up. As she later told the *Sheffield Star,* it was "hotter than the sun." She received calls from fans of Peterborough, United, Barnsley, Rotherham, Sunderland, Newcastle, Middlesbrough – even as far as Ipswich and Plymouth. By the end of the night she'd received 1,500 calls and as many texts, and it continued into the weekend. Correspondence ranged from good-natured to aggressive and in the end, Lisa had to cancel her phone number, at great cost and inconvenience. Compounded by the heartache of what she'd watched on the television, what had started as a fun-filled mistake had become a nightmare of her own.

Darren Moore's assertion that the tie "wasn't over" had drawn a sarcastic line or two from the reporters he was speaking to. An uphill task? "More like an Olympic climbing wall, coated in oil and set on fire," as one reporter quipped after the Owls boss had turned his back to make his way back down the tunnel. On social media his comments drew scorn and the "Moore Out" non-believers were back out in force, imploring Chansiri to pull the plug on what they saw as a second failed attempt at exiting the third tier by a manager who couldn't do the business when it really mattered. As he so often did, Moore described it as "noise"; noise to be ignored.

Wednesday had originally been due to have Saturday off, a recovery day designed to leave players to digest what had happened the night before. Such was the enormity of the defeat at London Road, those plans were called into question in the mind of Moore, who had planned to head back to see his family in the West Midlands after the game but instead found himself deep in thought, plotting next moves. Instead, he drove straight back to Sheffield. Long after midnight, not long before they pulled into Middlewood Road, players on the coach received a text telling them their day off was cancelled and that they were to report to Middlewood Road at 11am. It left one or two who live further afield with a desperate scramble to secure late-night hotels. No time to digest. No time to waste.

Without sleep, Moore re-watched every painful moment, every moment of encouragement. He made notes, hatched plans and caught brainwaves, pushing them around the mental corridors of his years of development as a player and coach. Wednesday had to win, and win well, against Peterborough just six days later but before then, Moore had his own players to win over first. Some had all but lost hope, it was later admitted. But while some in the camp quite understandably sulked, moped, keen to sleep off the remnants of an evening unhinged and close in on grief, Moore reverted to his favourite pastime; work. You'd have forgiven one or two close to him for wondering what on earth was the point.

By the time Wednesday arrived back in Sheffield it was well into the early hours. Home and through his front door, Moore continued, his determination unabated. By 3am he had an outline gameplan and by 4am a set-up for the week. A senior staff member remembers the darkness of his bedside table interrupted by a text at 5am. It was Darren. Incredibly specific instructions were handed over. Moore believed they could do this.

Moore finally got his head down between 6:30am and 7am; exhausted, excited, determined, the commentary of Don Goodman – the man he had stolen glances of training on his school astroturf over three decades earlier – perhaps bouncing around his skull over and over, as it had done for thousands of Wednesdayites robbed of sleep by a far more defeatist mood. The nightmare was over. It was time to dream again, time for their collective sympathetic nervous system to decide one last time; fight or flight?

"Two-nil was bad, three-nil was a mountain," Goodman had said on *Sky Sports* after Clarke-Harris' seemingly tie-sealing fourth goal, an inflection of hollow reality injected into every word. "I think four-nil is a mountain that will be insurmountable."

Insurmountable; adjective
UK / US / ˌɪn·sərˈmaʊn·tə·bəl/
- *(Esp. of a problem or a difficulty) so great that it cannot be dealt with successfully: "The task was not going to be achievable. It was insurmountable."*

FIFTEEN

INSURMOUNTABLE

Sleep hadn't been top of Darren Moore's list of priorities as he rocked up red-eyed to Middlewood Road the following morning. According to most, Sheffield Wednesday were dead and buried. Their play-off chances were in tatters, and they'd been condemned to another season in League One. Most. But not all.

Tens of thousands of others would agree, but for now Moore didn't have to change the minds of tens of thousands. He just had to persuade those in front of him at Wednesday's training ground that they were not done yet. On less than four hours of sleep he outlined the way forward. According to Moore it was an uphill task, rather than an impossible one, and between the final whistle at the Weston Homes Stadium and his drive to S6, he'd hatched a plan that he was convinced would work.

It was a plan that would involve almost everybody at the club, from the youth players all the way up to the chairman – and if there was anybody who could get that buy-in on a human level, then it was Moore. But before anything tactical could come into play, he had to get into his players' heads. It was no good him believing if they didn't, and convincing his troops that they were capable of a comeback never before achieved in the play-offs was going to take some doing. On the first day back in, Wednesday's players were practising penalties and watching hard evidence of themselves that they had four goals at home in them.

"I didn't get to bed until six-thirty or seven in the morning," Moore explained. "I was re-watching and de-briefing the game, and then we were in on Saturday by 11 o'clock. I showed them 65 goals that we'd scored here at Hillsborough straight away. We broke it down, and it was short of three goals per game. We'd scored five goals here on three occasions, and scored four once – we showed them all that. We had to break the mindset straight away."

Everyone would play their part, but alongside Moore at the centre of it all was his captain, Barry Bannan, and renowned sports psychologist Tom Bates. Every morning the entire group would watch a historic comeback – finals at Wembley, Tyson Fury getting up off the canvas, Liverpool in Istanbul. The greatest comebacks begin with belief. That was the mantra. The Owls skipper had seen good and bad times at Hillsborough and was determined for the season not to fizzle away, while Bates – who had been working with the team for almost two years – would put forward his methods, which included plastering up Teddy Roosevelt's famed *The Man in the Arena* speech all over the place.

Despite being in his mid-thirties, the psychologist had over a decade and a half of experience in the industry, his work in football not to be outshone by the fact that his work with Team GB at the postponed 2020 Olympics played a part in British Swimming's most successful medal haul in history. He first met Moore in the Midlands and they ended up working together at West Bromwich Albion, their shared faith helping to cement both a personal and professional relationship.

Time spent with Cambridge United, Charlton Athletic, the FA, AFC Bournemouth, Birmingham City, Brentford and Aston Villa set him up nicely as somebody that could aid Moore in his mission to fix a damaged mentality at Hillsborough, and the fact that he also possesses a UEFA A coaching licence just added to his credentials when engaging with players. A light-hearted bite back at Massimo Luongo after the Australian joked about his first meeting being "one of 332" set the tone. "As Mass has said," Bates quipped, addressing the group, "this is meeting one of 332. But it might be the most important of your day, so switch on."

Evidence of his success had become increasingly obvious as time had gone by. The Owls were conceding less, maintaining focus more, seeing out games rather than throwing them away, and – most impressively – had started to finally fight back from losing positions, a trait that had gone missing for a number of years. "You can't have performance excellence without excellence in preparation," Bates believes. "It just doesn't happen."

Bates was already a regular face around the training ground before the Peterborough defeat but for the six days that followed, he became a mainstay – coming in every day, showing the players videos of improbable comebacks in the past, thrusting upon them his belief, and Moore's, that they had what it took to upset the odds.

"It is not the critic who counts," read the Roosevelt speech put up in the changing room and around Middlewood Road. "Not the man who points out how the strong man stumbles, or where the doer of deeds could have done them better. The credit belongs to the man who is actually in the arena, whose face is marred by dust and sweat and blood; who strives valiantly; who errs, who comes short again and again, because there is no effort without error and shortcoming; but who does actually strive to do the deeds. Who knows great enthusiasms, the great devotions; who spends himself in a worthy cause; who at the best knows in the end the triumph of high achievement, and who at the worst, if he fails, at least fails while daring greatly, so that his place shall never be with those cold and timid souls who neither know victory nor defeat."

When asked why that particular speech was so important, Bates remembered walking into a "cold and timid place" when he first arrived. "A hesitant group of passively anxious players, and that's part of the reason why we conceded the goals we did, and couldn't fight back. We had to change that over time, a consistent reconditioning of the mindset. In essence it was a reminder of how far we'd come, but also a reminder of how we weren't going back to that fucking place. That was the old self. Now we're a new beast, a new being. That old self was gone."

As a gift, the sports psychologist put a framed version of the speech on Moore's desk so that he'd see it every morning when he sat down. A constant aide-mémoire of their purpose and what they were hoping to achieve. As captain it was vital that Bannan bought into it, too, though that wouldn't take much doing. His work with Bates had, alongside Moore's coaching, helped him churn out the best two goalscoring campaigns of his career. His buy-in was already there.

So that week Wednesday's talisman was hitting the WhatsApp group harder than usual, pushing out messages of encouragement, showing them 'signs' that it was possible. Manchester City stuck four past Champions League behemoth, Real Madrid. Stick it in the group. Barcelona went 3-0 up against Espanyol in the first half. Stick it in the group. City got three early goals against Everton... You get the picture.

They weren't comparing themselves to those great sides, but – in relativity – it was further proof that their task wasn't as insurmountable as had been suggested. "These are doing it, we can do it," was the skipper's message to his teammates. "If they can beat us by four at their place, why can't we do it at ours?" Even the fact that the chosen referee's last game at Hillsborough was a 5-0 rout of Cardiff City was mentioned.

The key was an early goal. That was another message that was driven home all week. So meticulous was the planning that the game was split up into phases, stages where Wednesday would need to get their goals by. Nothing was left to chance, even as far as the fact that they'd decided which way they wanted to kick first. They'd need the Kop's roar, so if they could they'd go towards them at kick-off. On top of that, any attempt to time-waste, which they knew was coming, would be countered. Ballboys and girls were instructed how best to combat it, handing players the ball directly – gone over in a training session beforehand. No stone was left unturned.

"We worked on the whole idea of this R.E.S.E.T," Bates explained, "which was an acronym that I developed. Instead of getting frustrated with players sapping the clock, they'd come together and focus their energy and attention on the next part of what's going to happen. A case of: 'Come on lads, lets stick to what we said we were going to do...'

"Reconnect, Engage with breath, Send and receive messages, find your Emotional state, and then it's Time to rise. That's where the circle breaks, and it's a shared mental model designed to avoid distraction."

In camp the feeling was that Posh's youthfulness, which so exposed the Owls in the first leg, could be used against them in the second. They didn't have the experience that Wednesday did and it was felt that they could crack under pressure if enough was applied. That could only happen if they started on the front foot and burst out of the blocks. On the training pitches coaching staff looked at ways to exploit Darren Ferguson's side but Moore would not be trying to reinvent the wheel. The work they'd done all season had been enough to get them to 96 points, 19 more than their semi-final opponents, so much of the hard work was done.

Meanwhile, over in Cambridgeshire, there had been suggestions of complacency. It's understood that at least a couple of players had expressed a feeling of the job being done, and they were already looking forward to their day out at Wembley.

***

In Wednesday's canteen, a whiteboard sits on the wall. It had remained unused for who knows how long, to the point where the cellophane hadn't even been removed. Bates noticed it, baffled, and brought it into use. "When you arise in the morning, think of what a privilege it is to be alive, to think, to enjoy, to love," he wrote, quoting Marcus Aurelius. And as the week went on others added to it, that dusty whiteboard going from being redundant to becoming a wall of positivity that would be in everyone's eyeline as they drank their morning coffees.

You know that bit earlier about the youth team? Their role was also important. Stood behind the net at the club's training ground they were tasked with trying to put off those players that they were so desperate to emulate. They were told to go for it, but did have a "healthy dose of respect" in their screams. The staff that joined them, however, may have been a bit more loose-lipped.

The penalty practice was important for two reasons. Firstly because it once more hammered home the point that Wednesday would do enough to need them. And secondly, when they did, they'd be as confident as possible taking them. So with speakers blaring crowd noises after being brought onto the grass, and a rabble of teenagers given express permission to shout obscenities their way, Wednesday's players were told to walk up and pick their spot. It wasn't the same as doing it in front of a roaring crowd, of course. But there was still pressure. After all, what seasoned professional wants to admit that a bunch of youngsters stopped him from finding the back of the net from 12 yards out? The amount of research that went into it was also huge, with studies taking place to decipher who would take the penalties, and in which order.

"We did a lot of research regarding when the whistle is blown and contact with the ball in penalties – I took it from World Cups, etc," said Bates, outlining his theory. "If players respond less than two seconds between the whistle and contact with the ball, they are 65 per cent more likely to miss because the process is being rushed. So we worked hard on controlling the moment, control yourself, and control the clock. We selected the final five based on the stats from the week, for instance those who had mastered their time period. But, critically, it would also come down to who felt the most confident in that moment."

Now, with the players on board, Moore needed the supporters to do the same. And that could have proven to be even more difficult. In the minutes, hours and days that followed the first leg there had been a meltdown. Tickets for what had long-since been a sell-out were returned, many had said they weren't going to bother, and one fan even went viral after filming himself ripping up his ticket and posting it on social media while a girl in the background sighed. "Josh, you're so excessive," she said.

Wednesday's players had been kept away from the media for weeks as Moore looked to take all responsibility on his considerable shoulders, but post-Peterborough it became almost a blackout. No apologetic words on Twitter or pleas for forgiveness underneath photographs on Instagram. What many took as shying away would actually turn out to be as much an instruction as anything else. As players their focus had to be on the task at hand. *It is not the critic who counts.*

"What I've wanted to do, really, is to try and keep the players focused on the games," Moore explained. "I think that's what it's about, it's about channelling all their energy and making sure they remain focused."

On the day of the second leg a short post from David Stockdale, unlikely to feature, appeared on his page. "If we don't have belief, we don't have anything," it said. "Give everything. It could personally be my last chance and I still believe... Need our fans to raise the roof one last time this season at home."

On the club's official Twitter account, just 11 tweets were sent out between full-time at Peterborough and the day of Moore's pre-match press conference. Six of them were about a charity game for young Rio Spurr, the son of former Owl Tommy, as money was raised for his cancer treatment; two were regarding the club's community programme; another advertised a job vacancy for groundstaff, and was predictably swamped with comments about the manager, the players and chairman.

The other two, sadly, were down to something a lot more sinister. First, on the Monday, came a statement from the club expressing their disgust at a "repulsive" racist message directed at Moore following the game against Peterborough. Two days later they were forced to do so again, this time after an "appalling" post about Chansiri.

It was abhorrent, and roundly condemned by the fanbase, the vast majority of supporters putting the defeat to one side in order to rally behind the men in charge. The message from fans was clear – criticism was fair, but racism had no place whatsoever. In a strange way it almost served to galvanise things. There was now another reason to turn things around.

Hours after the Owls' Moore statement, another fan shot into the limelight. This time it was for the right reasons, and he wasn't even a Wednesdayite. Tom, a long-time caller on *BBC Radio Sheffield*, had just seen his Chesterfield heroes lose at Wembley in the National League play-off final and, engulfed with emotion, called into Rob Staton on the *Football Heaven* show.

"You go on Thursday or Friday, whenever your game is, and you get behind that badge," he implored Owls fans. "The badge you fell in love with, the badge that you would do anything for. You get behind them and you never know. You never know, because you've still got a possible 120 minutes to get to win that game or whatever it is. So never give in. Never give up. Never give in on your club. Never turn your back. Never ever say: 'No, I've had enough'. Because it's your club and you should be proud."

The words of Tom – who, it turned out, is actually a bloke called John Connaughton whose name was put down wrongly one day and never changed – went viral and for many fans, it was just what they needed to hear. All of sudden they weren't going out of blind faith, or for fear of missing out. They were going to cheer on the team that they love, come what may. Before Moore had even had a chance to do his press conference, part of the job had been done for him. By a Chesterfield fan.

When he did take to the stage he urged fans to get behind them, spoke of their importance, thanked them for their support all season, and expressed hope that they'd be able to spur them on once again. It's something he'd done all season. What he did next, though, was different. As the conference finished he looked towards the club's media team, Joe Braithwait and Mark Ruane, asked if he was done, and then revealed that he had something he wanted to say. They set up the camera and got to work.

***

Plenty will lie and tell you otherwise but waking up on May 18, the general view amongst the fanbase was that Wednesday would beat Peterborough, but not by enough. They'd battle, give a better account of themselves, but ultimately fall short. It was an entirely fair thought process. In total just under 32,000 turned up for the game, a good chunk of them Posh fans coming along in anticipation of celebrating a first trip to Wembley for the best part of a decade. But walking to the ground, something felt different.

"Av ad these seats years" and "Neva miss a game" reads one mural, painted by Owls fan Luke Horton, on the wall of Hillsborough overlooking Penistone Road. And there was a lot of that, supporters going because that's what they do. They turn up. As they filed in from Catch Bar Lane and Herries Road, with a Béres sandwich or Four Lanes chippy in hand, there was a sort of magic in the air. Despite it all, the vitriol, the abuse, the pessimism, tens of thousands of fans – old and young – were still turning up, with Tom the Chesterfield fan's words bouncing around inside their heads. They only needed a spark.

Inside, in the bowels of Hillsborough, Stevie Wonder's *Superstition* played in the changing room and Wednesday's players filed in from outside the Megastore because their usual car park was taken up by *Sky Sports* vans. Moore, as he strolled in front of the Kop, acknowledged the groundstaff with a nod and "Magnificent work, gents," commending their efforts on a Hillsborough pitch that was in a substantially better state than a year previous.

All in black, donning an iconic pair of blackout Nike Air Max 90s, he maintained a steely focus as he fulfilled his media duties. Many managers try to instil the idea of not getting too high with the highs or low with the lows, but few practice what they preach the way that he did.

The stadium was filling up and as hype music blared from speakers into the Sheffield night air, fans spoke amongst themselves with theories of when they'd need to score, how they'd need to be up 2-0 at halftime and so on. Then, as a video began to play on the big screen situated between the Leppings Lane end and the south stand, dramatic music played out and heads began to turn. Fans watched on, still talking, as goals against Plymouth Argyle, Portsmouth, Derby County played, one after the other. Then the video stopped.

Silence, for a second, before Moore's booming voice reverberated around the stadium. "To all you supporters, thanks for coming out tonight," he said. "We really appreciate it. Stay behind us." Calm but commanding. By now all eyes were on that screen. Hillsborough stood still. "If ever we needed you, it's tonight," Moore finished. "Come on, let's go."

It started as a rumbling, a realisation almost, but those words had shifted things. Then came the roar as over 30,000 Wednesdayites decided that, for the next 90 minutes, they had faith. *Never give up, never give in.* Darren Moore hadn't needed to get those tens of thousands on side at the start of the week. But at that moment, on that evening, he had them. That had been what he wanted to say and it was like a switch had been flicked. Hillsborough was alive. What Wednesday needed to do, overturn a four-goal first-leg deficit, had never been achieved before. But with that short speech, Moore had returned what so many had lost. Hope.

Pitchside he clapped along with *Hi Ho Silver Lining*, as he always did, but the decibels were louder than usual. His arms were aloft for the chorus, but there was no hint of a smile. In the centre of all the noise he stood composed, focused. Wednesday won the toss, swapped ends so they'd kick towards Penistone Road as planned. In their pre-match huddle Bannan spoke of how it could be the last game for some of them, how their fine season shouldn't end with a whimper. "Give everything you've got," he told his teammates, "and die on the pitch for this club."

Referee David Webb blew his whistle, and it was immediately clear that the Posh were going to be, understandably, cautious. But Wednesday chased down everything. From the first minute you could tell that, if they were to go out, then they'd be going out swinging. Liam Palmer was booked within the first six minutes, Lee Gregory and Michael Smith pressed high, and Callum Paterson was like a battering ram.

Palmer hadn't played in midfield for years but that night was right in the thick of it. The decision raised eyebrows, both inside and outside the camp, but the club's player of the season was no stranger to versatility. He'd gone home to research, watching videos of deep-lying midfielders and familiarising himself with the role that was about to be thrust upon him. Defensive positioning and plugging runs, thankfully, was second nature as a defender.

Seven minutes. Bannan slips a ball to Marvin Johnson, as he's done time and time before, and Johnson's first touch takes it past the onrushing Joe Ward. But the defender can't get out of his way, the Owls wide man flies into the air, fans rise out of their seats. Webb points to the spot. The Hillsborough crowd roars like Wednesday have already scored. It's the start Wednesday needed, and the one that the visitors desperately didn't want. Paterson picks up the ball, but it's clear he won't be taking this one. Smith has taken seven penalties since arriving at S6, scored all of them, and makes it eight from eight by casually sliding past Will Norris. S6 erupts.

That early goal they needed? They'd got it. Even Moore celebrated and as Smith gestured to the crowd, Josh Windass raced to grab the ball. No messing about; it was only one. Peterborough had plenty of possession, but the hosts wouldn't let them rest. They were putting Posh under constant pressure and when they did win the ball back, a surge of energy swept through the ground. Wednesday needed to keep the backdoor closed, though, and Cameron Dawson was on hand to do so – saving Kwame Poku's effort with his feet to keep his side on the front foot. 'Barmy Army' chants echoed about the place and Dominic Iorfa did a fine job of keeping Ephron Mason-Clark quiet. Every tackle, every block, was cheered.

24 minutes. Johnson whips in a dangerous ball into the box, Norris flaps at it, it falls to Paterson. He shoots, or crosses, nobody really knows, but all that matters is that his effort ends up at the feet of Wednesday's masked man, Gregory. He's only just got up after being flattened by the 'keeper, but is aware enough to stick out his left foot. There's no pace on it, but behind the goal thousands on the Kop suck it towards them and over the line. Norris tries to grab the ball but Gregory shoves him into the back of the net, grappling with him in order to get it back before pumping his fists as he makes his way back to the halfway line. Two goals within 25 minutes. You know what...?

Hillsborough was in overdrive by now and even Moore, usually so calm and collected, bounced around the dugout. Everything he'd planned was coming together. But the job was far from done yet. Blue smoke rose into the air after a flare was thrown onto the pitch and caused a stoppage, one that Wednesday couldn't afford. So over by the north stand, led by Windass, a number of Owls players urged for no more. Every minute was going to count. Every break in play would give Peterborough time to regroup, and Wednesday needed to stay at their throats.

Posh were flustered and while Wednesdayites lost their voices, the visitors in black lost all momentum. A Mason-Clark effort was saved by Dawson, but the pendulum had very much swung Wednesday's way. Peterborough were trying to slow it down, cling on, but by the break Wednesday had enjoyed almost double the number of shots, won more than twice the tackles and had more than triple the amount of corners. The towering Michael Ihiekwe had won a whopping eight aerial duels. The Owls were in charge, and the crowd could feel it. There was another roar as the half-time whistle went, and off the players ran. They had more information to take on board.

In a break from the norm, *Hi Ho* belted out once more as the hosts disappeared down the tunnel. These small changes to the usual order could make all the difference, and it kept the buzz going. Half-time had seen fans' blind optimism turn to genuine optimism and as the sun went down on an unremarkable day in Sheffield, there was something truly special unfolding under the Hillsborough lights.

Whatever the Owls boss had said at half-time had worked. Buoyed by their first half goals, Wednesday came flying out in the second 45 and the crowd was everything Moore had hoped they'd be. The 12th man in every sense of the word. Dawson didn't make a single save in the second half. Peterborough didn't even have a shot. On field the battles weren't just footballing, they were mental. The youth that had served the Posh so well in the last game was left rattled as senior Wednesday figures got in their ears, over and over and over again, with sledging akin to an Aussie fast bowler. "You're not going to bottle this are you, lads?"

Moore kept at his side, stoppages were utilised. Any little chance to get in their ear again, to give them more information. Their time wouldn't be wasted, even if the visitors wanted it to be. "When their players went down, we got the players in so they weren't out there waiting on the pitch. We were talking to them, about the mindset and the game plan. That kept them on track."

Gregory saw a brilliant overhead kick superbly saved, Paterson's goalward strike was blocked, and Windass' fine volley was kept out as well. Wednesday needed a third, and sharpish. Missed chances on another night would have been seen as cause for concern but with every puff out of cheeks, every hands-on-head moment, every cry of: "You're kidding me?" from the crowd, it felt like they were getting closer.

71 minutes. Palmer, bossing his midfield role, picks up the ball about a third of the way into Peterborough's half and drives at their defence. He slips in Gregory who dummies it, masterfully letting the ball run through his legs after spotting Reece James slip in behind him. James takes one touch, steadies himself, and sees Norris closing the space. James has one option, and one option only. Ahead of him he sees the gap between the goalkeeper's legs, and with a flick of his left boot he finds it. Limbs, the kids call it.

Mayhem on the bench, mayhem in the stands. Jaden Brown leaped onto Simon Ireland's back, James – enjoying a fantastic evening in his return to the XI – sprinted back into position. One more. Out come the phone lights as Wednesday's old girl shook under the weight of so many bouncing supporters. You could physically feel the energy, the home fans together as one; a single organism, desperate to see the most impossible of jobs become possible.

Moore was bouncing with them, arms flailing, punching the night sky. They had split the game into phases and three of them were complete. Peterborough were in for a long 20 minutes as the loudest chant of 'We're All Wednesday Aren't We?' for years rang around Hillsborough. Whether they got that fourth goal or not, Wednesday's players had followed Bannan's advice. They were dying out there for this club.

In the top half of the Leppings Lane end the mood had changed. Drastically. Peterborough's supporters had come for a party, safe in the knowledge that even a defeat couldn't possibly have been enough to knock them out. They were Wembley-bound, as some of their fans had told their Owls counterparts on social media. But James' goal changed everything, and now they had a front row seat to a show they never wanted to see.

Time was running out for Wednesday, though, and desperate measures were required as the clock ticked down towards 90 minutes. Will Vaulks, owner of one of the longest throws in the league, was brought on with two minutes to go and man mountain Aden Flint was also chucked into the mix as stoppage time got underway. That felt like a combination that could work. Six minutes had been added on but with all of the stoppages due to injury, with the substitutions, it always felt like there could be more than that. Peterborough were playing for time, and they'd almost done it. Their fans were singing about Wembley as Ronnie Edwards booted the ball into the stratosphere, hoping to hear the whistle. Windass took a throw-in in line with the edge of the centre circle, and it landed at the feet of Palmer. No, said the ref. It went out closer to the Peterborough box. Up there, Vaulks was readying his towel.

90+8. A last throw of the dice. The Owls midfielder wipes down the ball in front of the north stand before launching it. It bobbles about before being half-cleared by Clarke-Harris, but only as far as Bannan. He fights off any thoughts of a wild strike to slide it instead to Johnson. He clips it into the box, with the sort of quality Wednesday had been been crying out for. Flint, rising like a salmon on steroids, gets his head to it and knocks it down towards a man who has seen it all at Wednesday – the good, the bad, the ugly. He can't miss, but it all happens simultaneously – both in slow motion and at 100mph. The next thing anyone sees is Liam Palmer sprinting towards the corner flag.

They had done it. They had actually gone and done it. The Owls' No.2 slid feet-first into the flag, before being piled on by his teammates. It had to be him. In the stands, some fans dropped to their knees. Others burst into tears, strangers embracing strangers. This wasn't just one of Wednesday's greatest comebacks. It was one of football's.

Up high above the dugouts, some idiot in the press box sporting a stupid Homer Simpson Christmas jumper turned to his converted colleague, a man in equal disbelief, and they hugged for far longer than is appropriate for professional journalists. First team analyst Liam Bracken reached out a hand in celebration, which was promptly grabbed. And Jimmy Shan, a man who'd become such a valuable member of the team, smiled and waved. Down below Moore clapped his hands, shouting: "Come on." He'd backed his side to get to extra time, and they'd done it. But now wasn't the time for celebration. They had another 30 minutes to go – and there were some tired legs out there.

The whistle went almost immediately after the equaliser. But instead of revelling in categorically the greatest play-off comeback of all time, the Wednesday boss was bellowing to his players to get over to him. By this time it was 10pm, the floodlights beamed down onto the Hillsborough pitch for what would be the last time in 2022/23, and in the centre of a huddle, with his players and staff locked arm in arm, Moore said his piece. The scoreboard read: FULL TIME (NOT QUITE).

As they split the stands erupted once again, Bannan and Palmer pleaded for even more – though they'd given everything – and Dennis Adeniran took his captain's head in his hands, offering words of support for a 30-minute spell that could still prove to be the last that they spent as teammates. *Hi Ho* played again, somehow louder still.

A thought for those of little faith, those who returned tickets or simply didn't attend, those who would now be sat elsewhere dealing with the fact that they'd missed their club's greatest ever comeback. A night that would be spoken about for years to come – they'd never be able to say: 'I was there'. One fan now remembers with a smile missing Palmer's goal, after deciding the dream was over and leaving his seat. He and his dejected family had reached the bottom of the steps inside the north stand before an almighty roar sent them rushing back up to celebrate the greatest goal they'd never seen live. Some weren't even that lucky. Not far away, somewhere outside the ground, another supporter sat in his car on the verge of tears, annoyed that he'd walked out. He'd got to his car door and heard the explosion of noise. Only his wife knows he left.

Back inside, the rumble continued. Fingernails had long since been gnawed off, shirts were up over heads, and some fans sat with their heads down still blown away by what they've just seen. These things don't happen to Sheffield Wednesday. Even those that said they believed couldn't really believe it. And Webb blew his whistle once again.

By now Wednesday should have been running on empty, but still they pressed. Gregory, Smith and Windass chased down everything, Paterson desperately trying to find that cross that would make the difference. Johnson was done, though, and on came Jaden Brown as another pair of fresh legs. Things had got bitty, Posh had nothing to hold on for anymore, and Wednesday were standing firm. Chances were at a minimum, but then Smith gave away a foul in a decent position.

By that point Ferguson's men hadn't had a shot on target for almost an hour but as Dan Butler whipped the ball into the box, there was an intake of breath. The back of Dawson's net rippled, the Peterborough fans burst from their seats, and the Owls were behind on aggregate once again. Gregory, so often the hero at the other end, was left thinking: 'Why me?' as the ball hit his back and flew past Dawson. Things fell flat, momentarily. But as the Wednesday stopper quickly picked up the ball and tried to get things rolling quickly, the home support rallied again. They had seen their side pull four back, so what was one more?

Before the game there'd been so much talk of 'The Wednesday Way'. What would be the most Wednesday way for the evening to go? Going 4-0 up and then conceding was on that list. But now, seeing it happen live, people had too much faith to give up. If nothing else the players deserved a chance to try so, as the half-time whistle went, fans rose to their feet. A standing ovation for the battlers in blue and white.

The second half started much the same, Flint could possibly count himself lucky not to have been penalised for bringing down Mason-Clark in a rare Posh attack, but then things returned to normal. Jack Hunt came on as Gregory made way – devastated that his final involvement may be the one that knocked his side out despite a terrific performance. Frustrated, he threw his custom-made mask under the seats in the dugout, maybe thinking he wouldn't need it again.

The visitors knew what they needed to do, knew how they'd have to hold on, so took their time with everything, went down at every possible opportunity, and tried to eat away at what little time they had left. It was 5-4, and their fans chanted: "You're not singing anymore" at the home support. The Owls supporters practically hadn't stopped singing for about two hours, and they weren't done yet.

112 minutes. Palmer, in the thick of things again, slots a wonderful ball through to Brown. His cross is good but Paterson's shot is blocked. Fortunately it bounces back to his feet. The Scot controls it with his right, pokes it with his left, and it rolls under Edwards' legs. Norris can only turn his head as he watches it pass him. And as Wednesday's versatile Swiss army knife wheels away to the north stand, tears begin to flow once more. These are the nights that create new Wednesday fans; the ones that reaffirm why others keep coming back.

If you want the rainbow, you have to put up with the rain. Paterson slid on his knees towards the corner flag and momentum was Wednesday's once again. But there was no bouncing from Moore this time.

Instead, as his bench went wild around him, he simply stretched out his arms and took it all in.

One final push. There were cramps everywhere, even up in the stands after what had been a long, tense evening, but still Wednesday rallied. Ihiekwe went close before making a superb block at the other end. Paterson, who must've covered every blade of grass, threw himself in the way of a Peterborough effort and cramped up immediately after. After 20 seconds on the ground he was up again, barging into another tackle before going down once more. The commitment of that 30 second spell summed up his night.

Penalties, then. Moore had predicted they'd need them, it's why they'd practised them so many times, and Bates – who had been celebrating up in the Grandstand earlier in the game – was immediately in his ear as the final whistle went. "If you prepare, then it'll all come together," was what he'd told the players. And they'd certainly done that. Not everyone had believed that the penalties at Middlewood Road would help, some had taken some convincing, but now they'd find out. Wednesday had won just one penalty shootout in the last decade – losing four – and by this time they had the eyes of the world on them.

As the realisation of what defeat would mean dawned on supporters, many haunted by 2017's shootout defeat to Huddersfield, Wednesday were huddled together once more on the pitch. "'Get in here!" Moore screamed, not wanting to waste his final opportunity to gee up his players. George Byers, so cruelly missing in action, let out a battle cry as they shored up who'd be stepping up to the spot and when. Bannan and Hunt both stuck up their hands. They'd done this before.

The penalty takers had been semi-decided beforehand, aside from a crisis of confidence in the moment, but there was no chance of that. The first five takers lined up in exactly the planned order, and it was up to the skipper to confirm it. "That's a leadership moment for him," Bates explained. "Who knows the players the best? It's the captain. So it's up to him to take charge."

For Dawson, a penalty-saver of note, there were some words in the ear from Shan, a chat with the vastly experienced David Stockdale, encouragement from coach Adriano Basso, and a heartfelt clasp of hands with Palmer as two players who bleed blue and white came together under the Hillsborough lights. It was almost 11pm.

Again the Owls won the toss, their skipper gleefully pointing to the Kop and raising his arms to urge supporters on. They responded. Smith went first, of course, placing it on the spot as he weighed up whether to go the same way as he did a couple of hours ago. He did, and scored. Clarke-Harris did the same, but only just, as Dawson came so close to keeping it out. Will Vaulks slammed home, and then came the twist – as Dan Butler's strike crashed against the bar and into the open arms of those celebrating on the Kop. Advantage Owls.

The skipper shared a moment with old friend Hunt, each telling the other how proud they are, before Bannan stepped up and scored. As did Oliver Norburn – again, only just. Windass was next. Lads hugged dads, others couldn't bear to watch, but the forward dispatched confidently, sending Norris the wrong way. Kabongo Tshimanga would score the fourth, making it 4-3 to Wednesday. Fans immediately looked to those standing on the halfway line, fascinated to see who'd be taking the fifth – and hopefully decisive – kick. They got their answer quickly, as club favourite Jack Hunt broke ranks and began his stroll down the penalty area. If he was feeling the pressure, then he hid it well.

Hunt was there for a reason. Throughout the week he'd been one of the most consistent from the spot, effortlessly putting them away from 12 yards out, sticking panenkas past the goalkeepers. He'd also got priors when it came to shootouts – so the coaching staff knew he had the mentality for it. His comments afterwards were testament to that.

"When a man has got nothing to lose it's almost dangerous at times," he said. "That's how I felt going up to take the penalty. In my career I've taken four or five in shootouts that have meant something. I've always been the sort of person who would rather fail myself than watch someone else fail. Luckily for me, the times I have taken a penalty I've had that chance. If Cam had saved their fourth penalty we would have been off and I would never have even stepped up for that penalty. I'm glad it happened the way it did."

So there he stands, just behind the spot, looking directly at Norris. Nonchalantly he tosses a piece of chewing gum around his mouth, glances at the ball, then at Norris again. One big step back, and then five smaller ones. The whistle goes and time seems to stand still, every face in S6 fixated on one man. The slightest of slips causes a sharp intake of breath, but then it happens. The net ripples. Hillsborough descends into madness. Fans barrel their way onto the pitch. In the midst of it all, Hunt turns to his teammates as they hurtle towards him and a casual smile spreads across his face, just in time for the cameras to catch it before he's mobbed. Wednesday have done it – the greatest ever play-off comeback has been completed. Within seconds, thousands have swarmed the field. The Owls were off to Wembley.

In the dugout Moore didn't even smile. His face was one of relief and as he gave Bates the most almighty of hugs his shoulders visibly sank, as if the weight of the world had just left his body. A hand reached out to Ireland, grasping it tight, and amidst the chaos of Hillsborough he had a moment of calm that his work so very richly deserved. "Every second was worth it," they said to each other. The average time between whistle and kick for the Owls' takers was five seconds.

The identity of the unused sixth penalty taker, he who would have taken on responsibility untold had things gone differently, seems to be a source of confusion. Some suggest it was Dominic Iorfa, though Callum Paterson would later make his claim rather confidently in a press conference the following season. It would have been his first-ever spot kick in professional football. Another player went as far as to recall it was Tyreeq Bakinson. Bakinson wasn't even on the pitch. Gladly, there was clarity of mind when they needed it.

Journalists rewrote their match report for what felt like the 50th time, players were lifted aloft, Flint ended up with a Wednesday bucket hat on his head and for a spell, the pitch was completely covered with supporters. Such pitch invasions are frowned upon by the league, of course, so any pictures or video seen to be glorifying the scenes officially would be condemned, but in the age of smartphones that didn't matter – they're all on the Cloud now anyway.

There were tears, oh so many tears; Jon McClure, the lead singer of the band Reverend and the Makers, grabbed a few blades of grass and stuck them in his pocket. One fan who'd opted not to run on pointed to a message on the scoreboard. "Please refrain from entering the pitch," it read. "Fat chance," he laughed. Among those drifting out of Hillsborough, one Beighton woman slid her old SIM card into her phone.

"Sorry, Lisa," read the first text. This night would be remembered for years, decades, to come. *If you prepare, then it'll all come together.*

Bannan's emotions spilled out as he made it out of the other end of the tunnel. "I told yous, I fucking told yous!" he shouted. "What a man," he exclaimed as he wrapped his arms around Dawson. The heartbreak of London Road and ecstasy of what he'd just been involved in bubbled over, but he had to compose himself to speak to *Sky Sports.* Behind him his teammates chanted his name, Johnson hopping on one leg after being forced off the field earlier in the evening.

After a warm embrace in the manager's room, gaffer and skipper made their way next door into the changing room together. The bottles of Madri were already flowing and before too long the singing began. A word of sympathy for the cleaners, here, because by the time they were done, that small space under the south stand will have been covered floor to ceiling in lager. The champagne was on hold, but the bevvies certainly weren't.

First team sports scientist Chris Brealey, a man who'd had his work cut out all season alongside conditioning coach Adam Yates and popular masseur Ben Parker, opened bottles with his teeth and passed them around while Oasis' *Don't Look Back In Anger* belted out – a fitting track, given Moore's previous talk about the club needing to start looking to the future rather than into the past. With promotion now just one win away, they still might find a better place to play.

The best was yet to come. "Listen in lads, give me two minutes," came Moore's voice over the rabble. He followed that up with a slightly more assertive: "A bit of quiet. Listen." Then came a speech that would change so much. "I'm absolutely just so proud of every single one of you," he said, giving a rare look at Moore the man-manager, rather than his usual head-of-the-family approach in interviews. "We had a bit of adversity in the first game and we knew we didn't perform. It just goes on to show you what preparation does. We've prepared all week the mindset, mentality and in training.

"The belief has been there from day dot and I can't commend you all enough in terms of what you've produced out there. It's absolutely incredible and you deserve it. I'm absolutely delighted, what we've had to come through this season. But listen, boys: we've got one more. We've got one more. Enjoy tonight, but we've got one more. I'm so proud."

And enjoy it they would. But first, their captain had something to say. It was short, but Bannan's words flew in the face of old cliché that Moore had lost the changing room. The video, which lasted less than 90 seconds, has been viewed over a million times – and couldn't have offered stronger proof that they were all very much with their manager. "This last week, what you've done to change our mindsets, with the staff, has been unbelievable," Bannan said in Moore's direction. "Because there were some people doubting it... What you've shown us and the work you've put in has been second to none and we wanted to thank you and the staff."

With that the formalities were done. Mere seconds later Moore had a bucket hat on his head, had been doused in beer, and Vaulks was in his pants as Wednesday's history-makers posed for a famous team photo.

Once the crowds dispersed, many of them made their way out onto the pitch again, savouring the moment as the remaining members of the media discussed how they'd never seen anything like it – and probably never would again. Palmer, who'd just made his 396th appearance for the club, sat alone on the centre circle on a video call with his family, who sadly couldn't make it due to a family holiday likely booked at a point when the play-offs weren't really on the table.

A topless Adeniran emerged. He didn't play a minute but you wouldn't have guessed it by his beaming smile from ear to ear. Windass took a selfie now immortalised as a Wednesday meme. "Piece of piss," the caption read.

Moore, in typical fashion, deflected all attention away from himself as he discussed the win. "I've never seen anything like it," he enthused. "I've been out in the community... Everybody I saw, every Wednesday-ite was phenomenal. This morning I went for a walk on my own and a gentleman in a car shouted at the top of his voice: 'We can do this, Wednesday.' Every step of the way we've had that encouragement. It's been one big joint effort and there was huge belief."

Midway through his press conference a former Owl interrupted him. Clinton Morrison, who enjoyed some good times at S6 himself and was on *Sky* duty, gave Moore a bear hug and told him: "You're an inspiration to us, man," just audible enough for those in close proximity to hear. The Owls boss broke away to continue his media duties with an almost embarrassed smile on his face. "Oh, Clinton," he said.

Bannan, now feeling the after-effects of 120 minutes on those legs of his, leant against the wall by the tunnel as he spoke. Praising the fans, those who'd battled with him on the pitch, and especially the technical team, he broke down how they'd prepared, how they'd pulled off the impossible. Over one journalist's shoulder, a teammate popped up. "Baz, Baz, tell them what Peterborough just did?" he said with a grin. His captain looked bemused, so was given the answer with a chuckle: "Shit their pants." That bit didn't make it onto *Radio Sheffield.*

"The game wasn't about tactics, we didn't play great football – we knew that it wasn't a game for that," said Bannan. "We just needed to find a way to win. It was just about who wanted it more, and we did... We'll enjoy tonight, but then it's onto Wembley." And enjoy it they did.

After the Madris at Hillsborough they made their way into town, ending up – eventually – at Firepit Rocks on West Street, a haunt known for good music and a late closing time. Partiers must've got the shock of their lives seeing half of the Owls team walk in, still in their Wednesday gear, as they desperately tried to get served. Vaulks was up on the table, Hunt spoke to those next to him of his penalty heroics, and Ihiekwe enjoyed a well-deserved drink after his mammoth performance a few miles away earlier in the night. Bannan, having just added another moment to his club legacy, sang along to chants about their red and white neighbours, and Dawson revelled in what is likely a rarish night out in his own city.

It went on for hours, players and fans clinging onto one of their finest moments in years for as long as they possibly could. Daylight started to creep in through the Firepit windows to signal the approach of closing time and out on the West Street pavement, those in Owls training gear said their goodbyes. Those two old friends Bannan and Hunt, with the battle scars from Wembley 2016, embraced once more, knowing their story together wasn't done yet. The hangovers would arrive later on, and would be absolutely worth it, but would need to be shaken off sharpish. Wednesday had a final to prepare for.

Insurmountable? Apparently not.

SIXTEEN

QUE SERA

I t's quiet. Peaceful. Still. As the sun breaks its way through the short darkness of summer and begins to glisten on the glass exterior of Wembley Stadium, a bird takes its morning sojourn to the Wembley arch to survey the scene on Wembley Way. It looks down on delivery men clunking, clanking and rolling their wares into bars and cafes, early-rising bank holiday joggers rolling their way around the stadium in half-asleep effort to get their exercise in before temperatures soar. The remaining evidence of the previous day's League Two play-off final is swept away as the world prepares for something bigger. Security staff clock out and colleagues clock in. Otherwise, nothing. A picture of perfect calm and creeping sunrise.

Much had happened since Jack Hunt's penalty, pitch invasions and rowdy sunrise beers at Firepit Rocks. Half the Sheffield Wednesday squad had continued their celebrations, as had been organised in the days earlier, by going for drinks in Manchester, snaking their way through the city on a bar crawl before those that were able to watched Barnsley sneak their way past Bolton before the last train back home. A small number had cancelled, some looking ahead to a Wembley final and others a little too dusty given the travails of the evening before, which had been far more spontaneous. The idea had been that depending on whether the second leg had ended in glory or sadness, a trip to Manchester would provide something for the squad; either a celebration or a chance for those likely to leave to say goodbye before all and sundry headed off on holiday. Thankfully, it was the former.

An 11-day break between second leg and final meant time to plot, time to recover and time for the world's eyes to fixate just for a day or two on Sheffield Wednesday Football Club after many, many years a long way out of focus. Social media was ablaze and as hangovers drew deep, Pep Guardiola broke from a press conference to lead the tributes to a remarkable comeback, launching into a surreal love letter to the depth of the English football pyramid and only slightly letting himself down by referring to the home team as "Sheffield." He was roundly let off. "This is England!" the Manchester City boss, on his way to winning the treble, exclaimed. "That's why it's unique! That's why it's so special."

Paul Hirst, *The Times'* Manchester football correspondent and a passionate Wednesday supporter, proudly answered Guardiola's query as to how many people were in the ground. "You are from Sheffield?" the legendary Spaniard asked in reply, gesturing with a thumbs-up and smiling warmly. "Well, congratulations." Hirst's heart burst with pride.

It had been seven years since the Owls' last Wembley appearance and only their second since the new stadium, arch and all, was completed in 2007. The club itself holds some of the old stadium's most iconic moments; Waddle and Sheridan's early-90s pearlers against Uniteds Sheffield and Manchester; a 1966 FA Cup final defeat in which they fell the wrong side of a 3-2 comeback win for Everton before Don Megson took them on a lap of honour to thank supporters for their commitment; the agony of two domestic cup final defeats to Arsenal in 1993. It's a special patch of land that has thrown the full breadth of life's highs and lows at Wednesday supporters, those who had made the walk down Wembley Way both in tears of joy and despair. Whatever the fixture, though, the feeling is that Wednesday fans do Wembley weekends right.

With the sunshine of play-off weekend beckoning, an initial allocation of 36,634 seats was boosted by a further 1,355 shortly before the club put them on sale. Wednesday fans aghast that Barnsley had actually been awarded a larger share of the attendance needn't have been concerned. In the days leading into the clash, another 6,000 were taken from the Tykes and gifted to Wednesdayites on request of the club, taking the total number of Wednesday tickets to 44,000.

That final allocation switch was not without controversy. Angry at the EFL's decision to hand what would have been empty seats to the Owls, an eleventh-hour motion to dispute put the Hillsborough ticket office on pause and sprinkled a couple of hours of chaos on proceedings as word leaked out of the news. A strongly-worded statement released that evening made clear that Barnsley had opposed the decision, insisting they had had to be reassured of spectator safety. It all served to contribute to the tension of a clash that had hardly needed it. Wednesday staff later maintained they could have sold another 10,000 tickets had they been made available.

Moore's steadfast commitment to a "business as usual" outlook was impressive. Players had been encouraged to revel in the enormity of the semi-final comeback – as the next day beers in Manchester would testify – but arriving back at training, it was back to the job in hand. Nothing had been won yet and for all the emotion, for all the white-knuckle madness of a night nobody would forget, a defeat would render the heroics of Hillsborough wasted.

"We understand the focus a weekend like this will get," Moore said. "We've tried to embrace it, enjoy it. It's been nice to have eyes on us in such a positive way. But for us, it really has been about focusing on the pitch and in our work on the training ground. We've worked hard to maintain that focus, we know it will be a tough game and we've prepared appropriately. We have an army of fans with us, we have the players and the staff and we have a oneness about us now. These times are to be embraced. These are special times. I've told the players that they don't stand there alone, I'm not a lone figure as a manager. We have an army with us, all in it together. My message is clear; to embrace the moment and to do it together as Sheffield Wednesday."

In a football sense, the week itself was fairly routine. Training at Middlewood Road, Wednesday off as normal and a day off on Friday in which Moore fulfilled his final media obligations and spent some time in his office putting the finishing touches to his plans. His players reported to the training ground on the Saturday morning, where they boarded their coach and made the hour-and-a-wee-bit trip south to Ashby-de-la-Zouch and the plush Champneys Springs complex for a couple of days of training. The venue was never publicly disclosed at the time, Wednesday preferring to check into their own private bubble without fear of distraction.

It was an approach at odds with that of their opponents. Barnsley, a side younger in years and experience, travelled early and trained at Brentford's Premier League-quality facilities. They sought to sample the Wembley atmosphere – most for the very first time – by going to watch the Championship play-off final on the Saturday. Watching from Champneys Springs on the television, one or two Wednesday figures wondered whether two hours sitting in plastic seats in soaring temperatures might not have been the best idea. Given the number of Owls players who had already tasted the pressure of Wembley itself, the focus was solely and squarely placed on studious preparation for the match, rather than the occasion.

Moore himself had been successful at Wembley before, winning a Championship play-off final against his former club West Brom in 2007. But speaking ahead of the match, it was another experience that he felt compelled to draw on. In 2016, when Wednesday so narrowly missed out on a return to the Premier League thanks to Mo Diame's wonderstrike for Hull, he had been invited to the match by the EFL.

"I took my eyes off the game and looked into the Wednesday end," he said with a look of genuine emotion. "They were bouncing. It felt as if the stadium was shaking, it really did. It was such a joy to see. I remember pausing for a good while to just stare into the Wednesday supporters. It really was one of the best sights I have ever seen in the game. I saw that up in the stands, now I want to see it from the technical area.

"There have been times this season that the supporters have dragged us through. They're the ones, they're the key, they're the special piece of the machine that gets this place going. It's such passionate support, you speak to people and you can feel it. It's something to behold and it's a real driver. It seeps through them having been passed on from generation to generation. To hear the support we're going to have down there, it's a driving force. You hear stories of the lengths people are going to, to be there, and it can't help but drive you on."

A social media plea had thankfully returned Lee Gregory's face mask, which had gone missing in the chaos of celebrations after Peterborough and sparked concern given that a replacement would not be fitted in time for Wembley, and he had been able to train as normal. Elsewhere, key man Marvin Johnson had shaken off injury in the second leg to re-join training midway through the week and looked in good order, while Reece James seemed to come through his comeback appearance having been subbed off late on. Dominic Iorfa had hobbled off late on at Hillsborough – gladly only with cramp – and was fine.

One thing worked on heavily that week was based on analysis of the Barnsley defence. When opposing teams took the ball to the by-line, it was noticed the Tykes centre-halves had a habit of retreating crab-like towards their own goal-line, leaving space between the penalty spot and the edge of the area for players to run into. Work was done on encouraging players lucky enough to wriggle into space in wide areas to cut their crosses back into that area. It was drilled over and over.

Away from football, plans had been hatched among the fanbase. Golden tickets secured, haggled over and begged for, flights were booked from Australia, New Zealand, Japan and the USA at short notice and great cost. Holidays booked months in advance were cut short with the eye-rolls of spouses and apologies were made to brides and grooms hurriedly forced to bump up evening guests after sheepish apologies and the realisation that, yes, football, to some, is more important. Dennis Adeniran and Liam Palmer had combined to fulfil the pledge of a supporter who had tweeted that he would get a Palmer tattoo should the Owls turn around their 4-0 Peterborough deficit. The Wednesday vice-captain not only paid for the session, but sat through the whole thing.

Daydreams of a sun-kissed skip up Wembley Way were unthinkable as fans angrily shuffled their way back through the turnstiles of London Road but Wednesday travelled down in their thousands, and the capital prepared itself. From former players to a packed-out bus adorned with flags marked "Lisa's Coaches," the fanbase scathingly known to others as "the Massive" were on their way.

They were on their way early, too. Scaling the 193 steps up from Covent Garden tube station at any time from 2pm the day before the Bank Holiday Monday fixture, the noise grew and grew as tourists rose to ground level, scratching heads in confusion at what the gathered blue-and-white masses were there for and what on earth a Honolulu Wednesday was. Blue flares filled the air as the atmosphere built and as every car, coach and train arrived from the north, dropping a few more bodies into London's newest borough; Hillsborough South.

If concerns had grown over potential trouble in London that weekend, Sunday evening cooled them. The atmosphere in Covent Garden, spilling into Leicester Square, was overwhelmingly jovial and good-natured. Police kept their distance, watching on with no small sense of fun. A vast bottleneck of supporters formed outside the Nags Head, directly outside the Tube station, and between the Lamb and Flag and The Round House, but there was no feeling that things were in danger of bubbling over. It was joyful, as if for those gathered seven years of misery had been building to this point. "What team are you?" asked those confused tourists slapped with a very different reality of the quiet shopping district they had expected from Covent Garden, "and what did you win?"

Tuk-tuk taxis belted their way through the streets to deliver passengers and found themselves guided through the masses only on the cheeky proviso they would blare Jeff Beck's *Hi Ho Silver Lining* from on-board ghetto blasters. After pubs had been asked to shut at 10pm so as to guard against the threat of overly unruly behaviour, queues at supermarkets swelled with sweaty, quick-thinking football fans with crates of lager beneath their arms. When those supermarkets closed too, groups of young lads jumped onto Boris Bikes in search of the next borough, returning as Heineken heroes. A great sense of humour was evident throughout; Barnsley were fewer in number but joined in and a local leaning from his first-floor window to look down on the masses was greeted with chants of: "You're only here to see the Wednesday" before he was applauded back inside. Two passing Arsenal supporters were sent on their way with a chorus of: "Top of the league and you fucked it up," every word soaked in self-deprecating irony. And lager. Everyone was soaked in lots of lager.

It was at this point that the team news rumours started. "Vaulks in for Gregory" was a popular shout, question marks over whether Callum Paterson would start even after his classy performance in the Miracle. Journalists, some out enjoying the sights and sounds of a London painted blue-and-white, began to receive their own quiet whispers; that, incredibly, Darren Moore was to name a side totally unchanged, one sent out to spark untold chaos at Hillsborough 11 days earlier. Barnsley had run over Wednesday's midfield for large periods of their two league wins earlier that season – would Palmer really line up as one of the players tasked with calming that threat? Would Will Vaulks, a man brought into the club in part to deliver such results, again watch on from the sidelines? Josh Windass in behind two strikers in a three-man attack? It was bold, brave and – once a bolt of shock had worn off – exciting. Miracle rewarded, Wednesday were throwing caution to the wind. Wednesday were going for it.

Eight miles south west of the Covent carnage, Wednesday players were tucked up at the four-star Novotel Hotel on Wembley Way, itself just a five minute wander to the stadium itself. They had an entire floor of the hotel booked out. Smart but by the standards of some of the well-paid group somewhat unremarkable, the hotel represents one of a raft of differences to how the club's plans were put together for their 2016 defeat to Hull, such is the superstition of Owls chairman Dejphon Chansiri in particular. It was all-change. Carlos Carvalhal's men had stayed at the nearby Hilton and just about every bit of planning that went into the day was altered, such was the deflating blow-out of seven years previous.

The players spent the night before the match relaxing, the odd venture to Costa or Starbucks encouraged among selfies taken with Wednesdayites lucky enough to have stumbled across a booking at the same hotel. Momentary chinwags with members of the *BBC Radio Sheffield* team, who also happened to have booked on at the Novotel, were laid-back and revealed a squad at ease with themselves. There was a general feel of relaxation that belied the enormity of the day ahead; another peek into the mindset the backroom staff had built up over two years of toil.

The two previous play-off matches that weekend had ended in penalties, tough, rugged affairs that fell the way one-off finals so often do. Luton Town had edged past Coventry City in Saturday's second-tier final to earn their place in the money-spinning Premier League after a 1-1 draw after 120 minutes. On Sunday, Carlisle United snuck past Stockport County to jump into League One. Same scoreline, same penalty outcome. The reality began to draw that Wednesday's fixture list could look very different depending on the result of the final. Leicester City and Leeds United had joined Southampton in suffering relegation from the top-flight, taking their place in the Championship. The teams coming up from League Two into League One? Leyton Orient, Stevenage, Northampton Town and Carlisle. There was no comparison.

It's always sunny on play-off weekend. Hot, too. The splendour of remarkable moments, it seems, invokes remarkably splendid weather. Coming into view on the steps down from Wembley Park station, supporter hangovers subside at the sight of the stadium's iconic 436-foot arch and are flung by the roadside on the wander up Wembley Way. It's a moment of Instagram-filtered surrealism for any football supporter;

fans bump into old school pals, family friends and drinking buddies long since moved away from Sheffield as dads tell sons of the time they came to watch John Sheridan dink the Owls on their way to League Cup glory. "We'll be back someday, you know."

It's a daydream, an idyllic wander through sunshine shared with dancing butterflies and dolphins dipping in and out of the pavement. Owls heroes of old pose for selfies; Waddle, Bullen, Palmer, Llera. Wayne Jacobs stops for an ice cream wearing his Owls coaching regalia and chats to fans not as a member of Wednesday staff, but as a life-long Wednesdayite. As one of them. Recently-departed Atdhe Nuhiu, a cult hero of nearly a decade with Wednesday and who played in the final in 2016, reported for Wembley duty again, this time as a member of the media core alongside Rob O'Neill – the iFollow commentator who had delivered the brilliant "Who needs Tom Cruise? We've got Liam Palmer!" line after his goal in Wednesday's own *Mission Impossible* against Peterborough.

Another taking the trip to the stadium was one Dean Windass, the former Wednesday loanee and former teammate of Jacobs and Darren Moore at Bradford City but, most imperatively, father of Josh and a man who remembered the venue like he would an old home. On May 24, 2008 it was Dean who thumped home a volley from outside the area to take his Hull City side to the Premier League for the first time. He was 39 when the ball came so sweetly off his boot and it reigns supreme as one of the most iconic moments in Wembley's vast history. An award-winning after-dinner speaker well known as one of the great football characters, Dean had missed the Peterborough comeback to fulfil an engagement in Blackpool and having had updates funnelled through from his partner, could only scream at his car radio as he navigated the M62. A *Sheffield Star* feature published in the days leading up to the match drew attention to the idea that in scoring at Wembley, Josh could follow in the footsteps of his old man.

"I've not spoken to Josh this week," Dean told the newspaper. "I've just texted him. He's doing his thing and getting himself ready and I don't want to distract him. The text said: 'I love you. Don't walk off that pitch with any regrets and go get me the winning goal.' That's all I put."

No doubt, Barnsley were an excellent football side. Dynamic and energetic, they were a side completely reborn under a manager linked with Burnley in the weeks ahead of his Oakwell unveiling and who many were tipping for the very top of the game. Michael Duff had masterminded a Barnsley double over Wednesday, beating up the Owls midfield in a 2-0 win at Hillsborough before ending that long, long unbeaten run with four goals at Oakwell. The fear was that, perhaps, the Tykes had Wednesday's number.

Like his colleague in the opposing dugout, Duff had arrived to find a club broken and had made grand strides both on and off the field in banishing the hangover of not only relegation from the Championship, but from a failed Championship play-off campaign the season previous. In giant Dane Mads Andersen they had a fair shout at boasting League One's most impressive central defender, with Liam Kitching and Bobby Thomas impressing either side of him. In Luton Town-owned goalkeeper Harry Isted they had a hugely in-form goalkeeper. Nicky Cadden had jumped into the left wing-back role with ease following a move from Forest Green Rovers and in Devante Cole – son of Manchester United legend Andy – they had a 16-goal striker who had led the line with danger after a so-so career of oh-so-nearly.

But it was in midfield that the basis of Barnsley's fourth-place finish was built. If Wednesday had been unlucky to not earn automatic promotion with 96 points, the Tykes, too, could have felt hard done-by, their tally of 86 good enough to finish in the top two on many occasions. In Luca Connell they had a tidy and technically gifted young midfielder brought in off the scrapheap at Celtic; in Herbie Kane they had an attacking threat plucked from the obscurity of a loan switch to Oxford United the season before and in Adam Phillips they had a player discarded by Burnley who had spent the previous year with Morecambe. It was a talented, energetic, youthful odds-and-sods of a midfield that worked. And it worked because Duff had made it work.

The Barnsley boss may well have been surprised to be preparing to take on Wednesday. Making the short trip to Hillsborough for the second leg of the Miracle, it was later suggested he had left the game early, ahead of Palmer's roof-lifting equaliser, believing Posh had done enough and running through the early mental gymnastics of how to beat them – and not Sheffield Wednesday – perhaps until his car radio told him otherwise. Interpreted as a sign of disrespect, it was something that rankled one or two in the Owls camp, as had mid-season comments about the age of the Wednesday squad. Cole had taken the opportunity to take half a swipe at Cameron Dawson when interviewed on *Sky Sports* after their 4-2 win at Oakwell. There was just a touch of needle there.

As the celebrations of a semi-final job well done over Bolton took place over his shoulder on the Oakwell pitch, a hoarse Duff was seemingly keen to build on a well trotted-out image of underdog status Barnsley have embraced and harnessed over the years. "Wednesday will be very, very good," he said. "They've been up there all season and I think Darren has smashed every record going. So we know the challenge ahead, but the few losses they have had, we've been two of them.

"We know we can beat them. There'll be no arrogance, we know we'll be up against it. They'll be the favourites, no doubt, but my lads have been written off from the start. When I came in in the summer everyone said we were useless, we'd sold all the players, we lost a few games, we went a month without scoring and everyone wrote them off pretty quickly."

With the pre-match press conference player blackout rolling on at S6 – aside from Barry Bannan interviews with *Sky Sports* and *SkyBet* that the Wednesday camp were at one stage keen to pass-up on, before realising they were contractually obliged to acknowledge under risk of a hefty fine – it had fallen to Moore alone to deliver a dead-bat summation of the "favourites" narrative the Tykes were looking to push. His experience, he said, rendered the storyline a waste of valuable energy.

"They're going to see it like that," Moore said when asked about Duff's comments. "Look, I'm too grey now to suggest any of that. What we've got is two good teams competing in a final, two local teams that know plenty about one another. All we'll do is prepare for the game. Do I predict a favourite? No. There never is in a final, really. I can blow that one out of the water, it's up to us to approach the game with detail, precision and respect.

"Both teams have shown a degree of consistency to get to this point. Youthful or older teams, experienced or not, players that have been to Wembley before and those who haven't. You can't put all that onto the game. It's all about the game on the day, you can't predict the outcome. It's about going into the game with precision. That's where our focus is at."

So studious, so prepared. The memories of the Miracle banished from conversation, publicly at least. Wednesday's approach had been business-like, focused and clinical. They had arrived in London the day before the final as Stockport and Carlisle played their way out of the League Two season. There would have been individual anxieties, but the overall feeling was that they were ready and Sheffield Wednesday's players closed their eyes, visualising their roles in their minds, repeating their instructions over and over, playing out the match in their heads. Some slept better than others.

On Monday morning, that little bird settled on the Wembley arch and as the world woke up to what would be a special day no matter the outcome, Sheffield Wednesday players and staff stretched and yawned their way to breakfast, to team meetings at the Novotel and towards one of the biggest days of their careers. Looking out onto Wembley Way as the morning grew old, they saw a sea of blue and white only occasionally dotted with red. In front of them, Wembley Way belonged to Sheffield Wednesday. To their left, the stadium. The 3pm kick-off lay in wait.

After all they had been through – from Sunderland to the long wait of summer, from record-breaking runs and the gut-punch of missing out on automatic promotion, from London Road to the stuff of miracles – this, surely, was to be their day. The Wednesday Way had changed.

Hadn't it?

SEVENTEEN

A BETTER PLACE TO PLAY

To wander through the stands of any football stadium ahead of an important match is to get the true feel of a football club. You get the taste of the tension, the agony of nerves, the look in the eye of people for whom nothing on that day is more important. And as the first few bars of *Hi Ho Silver Lining* bounced from the PA system at Wembley Stadium on May 29, 2023, you felt what it was to be Wednesday. After a generation of toil, there was a humming excitement; pride that this lot would do them proud. The second leg against Peterborough had elevated the entire club to a whole new level of self-esteem.

Even those present that are most sceptical of such things may admit that there was something vaguely spiritual about the feel of it. Not in a gooey, sci-fi and ouija board, hold hands, close your eyes and hug a tree kind of way, but in the sense of communion, of half a city sharing the same experience through very different eyes. No two people in the Sheffield Wednesday end that afternoon had lived the same life and no two people had grown to love Sheffield Wednesday in the same way. Some thought of loved ones lost, some of the intensity of personal battles still ongoing, some of times in their life when it was the daft football club sprawled out around them that had held them together.

Break it down to its bare artefacts and the experience of being a football supporter is a ridiculous notion. For 10 months of the year thousands of people slavishly throw time, life and money into the well, praying for something memorable from some boys kicking a ball on some grass. Grown men sing songs of players half their age and youngsters wait hours for the chance to have them scribble on a shirt procured by parents who frankly could be spending their money on other things. Plymouth on a Tuesday evening? They're there. A rainy draw at Cheltenham? An early kick-off spent watching Forest Green Rovers outscrap your heroes? Sold-out allocations by grown-ups who really should know better.

Except it's not a case of knowing better. Football is the great culture of the world, an intoxication, the pursuit of happiness and the feeling of being part of something bigger than our own little lives. As Josh Windass stood over the ball at the centre of the world, waiting for referee Tim Robinson to blow his whistle and start the League One play-off final, the sense was that this was an afternoon not only about the men on the field, but those off it. This was a day for Sheffield Wednesday not just as a football team but as a living, breathing entity of tens of thousands. And on the other end of the famous stadium, slighter in numbers but not in passion, it was exactly the same for those gathered from Barnsley.

Piercing down with relentless intensity, the sun provided the spotlight for each one of those supporters as Wembley played host to those unmistakable strains of Jeff Beck and Co. Whistled and jeered by those in the red corner, veins swelled and sweat dripped from foreheads as the Owls faithful took it upon themselves to showcase the very best of the club to the *Sky* cameras and to the world outside. It had been a sight to behold.

Earlier that morning the club had confirmed the news that its former physio, Alan Smith, had passed away at the age of 74. A figure with hero status usually reserved for star strikers and iconic managers, he had played a monumental role in the guiding of some of Wednesday's greatest-ever sides, through the tenures of Wilkinson, Atkinson and Francis while balancing trips to World Cups and European Championships with England. Des Walker offered words of condolence to his family, watching from home in South Yorkshire, via a pre-match punditry turn on *Sky*. Such was Smith's status among those gathered at Wembley, social media was awash with tributes and later in the 74th minute a ripple of applause broke out in homage.

As Windass rolled the ball back to Cameron Dawson to get the 2023 League One play-off final underway, to guttural roars of anguish from both ends of the ground, all eyes centred on the pitch. But breathing in the tension that afternoon was to realise that this was a day as much about every single individual staring out onto it as it was Moore and his players. It is they that take the headlines as the stars of the show, and so they should. But behind every pair of eyes straining in the piercing Wembley sunshine was their own tale, their own reason for taking Sheffield Wednesday into their hearts. From Plymouth Argyle to Carlisle United the same is true, but every fanbase is slightly different in their quirks, cultures and customs. It is in these tales that makes Wednesdayism unique and therefore provides the oxygen that the football club lives on far more than any Barry Bannan free-kick or Michael Smith header.

Making shuffling apologies on the way to his seat just a few minutes before kick-off was Ashley, a civil servant from Dronfield, who less than four hours earlier had been sitting at Chesterfield Royal Hospital. A lifelong Wednesdayite of 35 years, a trip to Wembley was one he couldn't have fathomed missing, though life had conspired to throw a spoke in the wheels in that another major life event, one much more important, had fallen on that day. At 10.30am his wife was due for a 12-week scan. They were pregnant with their first child.

To the knowing eye-rolls of his wife and her family, plans were hatched. Ashley and his wife didn't want to let people know of their pregnancy until the scan returned safe results and mates waiting for him in London, curious as to why he hadn't made the trip south with them, were told simply: "I don't want to talk about it." A keen runner, the logistics raced in his mind. If the traffic behaved, if he packed his running shoes and dressed appropriately, if the scan ran on time and if the parking slot he had booked was secured without issue, he could make it to Wembley on time. Scan complete, at 11.30am he got the nod, kissed his wife like he never had before and ran to the door of his Volkswagen Passat. He drove with urgency, he parked up and he ran two miles to the stadium. He'd take his seat, in time to watch a cagey set of opening exchanges, with an ultrasound polaroid pressed deep in his pocket.

Wednesday had sought to go direct, much in the way they had in the second leg win at Hillsborough, arrowing balls forward to Michael Smith and Lee Gregory. While Barnsley would look to 'play' a little more, it became clear just a minute or so in that a keen mode of attack would be centred on diagonal balls aimed at exposing the height difference between their Manchester City loanee striker Slobodan Tedić and

Reece James, making only his second start in six weeks. Such was the thought process, Tedić had started ahead of James Norwood, so often a terroriser of Wednesday, alongside Devante Cole.

Tackles were zealous and mistimed, passes strewn and simple defensive tasks scrambled as teammates failed in communication, battling against the noise. Neither Wednesday nor Barnsley had lost after scoring first that season and shared the top two spots in a table of early scorers in League One. It was uncomfortable and nervous. Understandably so, given the magnitude of the task in hand.

That said, Wednesday had a real chance fall to them in the seventh minute. Good work from Smith – already three fouls in – allowed Windass to swing in a cross. It was too deep to find Gregory and Jordan Williams, under little pressure, headed unwisely into the direction of a lurking Barry Bannan. The Scot set himself, waited and saw the ball fizz from his laces as handsomely as he would have liked. Bobby Thomas propelled his head in the way in desperation. From the resulting corner, a scramble led to Dominic Iorfa bounding into the box to force a save from Isted – with no threat of hyperbole – that was as good as anything the stadium had ever seen. Wednesday had started to find their rhythm.

Praying they could make use of it was Shane, 35, a bank manager from Dronfield, who stepped his way up and off the tarmac at East Midlands Airport and boarded plane LS633 hot with stress and with phone in hand. It's the sort of stress any parent with three kids – aged 12, six and three months – will know all too well, on his way to a family holiday in Tenerife lugging bags and toys and snacks and hoping everybody just calms the hell down for five short minutes. But having booked the holiday when Wednesday were sitting pretty at the top of League One just a couple of months earlier, Shane was also bearing a different kind of stress. Flight LS633 was due to take off at 3pm on May 29, 2023.

Trudging onto the plane in his Wednesday shirt, he watched nervously until the 15th minute, risking the wrath of his wife as all hell broke loose around them. To compound matters, Shane found himself sat next to a family of Barnsley fans battling through a similar predicament. As the pilot made his announcements and those boarded were instructed to switch their phones to airplane mode, he motioned to a steward in anguish. "When there is a result, is there any way the pilot could make an announcement as to the score?" The plane set into motion. He might as well have been sat on the moon.

A stoppage to heal the damaged shoulder of the whole-hearted Paterson all but killed that early wave of Wednesday momentum. Bedraggled, hair formed into a misinformed mullet coloured salt and pepper, the burly Caledonian gave off the image of a man up for the scrap. In Nicky Cadden he was battling Barnsley's most ravaging threat on the day and coped admirably, contributing to the attack when invited. His wasn't the only break in play and such was the searing heat, drinks breaks had been scheduled to aid the safety of those toiling. It served to prevent any real flow to the game, apparent 20 minutes or so in. The physicality on show didn't help on that front, Robinson given no option but to blow up time and again as battle lines were drawn all over the field.

Iorfa, still reeling from his golden chance a little earlier, so mightily impressive when the season had come to shove, had been given licence to bomb forward by Moore, so too James on the left of the picture. Marvin Johnson saw plenty of the ball in a touch-tight first half hour, but was given little room to manoeuvre by a committed pair in Thomas and Williams. Though different in style, the approach provided a snap glimpse back to those early sessions in Portugal all those months ago, inviting overloads in wide areas designed to open up crossing opportunities. But the Tykes gave little quarter.

Gone was the approach Wednesday had started with in both league games against their South Yorkshire adversaries. Caught out playing from the back, this was an Owls side that would sneer and snarl their way through the match, turning Barnsley around with a brutal and relentless approach of direct football. It wasn't pretty, and to that point it hadn't been devastatingly effective, but there was a feeling that their opponents were being made to feel uncomfortable, stifled and unable to build any momentum of their own.

If the selection of Liam Palmer in Wednesday's midfield had taken some by surprise, he had set about proving why the decision had been made. As the match turned past the half-hour mark it became clear it wasn't going to be a day for rich technical mastery, something he would admit – in midfield at least – was not a string he could pull on. It would be a battle built on bitter concentration and a coursing will to win. Of those he had plenty.

A born Wednesdayite signed to the club from the tender age of seven, he had been a youngster when the club won promotion from the division in 2012, a fringe player not even named on the bench when the Owls had last graced the home of football in the Championship play-off final four years later. But there he was, at the very heart of the action, battling the Barnsley midfield with every sinew of his being. He had been instructed to cut off the runs of the dangerous Herbie Kane, who he rendered anonymous. Thunderous tackles ploughed into Luca Connell and Adam Phillips. In possession, he'd keep it simple. He was there to do a job and quietly, without the glare of the sort of spotlight afforded to his great mate Bannan, for example. And he was doing it expertly.

Palmer had scrambled his way through the second half of a gruelling campaign of which he was a star, playing through injury with a double hernia in a groin as tight as the final itself. He played knowing that in a matter of days he would be jetting off to Germany for surgery to solve the issue. He so desperately wanted to undergo the procedure as a Championship player. He may well have had moments of thought of his parents and his young family, whom he had spoken to on video messenger in the moments after his proudest moments as the hero of the Miracle. In the stands, family moments were being made, some tinged with unimaginable hardship.

As the first half rolled on Dom, 42, an advanced practitioner from Leicestershire, looked down at the two children beside him in the Wembley stands with tears in his eyes. With joy, with pride and with sadness. Above all, the feeling was one of awe. His children, brainwashed into a life of Wednesdayism by their dad from an early age despite growing up some 70 miles away, looked out onto Wembley with smiles on their faces, overwhelmed by the sights and sounds of their club at its very best, for an afternoon completely devoid of the struggle of their day-to-day lives. Dom's daughter, 11, and his son, nine, both have a rare form of medullary thyroid cancer. It is treatable, but as things stand, it is incurable. School, horse riding, football training; they go about every day with a sense of spirit unimaginable.

Circumstances meant tickets hadn't been easy to come by and for a long time, the family began to make plans to watch the final at home, hoping to make the afternoon as special as they possibly could. But the brutal, painful fact of the matter is that May 29, 2023 might well prove to have been the childrens' last opportunity to sample the experience of Wednesday at Wembley. This was before Dom's dad decided to chance his arm, stepped in to contact the club and explained the family's situation. Wednesday couldn't do enough. As the match continued in front of them, nothing else in the world mattered. This was their club, their players, out there playing for a prize that would belong to everyone. For the day, they weren't a family defiantly locked in battle against the cruellest, coldest, most isolating of circumstances; they were a family of 44,000, bathed in the joy and sunshine of Sheffield Wednesday at its very best.

By the time the whistle blew for the turnaround, Wembley had been beaten into a strange sense of tiredness, both on the pitch and off it. A brutal and demanding 45 minutes had been broken up and twisted by constant stoppages and beyond Wednesday's two chances in the first 10 minutes, looking past a couple of half-half-chances for Barnsley through Phillips and Cadden, a battle on the grandest stage had slowed to a trudge, a tired and tipsy pub fight held at Madison Square Garden.

Moore's message at half-time was consistent and unspectacular in tone, his players asked to make better opportunities out wide and to regain a sense of calm on the ball. Out of possession he was largely satisfied with Wednesday's work. If they could just tighten-up on their own work, the match, the prize, would be theirs. They had to showcase their undoubted quality. No changes would be made.

By now the sun was dipping lower, creeping its way down over the train station slowly to blanket Wednesday supporters baked in heat. They pulled their hands to their foreheads in an attempt to ease its glare. It was painfully hot and the break offered an opportunity to seek shelter on the concourse, where they were greeted by a mood of tension. There was plenty on the line, after all. As on Wembley Way an hour or so earlier, conversations were shared between Wednesdayites who hadn't spoken in years. "What do you reckon, then?" one would say to the other, "Tight, isn't it?"

One of those was Neil, 47, a police officer from Adelaide, who wasn't going to miss out on another opportunity to watch Sheffield Wednesday at Wembley. Having left Yorkshire for Australia in 2008, he had barely missed a match on iFollow, tuning in to watch YouTube-broadcast press conferences in the dead of night, scheduling trips home to see family around periods in which he could attend as many Owls matches as possible. He hadn't been able to make 2016, watching from home. As Wednesday completed the remarkable and secured their place at Wembley, he realised he had only three days of annual leave left to take, but no matter. Flights were booked, a ticket secured from a stranger via Twitter who was heading away on holiday. The whistle-stop visit would cost over £2,000.

In his pre-match press conference, Moore cited his efforts as an example of the powerful relationship the club shares with its supporters. Via a three-hour stopover in Doha, Neil landed in London on Saturday evening. He would leave on Tuesday morning at 7am, with enough time to squeeze in a night's sleep before reporting to work in Adelaide at 8am on Wednesday. He'd spend more time in the sky and in airports than he would in London. But his love for the club took over all semblance of logic. Feeling all the feelings he'd feel in his front room, squinting into an iFollow subscription at hours ungodly, Neil was at Wembley.

One change would arrive at the break, offering a tip of the cap to the job done by Reece James on the left of the Owls defence. Targeted by tall Tyke Tedić, James had won the battle with Barnsley tapping out on the tête-à-tête by turning to Norwood. Wide of jaw and shoulder, the 32-year-old – who had a year earlier mocked Wednesday in his Barnsley unveiling piece – strode out onto the Wembley playing surface with a point to prove. It was reported as a concussion substitution by Barnsley, which meant they retained their full complement of five substitutes left to make. Norwood would become Wednesday's tormentor-in-chief, driving powerfully at the Owls defence and leaving questions as to why he hadn't started.

The second half was less than a minute old when controversy reared its head. With Barnsley attacking an east stand dotted with their own increasingly vocal and comfortably-shaded supporters, Bobby Thomas launched a throw-in skywards like a soldier with a grenade, hoping to spark a little chaos. Chaos he got. A nod-on from Andersen dipped into a rare pocket of space in the Wednesday penalty area and with no figure from either side there to claim a header, Liam Kitching and Lee Gregory strained to swing a leg at the ball. Both were unsighted, both swung with full-force. And there was a collision.

The reaction was curious and typical of the cagey nature of the occasion. There were cries of anguish from the Barnsley support but nothing close to the sort of appeal you would expect from a game of such magnitude. It was because the collision had occurred in such a flurry. Legs seemed to twist into one another and in truth, in real time, nobody seemed quite sure who won the ball. It was Kitching who had come off worse, writhing in agony while Gregory hurriedly removed himself from the scene and slid his protective mask above his face with angelic confusion. With a word in the ear of referee Robinson, it was VAR that would decide whether he had left the scene of a crime.

It took 45 seconds for the decision to be made, a long time to hold your breath in that heat. Slowed down and in the high definition of several angles, it looked dangerous. Kitching had nipped the ball away from Gregory and the Owls striker, eyes focused solely on the ball, had struck his calf with force. Media assembled in the press box not far from the incident felt it was a call that could go either way and those working on the live *Sky* broadcast went further. No penalty.

Among those breathing a monumental sigh of relief was Mand, 42, a product manager from the Peak District who was diagnosed with autism in 2020. A proud and passionate Sheffield Wednesday supporter, she is faced with challenges in large crowds, in noisy areas and in places she doesn't recognise. When triggered, her autism presents mildly in the form of her bouncing on her tiptoes, or quietly clapping her wrists together. At Hillsborough, despite the crowds and the noise and the unsettling nature of football, she feels at home, like none of that stuff matters. It's her place.

Mand was sat in a Club Wembley seat, unable to miss the biggest match in her club's recent history at the home of football. She'd met the families of players and chatted to Wednesday figures of old. Her mood was one of contented bliss. The day was not without its challenges – something she has long since come to accept – and at half-time, with a crowd making its way towards her, she quickly U-turned to settle back into her seat and lost herself in a programme. Her condition means she is prone to episodes of crying as things become overwhelming but at the final whistle of the second leg at Hillsborough 11 days earlier, grown men sobbed in each other's arms as her football team did the unthinkable. At Wembley, she felt for the first time that she was feeling the same emotions of those around her. It's a feeling she will never forget.

Such historic occasions turn on moments such as this. From the moment Gregory's boot had crashed into Kitching, and including that breathless wait for Robinson's signal of safe passage, only 171 seconds had elapsed before Gregory's next action. Racing onto a heavy touch in his own half, the ball hung in time, an equidistant yard between he and Barnsley man Adam Phillips. Gregory won the ball and felt the full force of Phillips' lunging effort. As had been the case less than three minutes earlier, it was clear there was a big decision to be made as Robinson blew his whistle and jogged towards the incident. Once again, for those in the stands, time stood still.

What was interesting was the stark difference between the protestations of the two sides. While there had been wails from the stands, Barnsley's players had not made much of their penalty shout, preferring to get their heads down and regain their positions, such was the whirlwind of what had occurred. Phillips' challenge was much more brazen, much more aggressive. He'd gone over the top of the ball and with both men stretching off their feet, this collision looked far more clear-cut, more fierce and more dangerous. That sparked the Wednesday players into fury; Windass threw his hands at the referee in rage, Bannan blitzed into his eyeline with his arms aloft. Palmer, Johnson, Ihiekwe all screamed their thoughts into the vicinity and raced onto the scene.

It would result in a card, of that there was little doubt. Reckless is yellow, television commentators reminded their audience, and dangerous is red. And with Robinson having taken a beat of consideration, having backed away from the huddle of players and having gestured Phillips around him, he deemed it dangerous. Phillips was sent off. VAR saw no reason to overturn the decision and the 2023 League One play-off final had been turned on its head. James clapped his hands in delight. So did Johnson. Wednesday fans roared. Barnsley were furious.

Adam, 42, a rail signaller from Exeter, had secured a pair of Wembley tickets for him and his seven-year-old son Ralphy during one of the worst periods of his life. After 18 years of marriage that had brought

A BETTER PLACE TO PLAY

two children, in March his wife had told him that their relationship was to end. For him, the news came out of the blue. He had spent weeks in a daze, unable to process what he had been told. It broke him.

The bombshell had taken not only his marriage, but his love affair with Sheffield Wednesday. A 10-hour round drive from Devon was a journey he had been happy to undertake over decades of passionate Wednesdayism but all of a sudden, the thought of heading to Hillsborough was too painful a prospect. On his journeys home, routine dictated that he would enjoy long conversations over the phone with his wife, killing time and sharing stories of their days. With that gone, his enthusiasm waned. He'd watch games on television, but in truth he was merely looking at them, devoid of emotion.

Making his way up the steps to his seat on May 29, 2023, Adam watched down on his young son, a sense of being overwhelmed making way for excitement in his face as the splendour of Wembley was revealed before his eyes. This was their club, passed down from Adam's dad, through him to Ralphy. This was their day together, a tiny pocket of joy among a sea of stories similar, at a time when Adam felt his world was falling apart. Watching his son's mood move like the tide as the game went one way then another reaffirmed his passion for a lifetime love. That little boy, together with Sheffield Wednesday, had pulled his world back together.

It was in the moments after Phillips' red card that the match seemed to turn. And in the most curious direction. With a man advantage on a large pitch – the same size as that at Hillsborough – with technicians such as Bannan in midfield and with the pace of Johnson and Windass going forward, this was Sheffield Wednesday's match to lose. But it was Barnsley that stepped on the gas.

Boss Michael Duff, apoplectic in the background of Robinson's decision, had collected himself to make a big call himself. With 10 men on the field, there would be no major system change, no immediate substitute. Barnsley would continue in a 3-4-2 formation, foregoing the extra body in midfield with so much of Wednesday's most dangerous moments having gone from back to front. It would be up to the men in blue and white to make better use of the ball, to move it quickly and to utilise such a major advantage in space. Barnsley would not cower into defensive submission.

Kane dried the ball off with a towel and Thomas launched it back into the box once more. A headed clearance, a sweetly-struck Cadden volley from outside the box. Kitching, so influential in matches between these two sides, craned himself backwards to deflect the ball goalwards. With Dawson beaten, it bounced off the overside of Wednesday's bar. The Barnsley crowd behind the goal rose as one. It seemed to serve only as a further knife twist of nerves for their Wednesday counterparts. The red card had blown the match into a new realm, Wednesday dragged from a position of stoic control to a blitz of blow-trading. Life was suddenly uncomfortable.

Matt, 38, a video editor from Wadsley Bridge, had wandered through the turnstiles of Wembley stadium a little nervously, a flag wrapped around his waist akin to a sarong. Told in no uncertain terms hours earlier he would not be able to take it in, on account it had not been pre-approved, it had become something of a personal mission. Something he simply had to do after one of the toughest 18 months any person could begin to imagine.

Emblazoned on the flag was an image of his father Ken, who at the age of 78 had died of cancer in the hours after Wednesday's win over Portsmouth on the final day of the regular season the year previous. Football and days out watching Sheffield Wednesday were the bond that held the pair tighter, a shared obsession; one that would see them taste the highs and lows and everything between as father and son. His day out at Wembley had to be spent with him. With Ken gone, Matt found solace in the thing they'd loved together.

Approaching the family's first Christmas without their patriarch, Matt's sister Michelle made the decision to take their mother Ann out on holiday to Tenerife for some rest, relaxation and a break from the stress of that first difficult festive period. They walked home on the final night of their winter break with suntans and laughter. Michelle, a mother of two, would never make it home.

A white van careered onto the pavement, badly injuring Ann and leaving her hospitalised for several days. Michelle tragically died of her injuries not long afterwards. Football and Sheffield Wednesday, such a constant in Matt's life before the bitter taste of such double tragedy, was providing the glue that held him together through a period of time few would have managed. And with Ken's unfurled flag hung by his side at Wembley, with memories of Michelle at the forefront of his mind, he watched the game unfold as the two sides wrestled.

The last two matches of the season had witnessed a departure in style from Moore's modus operandi. At West Brom and Doncaster Rovers he had sought to play attractive passing football, itself a stride or two away from the no-nonsense way he'd played the game himself. He'd spoken about the virtues of playing out from the back for much of his time at Hillsborough and the start of the season had seen green shoots of success on that front. By the time Wembley came around, Wednesday had scored 81 goals in their league campaign, five at the play-off stage and 19 across the cups to build a fearsome tally of 105. They'd conceded only 52.

As the months had grown on, as injuries had stuck pins in plans and as the pressure of a monstrous promotion battle weighed heavy, Wednesday had seemingly gone more direct in the latter stages of their campaign, leaning on the abilities of Smith and Gregory. Opposition managers, such as the ever-diplomatic Joey Barton, spoke publicly about Wednesday's style of play being unsophisticated, questioning whether it would stand up in the Championship. For the second leg and for Wembley, it had become an all-out aerial assault.

Effective as they'd been, the ground-out nature of the final weeks had welcomed groans from some Owls supporters, particularly those wading in the mire of social media hashtags. Was Wednesday's squad not capable of producing more glittering stuff? Were 1-0 wins at less fashionable clubs acceptable? Did any of it matter? It was a question that seemed cruellest during the period without Byers and Windass, when the world seemed to be crumbling in on them. In the age of *Sky Sports* analysis packages and non-stop access to the wares of Manchester City and Liverpool, style had become as important as substance through the eyes of many supporters. Within the camp they were simply satisfied at getting the job done with rugged efficiency and getting matches ticked off.

What was clear at Wembley was that the new style – put in place by a manager critics would routinely surmise "had no Plan B" – did serve to marginalise Wednesday's most technically gifted. Bannan had had moments and was a key man in terms of striving for quality in delivery, but Windass was a man lost and unable to claw his way into the game, later admitting that at each substitution he would look nervously to the bench expecting to see his number on the board of the fourth official. Playing in the No.10 role, his touches were limp, few and far between. Barnsley keeper Isted would end the match with only seven fewer. Windass cut a frustrated figure as he darted about, desperate to enter the family business of Wembley heroics. But it wasn't happening. In truth, in terms of grabbing hold of the occasion, with that man advantage seared into the forefront of their minds, it wasn't really happening for anyone.

Moore had stood on the touchline largely motionless for much of the second half, arms folded, fingers placed to his chin, deep in thought. Barnsley courted the more meaningful possession, their end of the stadium raucous as sunshine and stress sapped a little life out of those in blue and white and yellow. Duff had turned part-cheerleader, gesturing into the crowds of red and appealing for more noise. Paterson, a sweat-drenched warrior, had swapped places with Palmer to shuffle into the middle of midfield. On 78 minutes the Owls made their first change and the Scot was replaced by Vaulks. There would be no late drama, not yet at least, and the final whistle was blown after final throes that had petered out into nervous nothingness. The match would go to extra time.

Peter, 40, an administrator from Aarhus, Denmark, took the opportunity to sit down and relax during the break at 90 minutes , bearing the weight of an arduous 20-hour train journey via Frankfurt and Brussels. But with his 10-year-old son Svend in tow, watching the team he had fallen in love with himself at the same age, it felt as if he was walking on air. Peter's love of football was brought about in the wake of Denmark's against-all-odds 1992 European Championship win. Peter's love of Sheffield Wednesday was born watching matches piped into Danish television during long winter breaks that left him without access to the sport he adored. The shirt, the name, Chris Waddle. For Peter, there was no Danish team. It was always Wednesday.

The world has changed and through the kaleidoscope of computer games and Premier League domination, Svend's first love is Manchester United, an adoring romance carried out on television screens. Svend suffers from time to time with anxiety in large crowds, but in the bosom of his father's club, he felt entirely at ease at Wembley, experiencing football live; the sights, the smells and the drama. For an afternoon, satellite television images of Bruno Fernandes were a distant memory as Peter's little boy kicked every ball. Such was the tension playing out before them, at one stage he recoiled with cramp. The afternoon was real. And 543 miles from home, tired from rail travel, the afternoon was theirs.

This was Wednesday's 60th match of a long and gruelling season. At Oakwell in March, Barnsley had made a point of the difference in ages between the two sides, hinting at deeper resources of energy and exuberance as matches rumbled deep. Wednesday had the oldest average age of their starting 11, Barnsley the third youngest. But in extra time at Wembley, experience counted. With Barnsley's remaining 10 sharing the work of 11, with Phillips sat lonely on the sidelines, their second-half dynamism was diminished. And so it proved.

With Vaulks in midfield, Wednesday began to move the ball more effectively. They were sharper and more fluent as Barnsley tired after 40 minutes operating a body light. The Welsh international produced a cross for Michael Ihiekwe, so calm and so robust at the heart of defence throughout the afternoon, to register a header on target. The Tykes were pinned deep in their half as Wednesday grew and grew. Bannan, beginning to show signs of cramp, had Isted beaten with a spinning shot from 25 yards, but saw it curve over the bar.

Eight minutes into extra time came a breathless chance as the Barnsley keeper reacted fast to spread himself in the direction of Smith's poked effort just a yard from his line. He'd make another sprawling save moments later, touching Bannan's curling strike onto the post and to safety. The Wednesday skipper crouched forward, sensing the moment, desperately rallying his team towards glory. Finally, mercifully, it was Wednesday who were rising in the battle, asserting themselves on the occasion as they had done on so many occasions over the past few months. It felt as though the match was only going one way. Until it didn't.

The clock at Wembley ticked over to the 12th minute of extra time and Barnsley were on the break. Fresh air breathed into them by Isted's heroics, they moved the ball from the left-hand side of their own half, blitzing through Bannan's desperate cramp. Cadden pushed it through to the onrushing Kitchen, who took the ball onto his instep and sashayed towards a back-peddling Wednesday pair in Johnson and James, shrugging an unbalanced Vaulks to the ground. As play continued to break, the picture revealed a three-on-two in Barnsley's favour; Luke Thomas in space to Kitching's right, Luca Connell in space to his left.

Moments in time. The vital seconds that determine success or failure, glory or destitution. Thomas retrieved the ball and with icy calm took two touches before sliding it to Connell. The globe stopped spinning. Wednesday's defenders froze in motion with the goal at the youngster's mercy, Dawson scrambling in an attempt to get back into the picture. So fast was the move but so glacial the moment as Sheffield Wednesday's season hung by a thread. The ball slid across Connell as he looked to rest on the shoulder of his preferred left foot. Camera angles would later show a chance easier to score than miss; an open invitation of all-time hero status at Oakwell and a ticket to the Championship.

Somehow, Luca Connell missed.

Somehow, after 105 minutes, the 2023 League One play-off final would enter half-time in extra time with the score at 0-0. For a match that would later be described as something of a shocker, there weren't half a lot of white-knuckle moments. Short on quality? Perhaps. Short on the sort of slick passing play more routinely displayed on *Sky Sports* week-on-week? Most certainly. But for the star turns of Isted and Dawson, though, the match could easily have seen five, six goals or more. The red card had yawned open an occasion that had been touch-tight and against all semblance of logic, a revitalised Barnsley had had the better of the second half. Aside from a moment you rather suspect the freshly-turned 22-year-old Connell will remember for the rest of his career – in fairness, the most brazen chance of the match – extra time had belonged to Wednesday. It had flipped and flopped one way and then the next.

Chris, 37, an occupational therapist from Hillsborough, watched over the Wembley pitch with the colours of the occasion bright and vivid. He looked around at the faces around him, faces he'd grown to know from years of travelling up and down the country following Sheffield Wednesday. They'd puff out their cheeks, increasingly unsure of whether today would be their day. He puffed back.

Chris' last drink had come on May 3, 2019. His relationship with football hadn't always been the healthiest, for many years representing a vehicle for long and often painful weekends racing to the bottom of a pint glass. The experience of "doing the play-offs" with Wednesday holds uneasy memories. During an attempt at getting sober in 2016, having stood on Brighton seafront panicking as to what to do, he drank vodka disguised as soft drinks all evening, unable to fight the impulse to drink, hiding it even from his brother. He describes it as one of his lowest memories. There are matches he doesn't remember and matchdays he wishes he doesn't.

By May 29, 2023 he breathed in the air of north west London four years into recovery, knowing football had taken the place of alcohol in his life. Sheffield Wednesday – and more pertinently the people around Sheffield Wednesday – were the new constant. With his first child on the way, he had taken the decision that life as a home and away Owl would have to take a backseat for a while. Wembley was the full stop on that life; a door into his new one. He looked down at the pitch knowing he'd remember, breathing in every excruciating moment as it came. And painstaking as it was, it was glorious. And less than a minute into the second half of extra time, he found himself jumping into the air with crystal clear emotion. Wednesday had done it.

It came in a flash. In a moment, a perfect, dream sequence moment less than a minute into the second half of extra time, Wednesday had done it. The ball came off Vaulks' boot sweetly, in one touch and in perfect trajectory towards the top corner. It was going to take something special for Isted to be beaten, that much had been made clear, and Vaulks had done it in the most glorious delivery.

In the stands, delirium. Vaulks, the energiser bunny of the Wednesday changing room, took leave of his senses, racing towards the dugout. Teammates were in his vicinity, but nobody could lay a hand on him. He parted his arms to the crowd, took a step and launched into his famous acrobatic celebration, the one seen at Port Vale and fudged at Wycombe. On the grandest stage in rich, beating sunshine, it was perfectly executed in front of the world. Teammates bounded from the bench, mobbing their hero. Bannan punched the air and Fisayo Dele-Bashiru grabbed hold of history. With 15 minutes to go, Sheffield Wednesday had taken a precious lead and had planted one size nine into the Championship.

Moore had earlier turned to his bench for the second time in an attempt to deliver fresh legs and savvy use of the ball. Palmer was shuffled into the third different position of his day, on the left of the back three, allowing James, a pint-sized giant of the afternoon, to rest legs that had grown weary. In his place, Jack Hunt stepped onto the field for what was widely expected to be his last of 180 appearances for the club at which he had enjoyed such huge success and connection, the one he'd called home on the phone to his wife in a fit of emotion two summers previous. Marginalised to no little frustration for so much of a historic campaign, he had slotted himself into the annals of club history 11 days earlier by striking the penalty that took Wednesday to Wembley. He had one more chance to do it again and having laid on the assist for Vaulks, it seemed he had done it.

So cold, so cruel it was, then, that the moment was stripped away from him. VAR doesn't exist in League One football and in any other match over the last 10 months, Hunt's darting run behind the Barnsley defence would have been flagged for offside instantaneously. In the interest of allowing the play to be completed, linesman Akil Howson had to wait to raise his flag for an offside pass in the build-up. Vaulks had been the man to start the move and in struggling to drag the ball from under his feet, with Hunt unable to hold his run, the wing-back had strayed just a step beyond Kitching. In the faraway melee, Marvin Johnson was the first to look over his shoulder and set about spreading the news to his teammates. David Stockdale wasn't far behind. Moore called to his players and staff to regain composure and Vaulks raised his hands to his face in ashen bewilderment, the highlight of his career torn from his grip. Sheffield Wednesday would have to go again.

Ryan, 40, a teacher from Killamarsh, gripped his craft ale a little tighter as the night grew longer. Having left South Yorkshire in 2009, he now works in Kowloon, Hong Kong and with school to navigate around the Monday final, a trip to Wembley was never on the cards. Watching a screen in his local bar showing 44,000 Wednesdayites in shared pandemonium, life as an expat Owl on May 29, 2023 was a bittersweet experience; lonely in some respects, part of something enormous in others. The match was watched by Wednesday fans all over the world, in every continent; so far away, so tightly knitted together.

Wearing his 1980s Wednesday shirt, sweat dripped off him in stifling 98 per cent humidity. He makes no secret of his Wednesdayism.

Nearly 6,000 miles from Sheffield, he'd long since made sure hundreds of Cantonese children know of the untamed power of a David Hirst shot, and are aware exactly which Wednesday player is "better than Zidane." A colleague, a Forest fan whose grandmother was from Sheffield, had agreed to watch the match with him and as the evening stretched, as Vaulks' disallowed goal sparked despair and celebration, scores of locals gathered closer around the television, tangled in the ebb and flow of every attack of two teams they had never heard of. The two Englishmen looked at their watch as it passed midnight, as it passed 1am, as their start time at work trudged closer. They were in it until the bitter end.

It would all come down to this. In the 2022/23 season, including added time, Sheffield Wednesday played 11,438 minutes of football. They'd attempted 24,720 passes and 19,560 had found a Wednesday shirt. A total of 813 shots, 284 on target. One hundred and five goals, 96 points. Immeasurable pints of sweat spilled in every moment on the training ground, every stretch for a tackle on the pitch. Miles on the motorway and thousands of pounds for those sat in the plastic seats. Records, wobbles, a night that surpassed all others at one of the most famous football stadiums in the world. With a few minutes of their season left, it felt as though the fate of Wednesday's oh-so vital promotion attempt would end in the lottery of a penalty shootout against a team who had finished 10 points below them.

They'd tried and toiled and against 10 men Barnsley, had risen. Across the course of the match Wednesday were the better team, as proven by the numbers and the eye test, but the Tykes had stuck in and were defending every wave of Owls attack with exhausted desperation. Saves from Isted, blocks from Andersen and Kitching. The score remained 0-0 when Wednesday lost their talisman.

Bannan had been battling cramp since the late stages of the second half. He'd pulled up once, twice, three times. He'd been taken off the pitch for treatment and attempted to carry on. But with the final throes of the season in their grasp, with a vital penalty with his name on it, he simply couldn't continue, such was the sheer amount of work he'd put in. With tears in his eyes, with four minutes of the season remaining, he left the field to rapturous applause. He'd watch the end of his team's season from the bench. Palmer, man of the season, groin aching from the strain of a campaign of toil, would finish the match wearing the captain's armband.

One of the Wednesday fans to offer Bannan a standing ovation had been Paul, 44, a business owner from Mexborough. Eleven days earlier, Paul had attended the Peterborough second leg with eyes tired from a day spent in tears. He had travelled to the match from the wake of his mother's funeral with his family desperately clinging to hope, knowing she would have wanted them to file through the Hillsborough turnstiles – such was the appreciation she had for Sheffield Wednesday's ability to pull her most beloved together as they followed them up and down the country.

Pat to most, 'Nannan' to her grandchildren, a matriarch to all, she'd died of heart trouble while undertaking her weekly shop at the age of 73. She'd died the day of Wednesday's gnarled win at Bristol Rovers, a performance that carried the characteristics she'd exuded throughout her life; grit, determination and will to succeed. Paul's family gathered to watch that match just hours after her passing, and sobbed at the final whistle.

Taking their seats at Wembley on May 29, 2023, they thought of her, of the day of her funeral when Tina Turner's *Simply The Best* played out over the speakers, of the journey they had been on as a family and with Wednesday over a brutally difficult few weeks. Sheffield Wednesday were the family's vocation and the Miracle, they felt, had been down to Pat. Looking to the sky, they asked her for one more favour as the final entered the very final seconds of extra time. "Come on, Nannan." "Come on, Mum."

Three minutes of injury time had been added on to the 120 as the teams strained to finality. It had become attack versus defence as exhaustion raided Barnsley. The boys in red had just about done enough in what had been a titanic effort. Two minutes and 48 seconds of those had elapsed when the ball thundered from the boot of Fisayo Dele-Bashiru, Bannan's replacement, into the instep of Lee Gregory. One more go. The 34-year-old, who just over a decade earlier had watched famous moments at this famous stadium as an electrician who had all but given up on football, twisted and turned his way into the Barnsley defence. Nine seconds left.

Space opened up where there hadn't been any and he thought back to training sessions at Champney Springs earlier that week, the advice of his coaching staff ringing in the back of his head. As he was told, he crossed the ball back from the by-line and into the area around the penalty spot. As he'd been told, Barnsley shuffled crab-like towards their goal-line and the ball floated into space. Seven seconds.

Josh Windass, the running boy, the one-time part-time builder, ran on once more. He bounded forward, perhaps a little surprised at the space afforded, body filled with the adrenaline of opportunity as the picture became clearer. The ball hung in the air breathlessly, invitingly. And with six seconds left in a season made up of 686,280 of them, Windass dived forward, launching his head towards the ball.

There was a momentary hush in a moment such as that as the world slipped into slow motion. Supporters rose to their feet to the sound of plastic seats folding up themselves, of loved ones gripping the shirts of other loved ones in shared, silent prayer that the moment goes their way. And then a feeling only football supporters know. As Windass' diving header hit the back of the Wembley net, the clock read 120+3. Sheffield Wednesday had done something remarkable. Again.

In the stands, 44,000 people joined in public ecstasy. Ashley held his friends and gave a tap to the polaroid in his pocket, Chris celebrated with a perfect clarity and Peter held Svend high into the air, as Adam did Ralphy. Matt thought of Ken and Michelle, taking the time to look down at the flag he'd smuggled into Wembley a few hours earlier with tears forming in his eyes. Bannan jumped from the bench to celebrate with Dean Windass, whose son had repeated the sort of iconic moment he had for Hull 15 years earlier. A few metres away, Mand jumped around and embraced family and Neil clenched his fists in the air, knowing his long trip back to Adelaide would be spent flicking his mind through the memories of a lifetime.

As Shane's plane approached Tenerife, a ding was played over the announcer system. "I know we've a couple of Sheffield Wednesday fans on board," said the pilot, pausing for the effect of an *X-Factor* judge before explaining the circumstances in which the Owls had achieved the barely imaginable less than two weeks on from scaling the impossible. In Kowloon Ryan threw himself into the air and hugged Cantonese strangers. A few minutes later, *Simply The Best* would burst out of the Wembley speakers and a teary Paul gripped his daughter, thanking

Nannan for one last gift. High in the stands, Dom held his two children tightly, in tears, knowing he – and his barmy little football club – had been able to give them an afternoon they would never forget.

The final whistle blew and Wednesday's players looked out on those stands, knowing each of the 44,000 were celebrating their own stories in their own way. Their own reactions ranged from dazed, relieved bewilderment to crazed excitement. At that moment they became Championship players.

Still battling cramp, emotion in his eyes clear for all to see, Bannan led his players up the Wembley steps to lift the trophy. The players were at the centre of it but this was an achievement that spread far beyond the confines of a changing room. It was an achievement delivered by Sheffield Wednesday as an entity, the army Moore had described. A triumphant Dejphon Chansiri embraced players and staff as they walked past to collect their medals, wearing the expression of a man overcome with relief. Hugs also went to emotional club secretary Lindsey Hinton, a figure unknown to most supporters but who does so much to hold the club together day-to-day. When they got to the trophy, Bannan insisted Palmer lift it with him while Darren Moore shuffled himself backwards to stand behind them, clapping. He'd have his moment with the trophy later.

Sheffield Wednesday had achieved promotion with the sort of storyline Hollywood would reject on grounds of silliness. It was an achievement that belonged to everyone.

EIGHTEEN

ALL THE GLORY

Darren Moore made his way back down the Wembley steps to the adoration of those around him, accepting the high-fives and fist bumps of those lucky enough to get within touching distance of a man with an air of a mission complete. A scream from his left caught his attention and in a glorious moment of realisation, he dived forward into the crowd, embracing a young girl in a hug that released over two years of hard work, stress and so much time away from the family home. It was his daughter. "All the glory," he emotionally repeated into her ear, true to his faith in the most emotional of circumstances. He kissed his wife, held his mother and after a few moments snapped back into business, continuing his way down towards the pitch to join his Sheffield Wednesday players in celebration.

When gauging the emotions of Sheffield Wednesday's players in the minutes after Barry Bannan and Liam Palmer lifted the League One play-off trophy aloft at Wembley, it depends on who you asked. Some remember a feeling of contentment, some sheer adrenaline, some a state of bemused relief. One player remembers holding back tears as he made his way down the steps, fighting them for fear of embarrassing himself. He too had seen a family member in the crowd, eyes wide with pride and motioning the words "I love you." His chin went wobbly.

Once on the pitch, they pulled ticker tape from their mouths and grabbed bottles of champagne. They undertook obligatory photographs in front of sponsored hoardings, bubbly sprayed into the air while more ticker tape rained down. Dennis Adeniran had commandeered a bucket hat – nobody quite remembers where they came from – and Aden Flint followed. Within minutes more players were wearing them than not. They held flags bearing the phrase "We Stepped Up" and draped them over their shoulders drenched in sweat, booze and satisfaction. Will Vaulks poured the remnants of a bottle over his captain's head and the pair held one another. There was a lot of hugging. On the side of the scrum stood Moore, looking on joyously with the expression of a proud dad, satisfied.

Not a Wednesday fan had moved from their seat. They gazed onto the pitch, into the empty Barnsley end, knowing all too well that had things gone just a little differently, had Luca Connell not shanked his tap-in, had Lee Gregory's cross not been quite as pinpoint, had Josh Windass fluffed his header, that it could have been their seats that were bare and lonely. But they weren't. It was party time. And as Wednesday's players walked towards the stands to share their moment, singing along to *Hey Jude* and *Hi Ho Silver Lining*, it struck that the achievement belonged not only to those in football boots, but to Sheffield Wednesday as a collective.

Gone were memories of Forest Green, of season-long edge-of-the-seat anxiety and of furious chants at London Road. Wembley was plunged into a state of shared euphoria, as if all the suffering of the last generation had been worth it. Wednesday players were holding a trophy for the first time in 18 years. Vaulks draped a Jamaica flag over Moore's shoulders as he spoke to *Sky Sports,* before wandering off like a cheeky schoolkid.

Dean Windass scaled the steps at Wembley mobbed, face red and tears rolling down his cheeks. He briefly entered the pitch for a media interview and embraced his son. "My little boy," he'd later sob, proud as punch and as emotional as anyone within the stadium. He shared a word with his ex-wife in joint ecstasy at what they'd just watched. History had repeated in the most glorious of circumstances.

Atdhe Nuhiu stood to the left of the tunnel and as the players he had played with over so many years drifted past, they each stopped to share a word and a hug with the big Kosovan. "You did it, man!" he told Palmer, gripping him tight before pulling him away to admire his medal. Bannan and Josh Windass posed for photos and Dominic Iorfa was locked in conversation with him for several laughter-filled minutes. Nuhiu greeted backroom staff and non-football staff with warm words before heading off to the airport and a return to Austria. He had a game to prepare for, after all.

Blowing kisses and waving to family members in the seats above the tunnel, the players stepped into the vast Wembley changing room to the strains of Oasis. As it had done 11 days previously, *Don't Look Back In Anger* railed around the room, veins straining from the necks of each individual as they screamed every lyric. Staff members stood on chairs, recording the scenes on their phones, and Vaulks poured the bottom half of his Budweiser over Reece James' head – it's unclear how many bottles he actually completed. They wandered around in a daze, embracing whichever teammate happened to be in their path. They posed for photos, champagne replenished and treated appropriately. They sang terrace chants of Iorfa, Byers and Gregory.

Television commitments done and dusted, a couple of rooms away Darren Moore settled into the auditorium-like press conference centre wide of chest, laying back in his chair for a moment, medal rested over his shoulder as it would an Olympian. Minds couldn't help but hark back to how he had looked 751 days earlier at Pride Park, after his side had been relegated from the Championship in the hollowest of circumstances. He'd looked gaunt and unwell, croaking through answers. Deep in the bowels of Wembley, he looked healthy. He looked bigger and stronger. He looked happy.

Derby was one of many low moments in what had been a manic journey for Moore and Wednesday. Two squad overhauls, dire results and rabid criticism in some quarters looked to have taken a toll at stages. Within the last fortnight, he had been racially abused online. After discussion around the match, a reporter asked Moore how he had found the strength to get through the adversity of tough times to return Wednesday to the Championship. He had done so without a buckle, in public at least.

"I have my faith," he replied without a beat, offering a rare insight into Moore's innermost thoughts. "I have leaned on that from a personal point of view. And I have a great belief in what I'm trying to do for the football club. I'm trying to give everything to the football club and I have a real belief in that. I have tried to re-energise my players, my staff and the supporters. You can't do it alone. You can't say I've done that on my own.

"From within, you get parts of the game where you're not going to please everybody, but what I want them to know is that everything that I'm doing, I do for the goodness of the club. That's the main aim for the football club. When the football club gets Darren Moore, they get everything from Darren Moore. That is in terms of trying to bring a football club forward, of trying to bring those good times back. This is a really special moment. There are so many people that are happy, positive. It brings a real feel-good factor and when a football club does well, you see what you can do within the communities around the city and that's a responsibility we have. I'm so pleased to share this with everybody."

Moore returned to the changing room to a hero's welcome, doused in lager and immediately swept up in the joy of the occasion, joining in with a riotous rendition of: "We are going up." Music continued to blare through the changing room as Vaulks flipped and wriggled his way through the full rendition of his considerable dancefloor repertoire; worms, Russian squat dances and all. He came to life as Robbie Williams hit the playlist while players and backroom staff leant from side to side, arm in arm, throughout *Angels* – which had become something of an anthem in the changing room after the Scouser's numerous renditions throughout the campaign. Having posed for photos in homage to the image of Lee Bullen celebrating Wednesday's last play-off win 18 years earlier, Bannan jumped fully clothed – bucket hat, boots and all – into an ice bath, losing his footing and briefly submerging himself.

In an adjoining corridor waited reporters in a 'mixed zone' interview area, where players are welcomed to speak to various media outlets. Holding half-empty beer bottles, several made their way out to bathe in the glory of the afternoon and speak publicly on the madness of the previous fortnight. Liam Palmer confirmed an extension clause had been triggered to ensure he remained a Wednesday player the following season – as if it were ever in doubt – and some took the opportunity to make a point, too, with match-winner Windass aiming digs at Duff's decision to leave the Peterborough second leg early in typically cheeky fashion while imploring the club to press on off the field as well as on it.

"It's one of the best fanbases in the country. I've played for a couple of big clubs but look at this, it's unbelievable," said Windass. "We've been good on the pitch this year. The club's got a lot of work to do to catch up with the other clubs off the pitch, but hopefully we can do that and start being the giant club that we are."

Barnsley chief executive Khaled El-Ahmad sought out reporters to make public his disgust at decisions he felt had gone against his side. It was a theme followed by boss Michael Duff, who felt both the major calls – Adam Phillips' red card and the decision not to award a penalty for Gregory's challenge on Liam Kitching – had seen his side harshly done to. While congratulating Moore and Wednesday on a job well done and making clear he felt that across the course of the season the Owls had been the third best side in the division, he also said Barnsley had been the better side on the day. His was a look of biting anger as well as disappointment. It would prove to be his last public commitment as Tykes boss, leaving for the Championship and Swansea City three weeks later.

Interviews complete, Wednesday's players returned to the changing room to crank up the sound system and crack open more Budweiser. In a display of the cruel margins football delivers on big occasions, a Barnsley staff member emerged from a despondent changing room to forlornly roll crates of unneeded, unopened lager through the mixed zone with a look of dejection.

The plan for the evening had changed. Originally, it had been decided that Wednesday would travel back to Sheffield for their celebrations, though that had been shelved when players made it known that family and friends had booked hotels in London and that they would rather stay put in the Big Smoke. A conference floor at the Novotel had been reserved and the victorious players and staff revelled with their loved ones, Chansiri picking up the bill for a bar that flowed all evening. The mood was one of relief, satisfaction and joy in a room that was steamed-up with heat, probably not designed for the purposes of well over 100 guests jumping around and singing in celebration of a career highlight. Bannan delivered a speech to thank all those present and Moore spoke beautifully to salute the loved ones of his players; those who had not only supported them through the stress of a promotion campaign, but who had bought them their first pair of boots and taxied them to matches in their youth.

As events at the Novotel fizzled out, several players went to continue their celebrations in a London nightclub while others retired to their rooms, keen to catch up with family away from the hustle and bustle of a promotion shindig. Jamie Smith was not at the party, having had to head off home before a well-earned family holiday, while Ciaran Brennan footed the bill for an Uber back to Sheffield. On a sleepy, reflective coach originally planned to have carried the entire team back to South Yorkshire, Darren Moore laid back in his seat, draped his arm over the trophy and rested his eyes. Captured by legendary Owls snapper Steve Ellis, the image would live on as the ultimate snapshot of a mission complete.

Alongside the bus driver, Moore and Ellis, only four other souls were on board; Simon Ireland, soft tissue specialist Dom Millward, sports science chief Rob Lee and Fisayo Dele-Bashiru, who it later proved had said his goodbyes to his teammates for the final time. The rest of Wednesday's promotion-winning heroes remained in the capital and wherever they ended up, and in whatever condition, they rested their heads on pillows as Championship footballers and coaches after playing their part in the most remarkable fortnight.

Those celebrations continued for many into the following day. Perhaps the dustiness of a hangover didn't help, but Bannan remembers a feeling of melancholy; the pressure, adrenaline and exuberance of two years fighting to get out of League One leaving his body to leave huge satisfaction, but also a bizarre sense of emptiness. It's one described by many elite sportspeople after a soaring high and the achievement of an all-important goal.

Two days after the final, on Wednesday, May 31, Hillsborough South gathered once more, this time much closer to home as Sheffield Wednesday prepared for a celebratory bus tour through the city – and a civic reception at the Town Hall. It's a rite of passage for any Sheffield football figure, a sign of genuine achievement, one enjoyed by Owls legends aplenty down the years. It's a line drawn under the season and an opportunity for thousands of supporters to gather in joyous thanks. It's one last opportunity to see the class of whenever-it-was together for the final time.

The majority of Wednesday's Class of '23, families in tow, met at Hillsborough in the afternoon and kicked into a mood of relaxed celebration mode early doors, gathering at Dooleys Bar, a matchday hospitality room set on the first floor of the south stand just off the stadium's reception area. Some seemed to enjoy the taste of their beer better than others given the travails of the days before, while some swerved the taste of alcohol completely. A couple of senior players had woken that morning intending to drive and keep things sensible, but had rubber arms tugged via WhatsApp and chose instead to accompany the day with more than a few drinks.

Out in the world – their own little blue and white corner of the world for the day – excuses were being made across South Yorkshire as Wednesdayites gathered their belongings up in their arms and left the office early, desperate to catch their glimpse of the group of men that had overcome the insurmountable. At 5.30pm the players were carried to Devonshire Green at the top of Sheffield city centre to be met with their open top bus, bounding aboard with excitement, many dressed in appropriate party get-up.

The bus itself was, shall we say, a little understated in appearance. Some from across the city sought to poke fun at its image, suggesting it looked like a rubbish truck or a souped-up campervan. The social media banter wasn't exactly helped when a screen on the side of the bus, meant to show a video of goals throughout the season, glitched and was shown on its side. On a day such as this, who really cared?

Not the players certainly, who continued their refreshment on board and looked down on an adoring fanbase. Emotional interviews were completed on board by the club's media team, Bannan and Hunt – those two old friends – sharing a touching moment once more in which they described their pride at one another's achievements. Hillsborough, West Street, atop that bus. Callum Paterson wore an inflatable snake and comedy sunglasses to mark the occasion, gripping a bottle of Mad Dog 20/20, waving it at reporters and making good on the promise he would do so many months earlier. The Scot seemed to have permeated his delectations to his teammates, too, with George Byers and David Stockdale slurping from similar bottles of what looked to be fluorescent petrol.

Bucket hats continued in their vogue, worn by several members of the team at the outset of a summer in which they would also be widely worn by the Ashes-battling England cricket team, festival-revelling popstars, England footballers and other high-profile figures as manufacturers cashed-in on the must-have look of the year. That's not to suggest Aden Flint kicked off a nationwide fashion craze, of course. Reece James, one of several teammates clearly a little dizzy with drink, wore a blue and white jester's hat and was asked about speculation over a possible permanent transfer back to S6 that summer. Grinning widely into a reporter's phone camera, he replied: "We're all Wednesday, aren't we?"

Stockdale swaggered up and down the bus with the look of a man giddy with satisfaction, wearing a cowboy hat and drinking in every second of what he had described as his last chance of achieving yet another promotion. Stockdale had told Bannan earlier in the season that had they won the title, he would have ridden through the city on a horse. Promotion via the play-offs meant the hat would have to do. While the feeling of the time was that the in-out-in-out veteran would likely be one of the soon-to-be out-of-contract players released by the club come the end of June, it transpired decisions had already been made as the inevitable drew closer. Stockdale's career would go full circle when he took up the unique dual role of player/head of recruitment at his first club York City, in the National League.

Thousands had gathered at the top of town to watch their heroes board the bus while many more had centred at the Town Hall, keen to get the very best view of the celebrations. The bus wound its way into the city, hundreds following as if basking in the glory of its wake, flares pumping blue smoke into the air as they had done in Covent Garden just a few days earlier. It was a family affair, with kids thrown onto shoulders and older kids climbing lampposts to crane their neck and get the best possible view. Chants broke out from time to time and fans called out at the sight of their favourite Wednesday stars, who waved back with appreciative glee.

They reached their destination ahead of schedule and entered the Town Hall through a back entrance, emerging at the bottom steps of the handsome, 126-year-old building to unabated adoration from the thousands gathered before them. One Town Hall staffer claimed it was the biggest parade audience he'd seen – for either Sheffield club. Players danced and sang along to terrace favourites, some a little unsure of the words, and sat on Grade I-listed stone, drinking it all in. It became clear as they came closer into view that they were wearing the club's 2023/24 playing shirts in what was a low-key but effective unveiling that took all by surprise; a stolen glance at the future on a day designed to celebrate the immediate, magnificent past.

Of all the squad, the only face not present was that of Wembley assist hero Lee Gregory. Out of contract in the summer, any rumblings of conspiracy were stamped out as the club published an explanation behind his absence; simply that he was in Dubai on holiday with family. He'd actually left straight after the game. While nothing was guaranteed on his future – in his bit-part section of the season, it had been suggested his growing age might put the club off enacting an extension clause in his contract – the same remained for a great swathe of the squad within weeks of the end of their deals; Byers, Heneghan, Hunt, Paterson, Johnson, Iorfa, Adeniran, Brown, Stockdale, Dele-Bashiru. There were no guarantees even over man of the hour Windass, though the option to take a widely-reported contract extension clause seemed an obvious route for the club to take.

Upstairs awaited a civic reception and the players' families. Hosted by the Right Worshipful Lord Mayor of Sheffield Colin Ross – not how he was christened – beverages were laid out in the centre of the room and were gratefully accepted. But this was no regal stag do, more a pleasant family christening. Children darted around kicking blue and white balloons back and forth, occasionally knocking over an unwisely-placed glass of wine or beer bottle as players apologetically darted from chats with wives, girlfriends and local reporters to clear up the spillage.

The mood was polite but boyishly mischievous, Jack Hunt interrupting an interview with Will Vaulks to ask probing questions about whose fault it was that their goal had been disallowed, before a Michael Smith interview was hijacked by colleagues pulling faces over a reporter's shoulder. "You want a scoop?" one senior player whispered behind one reporter, recording device in hand, whose ears pricked up. "I'm gonna get steaming tonight!" This was Wednesday's squad at their most charming, at their most endearing; just normal lads, family men who just happen to be very good at kicking a football.

Wednesday figures were called out Noah-style, two-by-two to answer questions by legendary long-time stadium announcer Shaun Leigh on the Town Hall balcony. Lifelong Wednesdayite Liam Palmer took the opportunity to take his own little jab back at Rhian Brewster – there'd be more of that later – by leading a rendition of: "If you don't fucking bounce, then you're a Blade." Stockdale grabbed the microphone to launch into a one-man comedy turn. All thanked the gathered Wednesdayites for their remarkable role in a remarkable campaign.

Later, all the assembled Wednesday figures, including chairman Dejphon Chansiri, took turns to sign that infamous Christmas jumper worn in stifling heat at Wembley and throughout the bulk of the season by a certain *Star* reporter after the social media fanbase had surmised it was bringing the team good luck. A giddy George Byers took the opportunity to attempt to sign a journalist's forehead, managing only to poke him in the eye in the ensuing grapple. The sweater was dolled-up non-gratis by Sheffield-based Matrix Frames and over £2,300 was later raised in an online raffle, with proceeds going to local children's hospice Bluebell Wood.

The majority of players headed back with families to the stadium for a party that would reach late into the evening. Mallik Wilks danced with the children of teammates, speeches were made, embraces aplenty. For some, tucked in the back of their mind was the quiet thought that this was likely to be the last hurrah.

As the night grew on and the vibe shifted from family christening to that of a raucous wedding, Stockdale took a pair of scissors to the long, luscious locks of the club's partnerships manager James Todd, after a bet made some months earlier. A video was leaked onto social media later as Bannan took the mic and returned the favour of Brewster, leaning into the sort of back-and-forth that makes football in that city so passionate and virile. The wee Scot grinned while snarling: "Rhian Brewster, you are absolutely fucking honking son!" to cheers all round. With the soiree later having headed into town and back to the scene at Firepit Rocks, a similar video popularised a chant that Wednesdayites would lap up as the Owls skipper belted into a Barnsley-triggering rendition of: "Who put the ball in the Dingles net? Super Joshy Windass!" After the ups and downs of eight years in blue and white, and the largely unwarranted jibing of supporters of local clubs, Bannan was going to enjoy his success to the full. He'd give a bit back. And who could blame him?

As the crowds dissipated hours earlier and the Town Hall drained of the noise of the last remaining Wednesday figures, the room stood eerily bare, strewn with balloons and chairs and all the entrails of an afternoon of celebration. A look around the space, minutes before so busy and alive with joy and boisterousness, offered a feeling of finality, the realisation that the men who had fought tooth and nail across the highs and lows of 10 months of hard work would probably never gather in the same room again. Football is relentless; players would leave, players would come in and suddenly Wednesday's 2022/23 vintage would be no more, evaporated into memory and distilled into video vignettes of vital goals, heart-stopping moments, triumph and desolation. They were all of a sudden the teams of '91, '93, '05 or 2012; a thing of the past, gone in a puff of Wembley glory.

Taking his turn on the balcony, Darren Moore had stood tall to songs of his very own Barmy Army, regaling tales of the renewed bond between team, club and fans. He spoke of the need to build on what the club had achieved, of laying the foundations for what would come. Given the context of a generation of hurt, Wednesday fans, he said, were among some of the best in Europe. It was a foregone conclusion that some of his players would move on in the weeks that followed. But right there and then, with the Wednesday manager looking down on his public, the League One play-off trophy glistening to his side, it seemed scarcely imaginable that Josh Windass' header would prove to be the final contact of Moore's time at Sheffield Wednesday.

POSTSCRIPT

The news broke two minutes before 6pm on Monday June 19, 2023, the words reading short and cold on the club's official Twitter account. "Sheffield Wednesday can announce that manager Darren Moore has left the club by mutual consent." The announcement sparked a state of open-mouthed shock. It was three weeks to the day since Moore had lifted the League One trophy, a touch under that since he had stood on the balcony of Sheffield Town Hall and spoken about the future. A week earlier Moore had welcomed *Talksport* to Middlewood Road and spoke at length about his excitement for the challenge ahead, the fact that the club's recruitment drive was underway and spelled out his roadmap for success in the Championship. Moore and chairman Dejphon Chansiri had been pictured walking through Sheffield to go for dinner just a couple of days previous. The reaction was understandable. To those on the outside, it didn't make sense.

A Wednesday statement confirmed that Moore's coaching staff – Jamie Smith, Jimmy Shan, Adriano Basso and Simon Ireland – would all leave with him and included two sets of quotes; one from Chansiri and one from Moore. Both were appreciative in their appraisals of the other's role in achieving promotion, both detailed a mutual respect. It was clear the separation had not been especially acrimonious, as was so often the story in these parting of ways. No sacking, no resignation; it only added to the confusion.

The news took Wednesday's players by surprise. There had been no backroom briefing before the statement was released – not especially unusual – but the feeling is that they had been left as shocked as the wider world when the news was posted in their shared WhatsApp group.

The day after the news, Chansiri fulfilled a commitment to hold a fan forum in the 1867 Lounge at Hillsborough, which had been scheduled a week earlier. It was a long and winding evening of nearly five hours in which the Thai businessman made clear early on that he would not go into detail about the circumstances that led to Moore's departure, other than to repeat his expression of admiration for the manager. The two men, he said, had agreed not to speak publicly on the matter. He denied reports that recruitment ahead of the new season had been an issue and claimed that if fans knew the reasons behind his departure, they would better accept the situation. That line, as well as a swathe of ex-players and pundits attempting to fill the vacuum of information in the media, contributed to a whirlpool of increased speculation.

Two statements followed in the coming days; the first seeking to clarify certain details of the meeting more publicly, the second far more in-depth. Over 1,232 carefully-chosen words, Chansiri delivered his side of the story on the parting of ways, centring the issue on a disagreement over contracts for Moore and his staff. He said he could not "offer a minimum of four times his current salary on a three-year contract," adding: "I have to be realistic." Moore later gave an interview claiming the figure presented to Chansiri would have been around the average salary mark in the Championship and was merely intended to be the starting point for negotiation. He also cited differences in vision – that he preferred not to speak about publicly – were at play. Any insinuation of greed was vehemently denied.

"I didn't want to leave Sheffield Wednesday," he later told the *Sheffield Star*. "It wasn't about money, and I had already started working for the following season. I was prepared to negotiate; I wanted my agent to do that negotiation but the chairman wasn't interested in negotiating with my agent – he wanted to do it with me. But there was no negotiation, I was given a take it or leave it offer, and I gave my point of view."

Wednesday's retained list had been led by Moore and was cut-throat. Jack Hunt, who had gone from zero to hero in the second season of his second spell with the club, was released, leaving images of him chewing gum and awaiting the onrush of teammates having sealed the greatest play-off comeback of all-time immortal. Also gone were Jaden Brown, later unveiled at Lincoln City, and York-bound David Stockdale. Dennis Adeniran was perhaps the most surprising man released, in that, despite injuries, he had performed well in blue and white. Ben Heneghan was let go but would return for pre-season with the club initially as a "duty of care" act of goodwill, though consideration to a U-turn re-signing would be given as the summer ran on.

With extensions secured for leadership duo Barry Bannan and Liam

Palmer, the club exercised options to retain George Byers, Lee Gregory, Dominic Iorfa and Josh Windass. Marvin Johnson would sign a new deal, as would Callum Paterson. A new contract was tabled to Fisayo Dele-Bashiru, who would move on to the tax-free riches of life in the Turkish Süper Lig – and the prospect of away trips to some of Europe's biggest clubs – with Hatayspor.

A 16-day search for Moore's replacement saw the club sound out a range of prospective managers including Dean Smith, Slaven Bilic and Nathan Jones. They'd settle on former Watford manager Xisco Muñoz, a charming and ambitious 42-year-old Spaniard who had impressed with his Hornets side, achieving promotion to the Premier League in the 2020/21 season before being cruelly sacked as they sat 15th in the table.

It signalled a new start for Wednesday, promises of a bold new playing style and with only 17 senior players on the books in the depths of summer, the ushering-in of a new squad far departed from the all-British line up of the promoted cohort. The exit of Moore and his lieutenants drew a firm and distinct line under the 2022/23 season – one of intensity, of records smashed and of a number of moments supporters of other clubs can hope for once in a decade, never mind 10 months. Never mind 11 days.

It was over. It was mad. It was glorious. It was supposed to be insurmountable.

ABOUT THE AUTHORS

Alex Miller and Joe Crann are the Sheffield Wednesday writing team at *The Star* newspaper and, between them covered every key moment, on and off the pitch, of a remarkable 2022/23 campaign for the Owls. Joe is a lifelong Wednesdayite while Alex has slowly but surely fallen in love with the Owls since being seconded to Sheffield back in 2019.

A graduate of Leeds Trinity University, where he completed an undergraduate and master's degree in journalism, Alex wrote for newspapers including the *Yorkshire Post* and *Halifax Courier* before joining *The Star* and seeing his loan move made permanent two months later. A keen cricketer, Alex lives in West Yorkshire with his wife Naomi and their daughter, Edie. His first book - 91, the story of Wednesday's remarkable 1990/91 season - was published in 2021.

Joe has been covering football across the world for over a decade now and recently came back to his home city of Sheffield to write about the team that he grew up supporting. It didn't start off particularly well, with relegation in the first season following his return home, but the 2022/23 campaign made all of that worth it and offered up the perfect opportunity to co-write his first book with his most trusted colleague.

His journey has taken him from S8 to Johannesburg and back again, and with the continued support of his wife Steph and his family, he's hoping that it won't be the last time his name is on a front cover. His 'proper' place of residence remains up for debate.

Authors Alex Miller and Joe Crann take a minute to soak up the atmosphere at Wembley before the remarkable play-off final

ACKNOWLEDGEMENTS

Having followed Sheffield Wednesday my whole life, and worked as a football journalist my whole professional career, it made sense that my first foray into book writing should come as an amalgamation of those two things. After writing news articles and long-ish features for over a decade it has always been an ambition to do something a bit more long-form.

So with that in mine the first acknowledgment here has to go the way of my co-author, Alex Miller, who was kind enough to get me on board with *Is There Time For A Winner?* at the risk of us having a major fallout due to creative differences. Thankfully that didn't happen, and a large part of that goes down to him being a good bloke, a great writer, and the fact that neither of us mind a WhatsApp message at 2.03am. Without my wife, Steph, it'd probably have never happened either. Her support, when I doubted if book-writing was for me, helped me in my decision to take the plunge, and her ability to act as a springboard for ideas, hype-person and/or frustrations confidant was integral to this book coming to pass.

To my folks, Carol and Steve, thank you for the patience, and the understanding. And to my brother, Eddie, for pushing me on as well. These things don't happen without family – I just wish my Grandad was still here for me to give him a copy. A big thanks also to Danny Hall, our publisher and friend, who gave us this platform; our boss, Chris Holt, for his support along the way, and all those on the Wednesday beat that came on the 22/23 journey with us. Lastly, to the folks over at Sheffield Wednesday who gave me their time and their help throughout the process, it's greatly appreciated – but I hope they know that without me having to write it here. As a fan, having Barry Bannan do the foreword for something that I've co-written is still a bit nuts.

Joe Crann, 2023

ACKNOWLEDGEMENTS

The writing of this book would have been a much breezier task if Sheffield Wednesday had just bloody well behaved themselves and won the chuffing league, as they were expected to when Joe and I first met our publisher pal Danny Hall to chat over what direction we'd take on it.

First over a beer on March 17, with table-topping Wednesday imperious, 22 unbeaten and cruising with games in hand to boot. Wednesday drew 1-1 at home to Bolton Wanderers that evening and Josh Windass got injured. Then over a Meadowhall meal four days later; Wednesday lost 4-2 at Barnsley that night, continued a run of six matches without a win and ultimately fell out of the top two. Given the social media ribbing our great pal Dom Howson got for a flurry of mid-winter, red wine-inspired tweets, it's only fair we crawl out of the woodwork to admit our role in "the jinx". Still, it was more fun the way it panned out, wasn't it? League titles are for cowards.

Untold thanks go out to all the folk Joe has already mentioned, most of all Danny, who has now twice felt the brunt of my flagrant disregard for deadlines with the patience of a saint. Joe has become a great pal since we started working together at *The Star* and has been a pleasure to work with in this, our newest collaboration. Cheers pal.

Thanks to Harriet Massey, Steve Ellis and everyone who sent us photos, and to David Bond and Phil Kelly for proofreading. Thanks to everyone who took the time to speak to us as we pieced the story together – not least to the supporters in the Wembley chapter who trusted me with such personal things – and to the guys at Wednesday for their assistance. Thanks to my loving, supportive Bryett/Miller crew, both in life and in memory, and most of all to my beautiful wife Naomi – she was my fiancée the last time I wrote one of these – and my beautiful baby daughter Edie, who didn't exist. Elephants have wrinkles.

Alex Miller, 2023

ROLL OF HONOUR

James Abberley
Lewis Abrahams
Mark Adlington
Gary Adlington
Andrew Adlington
Mark Aistrop
Thomas Allen
Jack Allen-Scott
Philip Allsop
Rob Andrews
Lilly-Ann Conlen
Rachel Antcliffe
Richard Antcliffe
William Antcliffe
Iain Armitage
Denise Jane Arrowsmith
Mark Arundale
Graham Askham
Richie Atkins
Oliver Atkinson
Robert Austin
James Baboolal
Adam Baker
Jonathan Peter Baker
Mark Balaiss
Alex Ball
Paul Bangert
Jay Barber
Dylan Sebastian Barker
Jack Barker
Matt Barnes
Rick Barratt
Dan Barrett
Ryan Bartlett
Joseph Bates
Chris Beasley
Hollie Beastie
Naomi Beauchamp
Mand Beckett
Jonathan Bell
Chris Bellamy
Johnathon Bellamy
Jordan Bellamy
Rob Bellamy
Stephen Bellamy

Kai Benson
Dan Benton
Freddy Benton
Jonathan Benton
Nicholas Benton
Paul Benton
Alan Zak Berisford
Helen Berisford
Graham Berriman
Mick Berry
David Bertram
Josh Bibby
Jamie Biggin
Adrian Biggs
Hannah Billinghurst
Harriet Birch
Jeff Birch
Mark Birch
Marc Birkwood
Michael Black
Joe Blackburn
Ryan Blezard
Freddie Blood
Gary Bluff
Ash Boler
Chris Bolger
Dave Bolton
Robert Nobby Boocock
Adam Booth
Axel Booth
Dan Booth
Evie Booth
George Booth
Joshua Booth
Paul Bower
Simon Bowles
Graham Brace
Stan Bradder
Andy Bradley
Christian Brailsford
Dan Bramley
Chris Brammer
Callum Breese
Adam Lee Brewer
Wayne Bridgeman

Martyn Briggs
Donna Britton
Ben Danny Broad
Jon Broadbent
George Adam Broadhead
Dorothy Brodie
Malcolm Brodie
Sam Brodie
Izzy Brooke
Glenn Broomhead
Lewis Broomhead
Mikey Broomhead
Luke Brough
Amy Brown
Ben Brown
Bill Brown
Martin Brown
Mick Brown
Owen Brown
Stewart Brown
Ian Brownhill
Jonathan Brunt
Matthew Brunt
Peter Bryett
Paul Bulmer
Josh Bunting
Tom Burns
Thomas Burton
Stan Busby
Malcolm Bush
Finnley Butler
Robert Butler
Emma Butlin
Sarah Butlin
Stuart Butlin
Amy Callaghan
John Callaghan
Katie Callaghan
Vikki Callanan
Dean Calvert
Ken Cameron
Anna Campbell
Chris Campbell
Liam Capes
Andy Cardall

Anthony Cardwell
Debby Carr
Ryan Carroll
Devon Louis Cash
Cole Cawkwell
Graham Chadburn
Ben Chadwick
John Chadwick
Andrew Chambers
Peter Chan
Elliott Chappell
Finlay John Chappell
Matt Charles
Steve Charles
Katharine Childs
Mark Chilvers
Tommy Church
Dylan Clague
Rob Clague
Paul Clare
Michael Clark
Sam Clark
Simon Clarke
Stephen Clarke
Oliver Clay
Oliver Petar Cliffe
Louise Clifford
Peter Coleman
Stephanie Emma Coleman
Alan Coley
Nathan Coley
Charlie Colley
Chris Collindridge
Richard Collins
Darren Collinson
Dave Collinson
Martin Connolly
Morgan Conroy
Graeme Cook
Simon Cook
Stuart Cook
Dan Cooke
Josh Cooper
Evan Copeland
Henry Craig Cornwall
Richard Couldwell
Sophie Couldwell
Dennis Cox

Logan Craythorne
Joshua Cresswell
Rhys Cresswell
Daniel Crofts
Jeff Crofts
Brandon Crook
Richard Crooks
Violet Cropper
Xander Cross
Luke Croxford
Stephen Cullen
Dale Cunliffe
Jim Cutts
Luke Dando
Lucy Danks
Paul Danks
Mark Dauris
Neil Davey
Steven Davey
Les Davies
Rich Davies
Alex Davis
John Paul Davis
Joseph Davison
Daniel Dawson
Stephen Day
Garry Deakin
Tom Delaney
Sean Dennell
Simon Dennis
Reuben Dent
Janet Dickinson
John Dickinson
John Dickinson
Rafe Dickinson
William Joseph Diston
Thomas Dobson
Samantha Doman
Elliot Donkin
Elizabeth Donkin
Chris Dooley
Tom Dooley RM
Jack Doona
Kieran Doona
Jack Stephen Douglas
Matthew Doxey
Dave Drabble
Joanne Drabble

Robert John Drury
Nick Dunnington
Tom Durkin
Nick Durnan
John Dyson
Owen Dyson
Luke Earnshaw
Elliot Eason
Oscar Edwards
Oliver Ellerton
Philip Ellis
Steve Elwood
Patrick English
Alan Epton
Archie Eratt
Layton Eratt
Graham Evans
Michael Evans
Malcolm Eyre *RIP 18.01.23*
Louis Fairest
Ian Farr
Luke Fenlon
Steve Fennell
Richard Fereday
Matt Fern
Chris Ferris
Louise Fieldsend
Roger Finn
Joanne Firth
Paul Firth
Dan Fletcher
Luke Fletcher
Owen Fletcher
Steph Fletcher-Spence
Aaron Flint
Chris Foster
George Foster
Glyndon Foster
Laurence Fowles
Alan Fox
Charlotte Frisby
Alissa Frith
Chloe Frith
Steve Froggatt
Mark Frost
Adam Furneaux
Jack Gagen
Tony Gallardo-Vega

Craig Gamban
Dan Garcia
Noah Gardner
Tony Garfitt
Thomas Garraway
Charlie Gascoyne-Thompson
Matt Gerrietty
Paul Gibson
Andrew Gibson
Tom Gibson
Chris Gilbert
Lucas Glendenning
Jonathan Glossop
Michael Glossop
Jamie Glover
Grace Godley
George Godley
Michael Gothard
Richard Gould
Ruth Greaves
Daniel Green
Laura Green
Steve Green
Sawyer Greenhalgh
Steven Gregory
Ben Griffin
David Griffin
Max De Grunwald
Dave Gurd
John Hackleton
Adam Hadfield
Lyndon Hague
Riley Hague
Dan Hall
Ethan Hall
Joe Hall
Lowell Hall
Tom Hallows
Joseph Hamed
Dennis Hamill
John Hancock
Chris Hannan
James Hannah
Ben Hanson
Michael Hanson
Michael Thomas Hanton
Daniel Richard Hardy

John Hardy
Michael Hardy
Richard Hardy
Ollie Hargreave
Richard Hargreaves
Bridget Harrison
Lee Harrison
Matt Harrison
Sam Harrison
Harry Harrold
Danny Hart
Helen Hartle
Paul Hartle
Christine Haslam
AJ Hawley
Cam Hawley
Danny Hawley
Grampz Hawley
Mick Hawley
Simon J. Hayhow
Dave Haythorne
Andrew Heeds
Jack Heeley
Jamie Heeley
Simon Heeley
Cooper Hemingway
John Hendley
Walter Alfred W. Henshaw
Olivia Hewitt
Darren Hibbert
Craig Hibbert
Nathan Hickin
Dave Higgins
Harlow Connie Hill
Isabella Charlotte Hill
Jax Joseph Hill
Jack Hinchliffe
Scott Hinchliffe
Steph Hinchliffe
Terry Hinchliffe
Elliott Hirst
Paul Hirst
Jonathan Hix
Leon Hobson
Roger Hobson
Shaun Hockenhull
Tom Hodder
Chris Holcombe

Kevin Holcombe
Neal Holden
Esmé Holder
Rob Holland
Daniel Holroyd
Marcus Hopcroft
Shawn Hopkins
Terry Hopkins
David Hornby
Richard Hotham
Karl Housley
Joseph Howard
Emma Howe-Andrews
Elliott Howson
Joseph Howson
Charles Hoyland
Gareth Hunt
Owain Hunt
Rowan Hunt
Keith Hunter
Keely Hutton
Steph Hyner-Jones
Pasquale Iampietro
Jermaine Isherwood
Joan Jackman
Kevin Jackson
Leo Jackson
Keith Jagger
Robbie Jamieson
Finley Jarvis
David Jeffcock
Jacob Jeffcock
Monica Jeffcock
Joanna Jimenez-Owen
Toni Jimenez-Ramos
Dan Jobar
Arran Johnson
Craig Johnson
Kevin Johnson
Michael Johns
Michael Johnson
Nick Johnson
Steve Johnson
Damian Jones
David Jones
Mark Jones
Toby Ethan Jones
Curtis Jordan

Sandra Jowitt
Phill JP Shaw
Dilip Kanji
Matt Kelcher
James Kelly
Liam Kelly
William Kelly
Jackson Kelsall
Jason Kemp
Jake Kempton
Mark Kempton
Steven Kempton
Paddy Kenworthy
Dan Kershaw
Archie King
Jamie King
Keith King
Sam King
Jonathan Kinnear
Lee Kirk
Peter Kitching
Niamh Kitson
Jonah Klos
Mick Knapton
Chris Knight
Stephen Krall
Daniel Kristall
Marcus Krupa-Meisner
Bailey Laird
Riley Laird
Kevan Lancaster
Stuart Laver
Paddy Lavin
Blake Law
Peter Lawrence
Derek Lechner
Philip Lee
Andrew Lee
John Leigh
Ben Leonard
Charlotte Lincoln
David Lincoln
Harry Lister
Angus Littlewood
Owen Littlewood
John Liversidge
Tony Livingston
Peter Adolfsen Løhmann

Demi Lomas
Emilia Rose Long
Max Loukes
Will Lowry
Nick Lynch
Adam Lyons
Paul Lyons
David Machan
Louis Mahone
Shaun Maleham
Richard Mangham
James Manley
Eddie Marples
John Marples
Andy Marriott
John Marsden
Darren Marshall
Ian Marshall
Alex Martin
Sharon Massey
Andrew Mate
Alex Mathieson
Hedley Matthew
Annie Matthews
Tom Matthews
Glynn May
Vaughan May
Harry McClean
Chris McClure
Alyssa McGarrity-Taylor
Kian McGarrity-Taylor
Kian McGarrity-Taylor
Keegan McGuckin
Chester McGuinness
Kieran McKeefery
Patrick McKenna
James McKenzie
John McLaughlin
Nea Mclean
Ralphy McNeill
Jordan Meates
Howard Mellish
Alex Merrill
Alan Metcalfe
Robert Metcalfe
Cara Millar
Edie Miller
Rob Millington

Jamie Mason Mintoft
James Molloy
John Montgomery
Ben Moody
Robert Moody
Simon Moody
Adam Moore
Thomas Moore
Phil Moors
Dennis Morgan
Miles Morgan
Gav Morley
Henry Moroney
George Philip Morris
Jamie Morris
Joel Morris
Andy Morton
Shane Morton
Wednesday Morton
Ben Motley
Liam Mottram
Derek Mounfield
Peter Mounsey
Judy Moxon
Dec Mullane
Colin Muncie
Tony Munden
Fred Murray
Malcolm John Murray
Jonathan Nassau
Graham Needham
Mark Needham
James Nelson
Paul Newby
David Nicholls
Andrew Nicholson
Andy Nicholson
Chris Nickson
Katie Noonan
Jo Oakley
Joe Michael O'Hagan
Madison O'Hagan-Bulmer
Harry Oldfield
Richard Oldfield
Jamie Oliver
Rob O'Neill
Jason O'Rourke
Alex Oxley

Gary Palfreyman	Paul Queeney	Mark Rotherforth
Harry Palmer	Craig Quixall	Tim Rudland
Jack Parker	Andrew Ramshaw	Oliver Rushton-Smedley
Cobie Parkin	Claire Reaney	Steven Rymill
Dominic Parkin	Ben Reay	Adam Sadler
Ian Parkin	Dave Reckless	Tom Sadler
Richard Parkin	Alfie Redfearn	Nathaniel Salih
Steve Parkin	Shane Reeves	Ben Sampson
Ell Patman	Mike Relf	Luke Samuels
Lucy Peace	Harry Revitt	Chloe Sandall
Thomas Peace	Dan Reynolds	Andrew Sandford
Russell Peaker	Steve Reynolds	Charlie Saul
John Harvey Pearson	Eli Rhemtulla	Isaac Savas
Brad Peasgood	Harry James Rich	Fred Saxon
Ross Penny	Craig Richards	Sam Scarlett
Ian Pepper	Jonathan Richards	Graham Scott
Martin Perryman	Jordan Richards	Mick Scott
Callum Phelan	Evan Ridge	Ian Scrafield
Isabelle Phillips	Brian Robbins	Neil Seepujak
Daniel Plant	Chris Roberts	Mick Sellars
Joel Platt	Grant Ewan Roberts	Tom Sellers
Adam Pollard	Scott Roberts	Harry Senior
Simon J Pope	Chris Robinson	Carol Senior
Glenn Poulton	Tom Robinson	Bobby Serban
Mike Priddon	Wayne Robinson	Paul Sewell
Mark Priest	Lucas Roe	Ray Shabi
Jack Priestley	Freddie Rogers	Charlie Sharpe
Paul Prior	James Rogers	Dave Sheldon
Adam Pugh	Oliver Rogers	Darren Freddie Shepherd
James Pym	Steve Rogers	David Shepherd

Also published by

THE INSIDE STORY OF SHEFFIELD WEDNESDAY'S 1990/91 SEASON

A New History of the Owls' Darkest Times - 1973-1976

Morgan Shillito
Nobby Siddall
Archie Simmonite
Craig Simmonite
James Simpson
Jack Sims
Catherine Slinn
David Smelt
George Smith
Hannah Nicky Smith
Jenni Smith
Karen Smith
Lewis Smith
Mark Smith
Max Smith
Paul Benjamin Smith
Phil Smith
Roger Smith
Scott Smith
Tom Smith
Wendy Smith
Matthew Smithies
Jim Snowden
Jayne Somerset
Gary Speight
Pete Spencer
Jamie Spier
Neil Stain
Ethan Staniland
Kerrie Staniland
Kevin Stanley
Joe Staton
Isaac R. Stennett
Matthew Stephenson
Dominic Stevenson
Ray Stewart-Kelcher
Christian Stickland
Simon Stickland
Denise Stocks
Cobi Stokes
Dave Stone
Michael Straker
Callum Street
Taylor Street
Adrian Sutton
Ian Sutton
Kirsty Sutton
Karl Swain

Chris Swallow
Terry Sweet
Adam Swift
Graham Swingler
Mark Talkes
Ben Taylor
Deborah Taylor
Emily Taylor
Julie M Taylor
Katie Taylor
Rich Taylor
Jeremy Theaker, *in memory Of Jem Haytack*
Adam Thompson
David Thompson
Ellie Thompson
Josh Thompson
Riley Thompson
Mike Timmons
Kai Timms
Michael Titterton
Richard Todd
Matthew Tomlinson
John Topham
Mark Townend
Tom Travis
Bradley Truelove
Chun Tsang
Stephen Tufnell
David Tunley
Neve Turner
Richard Turton
George Tyas
Giles Ursell
Andrew Varns
Toby Ventham
Amy Wakefield
Ayrton Gavin Waldock
Rachael Walker
Mick Wall
Kel Wallace
Ray Wallis
Jowan Walters
Chris Walton
David John Ward
John Ward
Rich Ward
Gabriel Ware

Kelly Ware
Eileen Washington
Scott Watson
Simon Watson
Chris Watson
Finlay Alexander Wellwood
Andy West
James Whaling
Paul Whitaker
Darren White
Paul White
David Whitehorn
Liam James Whitehouse
Rob Whitelaw
Alan Whitley
Ben Whittaker
Jake Wild
Pete Wild
Sophie Wild
Liam Wildsmith
Henry Wileman
Ian Wiles
Clive Williams
David Williams
Elliot Williams
Antonia Williamson
Matt Williamson
Matthew Williamson
Oliver William Wilson
Tom Wilson
Andrew Winbow
David Winfield
Darren Winnell
Victoria Wood
Jack Woodcock
Gary Woodcock
Harry Woodhall
Daniel Woodhead
Mike Woodhouse
Bernard Woods
Sam Worley
Graham Wraith
Michael Wren
Chris Wright
Richard Wright
Tony Wright
Ruby Young
Joni Young